The Heart of the Elder

Good Elders and Their Influence

The Heart of the Elder
Good Elders and Their Influence

Lillith ThreeFeathers and Joy Marie Wedmedyk

Megalithica Books
Stafford England

Cover Art: Nemo Boko
Editor: Leni Hester
Layout: Taylor Ellwood/Storm Constantine

Set in Papyrus and Book Antiqua

MB0196
ISBN: 978-1-912241-04-0

A Megalithica Books Publication
http://www.immanion-press.com
info@immanion-press.com

Dedications

We dedicate this work to those who came before us, to our Elders, to the ancestors and divine ones, known and unknown, who have supported us on this lovely planet, our Mother Earth, and who continue to help us as we live and learn.

We dedicate this work to those we love, our children, and to their future.

We dedicate this to everyone who has walked these life journeys with us and to our students.

We dedicate this work to all of those who submitted to this book; their words added breadth and depth to our vision and brought the Elders to life in a tangible way.

Just as humans are in transformation so too is the Earth. Therefore, we dedicate this work to the Earth since she is necessary to our survival. This book is also dedicated to all of those people who teach and work towards the day when all humans will live in balance with the other beings who inhabit this planet.

Acknowledgements

To our teachers and Elders, we thank you for your patience, kindness, and commitment and for sharing your wisdom, teachings, and traditions with both of us. You shaped our thoughts, our understanding, and our lives in ways that continue to bless us every day. Thank you.

We would also like to acknowledge the work of those who helped with this book, those who talked with us, debated the topic, and answered our questions. We are indebted to those who shared their personal stories. We thank them for their time, energy and words.

Thank you to our wonderful beta readers: Rebecca Spencer, Karen Thoms, Doug Thoms, and Mowglellan. Your help was immeasurable.

We thank the lovely Drema Deòraich, writer and editor, for her professional comments and valuable assistance.

We offer our gratitude to Storm Constantine and Taylor Ellwood of Megalithica Books who believed in us and in this book.

Table of Contents

Pagan: Our Definition

With this book, we want to increase understanding of Pagan values and offer comparisons between various individuals and groups within that community. When we began interviews for this book, a number of Pagans claimed that no defining holistic Pagan affiliation existed. One of the reasons cited as an argument was the lack of cohesive belief system or unifying concept. We reject that thinking. In fact, it is that diversity that makes Paganism a vibrant and evolving culture.

As authors and as people who work in and serve this community, we believe that all humans and all ages of people have an important place in society. From this foundation, we can discover how Elders influence and carry the Pagan population. Despite the mainstream societal confusion about the place of older people, in both Pagan beliefs and culture, the roles filled by Elders remain valuable — and their positions may become even more important in the future.

If nothing else, Pagans believe in questioning dogma, searching for personal beliefs, accepting a human connection to something greater than the individual (whether "greater" is defined as animist, symbolic, transcendent, or immanent). They believe in following self-determination in both their everyday lives and spiritual paths. Paganism often includes a rejection of specific religious beliefs, such as those of the mainstream dominant society (for example, the Christian necessity for salvation from sin).

Regardless of their rejection of an overarching dogma, individual followers of the various belief systems do coexist, and they frequently gather together for rituals, festivals, and other events. Despite countless variations in terminology or distinctive and specific differences, Pagan community and culture does exist. As one example, Pagans value the Earth and the natural world, even those who seldom leave the city. Specifics of Pagan culture and community will be explained in more detail elsewhere in the chapters of this book.

For the purposes of this book, the term *Pagan* will be used to identify the countless groups that accept Pagan or Neopagan as their identity as well as those who prefer other historical or explicit labels. Just as the label *Christianity* includes countless forms of worship and numerous belief systems, so too does Paganism. However, Paganism is broader than a simple umbrella designation. Certainly it includes many people who follow comparable beliefs, for instance, participants of various Wiccan groups or those who follow an animistic belief system or those who believe in pantheism or polytheism. However, to limit the Pagan community to those with identical or similar beliefs is to ignore a large portion of people who find welcome, support and friendship there.

Truthfully, many of the people within this community do not call themselves Pagans or Neopagans. Individuals may use other titles, such as Heathen, Wiccan or Druid, and a few might reject designations altogether. In fact, Pagans call themselves by many labels, and most certainly, they would offer a variety of definitions for each of those labels. Yet, they are part of the Pagan people.

Our definition of *Pagan* incorporates the variety and range of polytheistic religious groups: those who practice pantheistic, dualistic or non-monotheistic religions, as well as followers of religions based on ancient indigenous, folk or ethnic traditions. Our definition includes Neopaganism, Neoshamanism, Animism, Spiritism, Reclamation Traditions, and other alternative spiritual groups. With this definition, we do not mean to slight unmentioned groups, nor do we ignore the many individuals who do not belong to an organization. We include as part of our definition the large number of individuals who identify as solitary practitioners of the various Pagan traditions and philosophies. In addition, the Pagan community encompasses the diversity of social groups that participate within the general Pagan culture, even those that would not call themselves religious or spiritual.

Rather than limit our survey to specific groups, we chose to involve as many individuals as we could, regardless of disparate or contradictory beliefs. In fact, we endeavored to contact a diverse population in order to include all of that diversity. You can find more details about our survey process in the appendix.

Unfortunately, we cannot mention all of the significant terminology used by specific groups or paths. Utilization of multiple terms, especially those that have not been translated into English — for instance, Seidh, Ovate, Stregha, Olorisha, etc. — would be extremely cumbersome, reduce understanding, and render assessment difficult. Therefore, we chose the word Pagan as a comprehensible term. We define Pagan inclusively and use the term for simplicity and straightforward communication.

The Beginning

We've been asked why we wanted to write this book. The simple answer is that both of us have been part of the Pagan community for more than forty years, actively teaching and counseling others, forming communities, creating and leading rituals. We experienced the social movements of the Sixties that offered people more freedoms, personally and politically, and began to shape the future. We also watched a spiritual evolution that took many different forms, including the rise of the various Pagan traditions. In fact, we participated in a number of those transformations.

Throughout that time, we sought advice from Elders, and through those connections, we realized that experiences with Elders were not only valuable but also necessary. Elders love to reminisce, and we do that quite frequently as well. We love to remember the Elders we have known, studied with, and shared our lives with. When we reached an age where others viewed us as Elders, people came to us asking about our experiences. As we shared meaningful events, audiences formed to listen to our stories, and they said they wanted similar associations. Over the years, during numerous discussions, we heard repeatedly that people wanted to learn from an Elder, wished for one, but had no idea how to do so. The idea for part of this book came from those conversations.

More importantly, we also wanted to honor those who had taught us — and those lessons turned into quite a journey as we traveled through life in search of ourselves, striving for personal growth and spiritual wisdom. Through our explorations and studies, we encountered a lot of synchronistic magic surrounding the people that taught, supported, and pushed us down our paths. This book was written to reveal part of that journey and to share a bit of what others have experienced.

Involvement with Elders help people to define themselves and to find their way in the world, which in turn makes it easier to define their roles in their families and extended communities. In addition, Elders perceive us from different perspectives: they view us differently than we see ourselves. Through that gift, they help move us past our limitations, whether those limits are spiritual, emotional, mental or physical.

Elders are a valuable part of any society, and that includes Pagan culture. They help us to define values, understand social order, explain morality, and offer freedom from sterile or limiting ways of thinking. Our Elders help us to prioritize what is important. Naturally, they provide continuation of teachings, culture, traditions, and social interactions, but they also provide guidance.

If you have the support of an Elder, you have someone to help you figure out the puzzles of life. In addition, Elders can teach you to trust your instincts. An Elder might simply tell you, "You're on the wrong path, walk over there." However, those words may point you to a true-life path; they change you because they move you from where you are to where you need to be.

Before the majority of the population could read, Elders were considered encyclopedias of knowledge and experience. Individually, they didn't know everything, but together they knew what the community needed; together they could help everyone prosper. During a drought, if you needed to know where you could find the deepest water holes, Elders remembered. They knew how to preserve an abundance of pears so the food didn't go to waste. Why do we boil a certain nut before we eat it? The neighborhood medicine person explained. What do we do when aphids invade our garden? Ask your old auntie. What about offering rites of passages to our teens? Your great-uncle and his peers handled that. The old ones could explain how to repair shoes, make a bowl, predict the weather, or teach a child to fish. They offered advice; they shared real knowledge based on experience, and in doing so, provided a connection between the generations. In small villages, they mediated disputes, and when necessary, explained proper behavior to children and adults alike. They held the family and society together.

> In African society, elders can be seen as positive mentors in the community. Old age is important in Africa because the older one is, the more they are respected and valued in the community.
> - Michael Banutu-Gomez,
> *Africa: We Owe it to Our Ancestors,*
> *Our Children, and Ourselves.*

Today, the majority of our interactions can be mediated; that is, they can be distanced by technology. We can interact with another individual completely online and never meet in person. For instance, we can obtain a recipe on the internet and watch a video to learn how to make cookies, but that cannot compare with the extraordinary experience of learning how to make your great-grandmother's brownies with your grandmother. The first offers only a basic recipe, which might lead to a tasty dish or a failure, while the second brings a sense of family continuity and permanence. Although technology offers a wonderful variety of learning experiences, the knowledge gained online cannot reach the levels achieved firsthand with an expert. After the death of a grandparent, how many people have struggled to recreate that special cookie recipe? They might come close, but they fall short of the special taste and texture. Perhaps she added a pinch of an ingredient that was never noted on the recipe card or maybe she stirred the mixture exactly 100 times. In any case, her cookie recipe evolved through trial and error — and how she perfected the recipe cannot be relayed through a piece of paper.

Just as an individual who learns cooking from a grandparent feels a connection to the family ancestors, each of us can benefit through training with a master whether we are studying crafts, spiritual traditions, or ethnic customs. Imagine trying to learn a foreign language with no one to talk to. The computer cannot tell you if you are pronouncing words correctly, only another human being who speaks the language can do that.

For centuries, that is how people learned: they were taught through interactions with grandparents and older community members who were valued for their knowledge. In many traditional cultures, especially in Asia or Africa, the Elders remain important even in death. That practice continues in countries as diverse as Japan and Nigeria. Following a practice handed down through generations, contemporary families offer prayers to them so that they can work on behalf of their families from the other side. Currently, religions of the African Diaspora, countless indigenous spiritual paths, and many Pagan traditions continue to honor ancestors and other dead.

Although Pagan and alternative cultures merge with mainstream society, they are vastly different. Pagan culture embraces old traditional viewpoints as it creates new ones. It accepts those who feel marginalized from the majority culture as well as those who succeed in the mainstream culture. Because of its evolution away from Judeo-Christian society, Pagan culture has no difficulty embracing unconventional or even unorthodox ideas. For example, consider the controversy over the right of same-sex couples to marry and raise children; Pagan groups embraced those families decades before U.S. "defense of marriage" laws were overturned.

Based on that distinction, we wanted to see if Pagans differed from majority society in regard to attitudes about Elders. Therefore, we created a questionnaire and asked many people to comment. We are thankful for those individuals who responded, and we included quotes from everyone who did. In addition, we interviewed individuals by telephone and in person. At public Pagan events, we talked with people, asked questions, and started conversations. We spoke to friends and strangers. The contributors came from a variety of traditions; they ranged from beginners to those with life-long involvement in the Pagan community. A few were solitary practitioners while others were leaders of spiritual groups and considered Elders. A number of people permitted us to share their personal stories. Our research process is further explained in the Method section of the Appendices.

All of those investigations were invaluable, and numerous quotations resulted from them. However, early in the process, we realized that we could only include a portion of those conversations. Once we gathered the answers, we discovered similarities and analyzed differences. Our discoveries gave us a few puzzles and a lot of hope. Repeatedly, we were reminded that interactions with Elders had helped people learn, heal, change and evolve.

This book speaks of the societal changes we have experienced regarding attitudes about older people. It gives a context for reclaiming, acknowledging, and supporting the diverse roles of Elders, especially in our spiritual communities. But more than that, the information gathered within these pages offers an adventure that can support your own personal path. You will gain insight into finding an Elder and learn how to create and maintain relationships with one. Additional topics include the cultural roles filled by Elders, help with navigating the ways they communicate, and how to be present for the experience. Finally, we cover how to create ceremonies to acknowledge your Elders and even how to say goodbye to them when your time with them is over.

This has been a labor of love, and it is an offering to all of you. We wish for you the same joy and wonder that filled our lives as we took the journey on our own search for wisdom, mystery, magic, and connection to our Elders. Step into the stories shared in this book. As you share in the stories and experiences of others, allow them to mingle with your own personal mythology. Through them, we'll find a definition of these distinctive individuals called Elders. We'll discover how special experiences with them have influenced others. We'll see how Elders have impressed their knowledge on culture and society, and understand how they will continue to do so.

Shifting Roles

In the decades since World War II, both US society and family structure have greatly changed. Prior to WWII, millions of people resided on farms[1], typically with three or four generations living and working together. During WWI and WWII, traditional gender-based employment plummeted because women grew to be indispensable in all areas of the workforce. Remember the famous poster of Rosie the Riveter? However, the core of society considered that a temporary fix.

After WWII, women were expected to leave their jobs, marry the returning soldiers, and begin families — and for the most part they complied. The concept of the nuclear family was born. Between WWII and the end of the Twentieth Century, society ranked it as the preeminent family structure; that is, the standard used to judge families became one female married to one male living with their children. No longer were older relatives included in the household (although typically they still lived nearby). After WWII, US corporations grew rapidly. At the same time, agriculture, no longer focused on small farms, moved into the realm of big business.

---

[1] US Department of Agriculture. "Ag and Food Statistics: Charting the Essentials" (2014).

However, during WWI and WWII, many women had tasted the freedom offered by having their own livelihoods. Even those who were happy to begin families no longer accepted all of the historical limitations projected onto them. Many scholars view this transformation as instrumental to the foundation of the Women's Movement — with its progeny to rise in the advancement of Goddess spirituality and the drive for LGBTQ rights. Eventually the changes in social expectations (especially among women) became linked with the financial downturn to influence the growth of two-income families.

Family structure was not the only change; in the same period, US economic potential shifted too. Throughout the following decades, cycles of inflation and recession led to deindustrialization. As the economic boom faded, US society became more mobile. These factors forced the family further apart because people moved around as certain areas thrived while other regions declined. While the shift away from family farms triggered dissociation between generations, now they were isolated by distance. For example, children no longer visited after school with grandparents; instead they went to latchkey arrangements.

Soon, families were faced with the banking and housing crisis. When finances became unpredictable and social expectations shifted again, these two factors merged together in people's minds and created an assumption that both the social order and economic opportunities were capricious. Reactions to these altered relationships and financial crises have been far from consistent. Even when the transformations were positive, they disrupted historical social structures.

Based on frustration and anger, countless people looked for someone to blame for their personal hardships and economic troubles. Certainly, their view of the world can be divided into a dualistic concept of "us versus them," an attitude that leads to the simplistic attribution of problems to a scapegoat. Some people found one in blaming the older generation(s) while others blamed people of color or women workers. Conflicting expectations have moved contemporary alliances towards exclusion. In other words, certain groups have begun to manifest simplistic definitions for those they consider qualified for membership and those within a specific faction have less communication and limited interactions with "outsiders" or between divisions. A few, longing for an idealized perception of the past, pushed for a return to the ideal of the nuclear family.

However, the nuclear family has now become an uncommon situation. Families are not in danger of dying (as politicians tend to rant) — far from it. However, the concept of family has changed. By 2013, the Pew Research Center found that not even half of US children lived in families with married heterosexual parents[2]. According to the US Census of 2010, families are made up of single parent homes as well as homes with unmarried partners; of homes with married partners, approximately half a million comprise same sex couples with children. In addition, households with more than two adults, including multigenerational families, are once again increasing in numbers.

Historically, our culture embodied certain clear-cut expectations in each generation. Elders rose from the oldest-living generation and stood as role models; they were living libraries of needed wisdom. Now many families have lost the family traditions that were taught by the oldest generation. Certainly, the proliferation of information through the internet has impacted that position too. Within the dominant culture, contemporary intergenerational relationships are rarely based on reciprocal need and respect, a situation that has further confused generational roles. Although some have reacted with fear, anger and anxiety, many people have embraced the changes, finding liberation in shifting roles and variable societal expectations. All of these transformations have created a society in which social expectations about gender roles and generational positions have shifted.

Intergenerational Healing and Paganism

While relationship interactions can influence ethical and moral concepts, many other factors impact those attitudes. Media,

---

[2] Gretchen Livingston, "Fewer than half of U.S. kids today live in a 'traditional' family" *Pew Research Center* http://www.pewresearch.org/fact-tank/2014/12/22/less-than-half-of-u-s-kids-today-live-in-a-traditional-family/ (accessed 1/26/2017).

religion, music, peers and education also contribute to individual or group beliefs. Still, no one culture or religion holds the key to morality and principles. In response to the realization that many of the previously accepted concepts are now ineffective, individuals discover that their earlier worldview is no longer functional or beneficial. Frankly, our society is struggling to determine what is important. Although a few individuals find comfort in returning to childhood religions, others completely reject inherited concepts, including the beliefs and symbols that arose from familial, cultural, or religious traditions.

When faced with a spiritual tradition, especially one handed down through uncounted generations from parent to child, each individual will eventually ask: "Should I continue to follow this path? Does this bring value to my life?" Although a few individuals find comfort in returning to childhood religions, numerous people completely reject inherited concepts, including the beliefs and symbols that arose from familial, cultural, or religious traditions. Often the seekers describe themselves as searching for what is missing. According to a Pew Research Center survey in 2010, 66 million people in the US were considering leaving Christianity for a different spiritual path. In the same survey, 59 million people were religiously unaffiliated, and many of those were also searching for a new faith.

As numerous people leave Christianity, quite a few of them will discover Paganism. In fact, many current members of our population have embarked on a similar quest (to use classical literary terms) before being welcomed into our community. When these individuals find a mentor, they will be given new or updated symbolism to replace the rejected religious imagery. This will invigorate their spirituality and offer a foundational worldview to support their health, assist with evolution, and establish a connection to the divine — or a concept of vast significance. This change brings revitalization to the individual as well as the community.

Pinpointing facts about the number of US Pagans takes diligence. Unfortunately, the largest religious research institute, Pew Research Center, redefines categories from year to year. In addition, it often groups together unaffiliated religions or conflicting faiths. Despite that confusion, numbers do exist. Consistently in the last decade, Pew's US surveys reported a growth in non-mainstream religions.

In 2007, a Pew Research reported that 1.5% of the US population identify with other faiths, including Pagan, Wiccan, Druid, Native American spiritual and other pantheist or polytheist religions[3]. Since the US population in 2007 was estimated at a bit over 301 million, Pew's report would imply that more than 4.5 million people were willing to identify as Pagans or Neopagans that year.

During the next survey in 2010, Pew rejected the previous categories. Rather than list specific non-mainstream faiths (and despite the statistics from 2007), Pew grouped Wicca and similar religions under the label "other religions." Further complicating analysis, the organization determined the definition of the category "other religions" separately for each country[4]. Even with that unclear cataloging, Pew projected that the category would almost triple in size by 2050[5]. In 2010, Pew also separated out folk religions, which it defined as being associated with indigenous peoples or ethnicity, such as Native American and African traditional religions[6]. At that time, the rate of growth for those practicing a folk religion was forecast to be 100%[7].

Recent research has supported both of those changes and indicated a reduction in people claiming to be Christian; in fact, the percentage of those reporting as Christians has dropped to half of what it was forty years ago. Certainly, this response appears in research even when alternative religions are lumped

---

[3] "Chapter 1: The Changing Religious Composition of the U.S." *Religion and Public Life* (Pew Research Center, 2017). Retrieved June 15, 2017, from www.pewforum.org/2015/05 /12/chapter-1-the-changing-religious-composition-of-the-u-s/.

[4] "Spotlight on Other Religions" *The Global Religious Landscape* (Pew Research Center, 2012). Retrieved June 15, 2017, from http://www.pewforum.org/ 2012/12/18/global-religious-landscape-other/#spotlight.

[5] "The Future of World Religions: Population Growth Projections, 2010-2050 North America." *Pew Forum.* (Pew Research Center, 2015). Retrieved June 15, 2017, from http://www.pewforum.org/2015/04/02/north-america/.

[6] "Appendix C: Defining the Religious Groups." The Future of World Religions: Population Group Projections, 2010-2050 (Pew Research Center, 2015). Retrieved June 15, 2017, from http://assets.pewresearch.org/wp-content/uploads/sites/11 /2015/04/PF_15.04.02_ProjectionsAppendixC.pdf .

[7] "The Future of World Religions: Population Growth Projections, 2010-2050 North America." *Pew Forum.* (Pew Research Center, 2015). Retrieved June 15, 2017, from http://www.pewforum.org/2015/04/02/north-america/.

into vague designations such as "other religions" or "folk religions."[8] These statistics (and others) support the claim that many people will switch to Paganism in the next few decades.

People who reject childhood religions and past spiritual symbolism are attracted to the flexibility and accommodating paths offered by Pagan practices. Especially when people perceive mainstream communities to be lacking in support systems, individuals enter the Pagan community searching for alternative viewpoints. In the Pagan community, they find fresh concepts, innovative philosophies, and traditions that offer renewed symbolic meanings. As Pagan Elders teach new concepts and spiritual practices, they provide rejuvenated and life-affirming associations. Because of the diversity within Paganism, Elders (by whatever title) fill a variety of powerful roles, providing guidance and stability.

In order to develop into a healthy society in the future, all of the generations will be required. Mainstream culture will need to embrace beneficial intergenerational relationships. To assist with that, Elders will be essential; they will need to move back into historically important roles not only in alternative groups but also in mainstream society. Due to the ancient wisdom at the foundation of their alternative belief systems, specific Pagan communities already recognize the place of Elders. However, Pagan communities need to define and clarify the functions of those Elders before they can extend their attitudes throughout the dominant culture.

Through experimentation with new ideas, Pagans discover liberating alternatives to dysfunctional interpersonal relationships and to inconsistent but standardized societal roles. Later they share those valid and vibrant changes with people uninvolved in the Pagan community. In addition, they are willing to investigate the shortcomings of their culture, specifically in areas of human rights, diversity, and inclusion. As a result, Pagan groups could be at the forefront of restoring positive intergenerational interactions. Their support of various

---

[8] "Appendix C: Defining the Religious Groups." Pew Research Center *The Future of World Religions: Population Group Projections*, 2010-2050 (Pew Research Center, 2015). Retrieved June 15, 2017, from http://assets.pewresearch.org/wp-content/uploads/sites/11/2015/04/PF_15.04.02_ProjectionsAppendixC.pdf .

alternative lifestyles has already influenced society, and so it is logical that Pagans are capable of extending their intergenerational acceptance and recognition of elderhood into mainstream society. In this way, Pagan communities have a rare opportunity to remind the majority culture that all people have a place in the circle of life.

People all over the U.S. have a dawning recognition that things are not quite right, and their discomfort creates a realization that we need each other in ways that we might not prefer. Pagan culture could very well show the larger majority how individuals can appreciate each other so that we can work together to create a beneficial future. For example, we might not always comprehend goths, hip-hop musicians, hipsters, hillbillies or even grumpy white-haired veterans, but the interaction of individuals from those groups brings vibrancy and strength to our civilization. By re-establishing beneficial ways to connect to the past, we can learn from those who came before us, use their knowledge to avoid past mistakes, and create the future we want to see in the world. That future requires that we reestablish respectful intergenerational interactions that value all the stages of life. In order to do that, we must examine and redefine the concepts embedded in our culture relating to the place of Elders in society.

With this book, we are not proposing a return to the old way of doing things (whatever that truly means), but a return to an old wisdom: the realization that the bonds that hold us together are necessary for society. Those bonds are not based on laws, but on relationships. In fact, the ties themselves will help us to develop holistically and harmoniously.

Our Pagan Culture

In order to define Elder status and determine their position within Pagan society, it was necessary for us to review the ideas that define culture and community. We are all descended from tribal societies and cultures. Many of us feel we have lost the connections to our ancestors and wish to rediscover that sense of community. Since human beings are social creatures, we desire to connect, communicate, and express ourselves within a group of like-minded people. Therefore, we search for a common kinship, fellowship, and a sense of belonging. This quest propels us to join together in small groups. Through those interactions, we design unique expressions of our worldviews.

As Pagans, we exist within the greater Western culture of our country. Yet, we create our own subculture as we search for and find others that are most in tune with our beliefs, chosen lifestyles, and personal self-expression. However, the Pagan culture is not always recognized as distinct from that of the greater society. When we began interviews for this book, a number of Pagans claimed that a defining holistic Pagan affiliation did not exist. We reject this viewpoint. Through a review of historical, sociological and spiritual viewpoints, we considered the pieces that combine to create our expanding Pagan culture. The subculture of Paganism is a unique evolving expression of our changing world.

A Bit of History

While it is difficult to pinpoint the contemporary rebirth of Paganism, many facets of it rose out of respect for the Earth, a desire to connect with nature, and an interest in ancient beliefs and folk practices. Another origin of the Pagan culture was a response to limitations in the dominant culture, especially in areas of social freedom and social responsibility. Although reconstructed traditions were uncommon until mid-Twentieth Century, the beginnings of the modern Pagan movement were earlier. In fact, prior to WWI, Druidic orders were well established in the United Kingdom.

Dion Fortune (1890-1946), was a prominent British occultist, mystic, and author. As a student of Western esotericism, she was influential in the modern revival of the magical arts. Students of Wicca and various magical traditions continue to study her works. Two of her novels, *The Sea Priestess* and *Moon Magic*, became influential within the Goddess Movement and Wicca. The best remembered of her magical books are: *The Cosmic Doctrine*, teachings on mysticism, *Psychic Self-Defense*, about protection from psychic attacks, and *The Mystical Qabalah*, an introduction to Hermetic Qabalah. The last book was first published in England in 1935 and is still regarded as one of the best books on magic.

Others were also very influential in the forming the Pagan culture and community. Sybil Leek (1917-1982) was an English witch, astrologer, psychic, and occult author. Known as "Britain's most famous witch," she rose to media fame in the 1950s after the repeal of the Witchcraft Act. Through her writings, she had an effect upon the formation of Neopagan Witchcraft, the religion of Wicca, and contemporary astrology.

Wicca as a revitalized modern practice originated in the early Twentieth Century in England with the influence of Gerald Gardner (1884-1964), who was initiated into the Craft of Wicca in 1939, and Alex Sanders (1926-1988) and Maxine Sanders (1946-), founders of Alexandrian Witchcraft. Soon it was propagated by organizations such as the Witchcraft Research Association. After the faith was transported to the United States, these pioneers were joined by a growing list of authors who expanded knowledge of Pagan practices. The names are now famous. Although there are too many to list, they include Raymond Buckland (1934-2017) and Doreen Valiente (1922-1999). They brought previously secret methods to the forefront allowing Wicca and Witchcraft to become new expressions of spirituality.

In 1968, Oberon Zell (1942-) and R. Lance Christie (1944-2010) founded the Church of All Worlds (CAW), the first Pagan church in the US. That same year, Zell created *Green Egg*. Originally printed as a newsletter, it developed into an international magazine and is still available as an e-zine.

Also in 1968, Gavin Frost (1930-2016) and Yvonne Frost (1931-), began the coven that would develop into The Church and School of Wicca, which gained federal tax exempt status in 1972. By 1978, their correspondence courses were well established. In 1985, their book and teachings were considered influential in a Virginia's District Court ruling that declared Wicca to be a legitimate religion, and in 1986, the Federal Appeals Court upheld that decision. The Church and School of Wicca still offers a complete curriculum of correspondence courses.

Throughout these decades, the issues of woman's rights and the political empowerment of women had an enormous social impact. This awareness boosted the establishment of Goddess worship traditions in the modern Pagan movement, resulting in the creation of associations such as the Fellowship of Isis founded in 1976 by Olivia Robertson (1917-2013), her brother and sister-in-law. Despite its name, the FOI is dedicated to honoring all goddesses and pantheons. The membership remains active and includes events worldwide.

Around the same time, other organizations were formed, such as Circle Sanctuary, an international spirituality resource center founded in 1974 and headquartered on a nature preserve in Wisconsin. Its leader, Selena Fox (1949-) continues to be a driving force in the Pagan and Wiccan communities. In addition, the Lady Liberty League (LLL), the political arm of Circle Sanctuary, focuses on religious freedom and civil rights.

Starhawk (1951-), a pioneer and author of many works celebrating the Goddess movement and Earth-based, feminist spirituality, describes herself as: "a peace, environmental, and global justice activist and trainer, a permaculture designer and teacher, a Pagan and Witch."[9] She was one of the founders of the Reclaiming Collective, a group that began to stage public celebrations in the Seventies. Influential authors of the collective have included M. Macha Nightmare, T. Thorn Coyle, Diane Baker, and Anne Hill.

Soon a drive emerged to understand the historical roots and esoteric underpinnings of Paganism. Publications expanded to encompass those areas too. In 1979, Margot Adler (1946-2014) published her sociological study of Paganism in the United States. As a well-known journalist, her book, *Drawing Down the Moon: Witches, Druids, Goddess-Worshippers, and Other Pagans in America*

---

[9] Starhawk. "Peace, the Environment, Global Justice and Magic" (2015). Retrieved January 8, 2015, from http://starhawk.org/.

Today, galvanized interest throughout US society. The following year, Michael Harner (1929-) published his influential work, *The Way of the Shaman*. In addition, Isaac Bonewits (1949-2010) not only authored many books on Druidism, Paganism, and magic, but also influenced a number of US Druid movements. In 1983, he founded Ár nDraíocht Féin. Ronald Hutton (1953-), writing as a scholar, published books focused on British folklore, ancient Druidry, and the pre-Christian foundations of Paganism. Also beginning in the Eighties, another famous author, Scott Cunningham (1956-1993), wrote for the solitary practitioner. With his books, Wicca could be practiced in private with no need for a group or an initiation. Thus, he made Wicca available to anyone.

Throughout the Eighties, the contemporary Pagan movement began to solidify. It incorporated early influences, a variety of spiritual beliefs, and social awareness into an evolving culture that continues to develop today. Everything that mattered to the individuals in the various historic subgroups merged together and evolved into unique systems. Each way progressed from spiritual questioning that experimented with methods of practice and study and incorporated community and environmental issues. All of them embraced the freedom to create new ways of being, expressing and becoming.

From these varied and independent influences, we now find a culture that can be recognized by diverse customs and behaviors. In fact, these early influential individuals, and countless others, became Elders for contemporary Pagans. By publicly sharing their spiritual philosophies and beliefs, a new movement spread. Not only did they transform religious views and create innovative spiritual paths, their achievements were foundation stones of what is now a vibrant Pagan culture.

Cultural Identification and Beliefs

In general, social anthropologists, sociologists, and scientists explain *culture* as "shared characteristics of a group." Typically, group qualities include similarities in language, music and the arts, food, social activities, religious beliefs, and beliefs about death. How does Pagan culture incorporate those categories?

Due to its diverse beginnings, Paganism is a collection of various subgroups or subcultures. Because it is possible to find acceptance and expression of personal life experiences, circumstances and personal choices, whether they are spiritual, political or societal, many different kinds of people are able to form supportive relationships with others in the Pagan community. Pagans strive to be nonjudgmental. Polyamory is viewed as a life choice and a personal spiritual expression. Pagan communities are accepting of LGBTQ community, that is, people who describe themselves as lesbian, gay, bisexual, transgender or queer. In addition, many Pagans will help with the political struggles of this group or at the least, they will offer emotional support. Children are afforded a place within the community, and many festivals incorporate children's programming. Most Pagans with children are raising them in the family's chosen spiritual path. In addition, Pagans who have special needs, health concerns or are aging, find that others are very willing to help them if they need it. Some festivals have designated special areas for camping for those with such concerns. Most importantly, spiritual subgroups that exist within the greater Pagan culture are generally tolerant of other groups, even those with different beliefs.

Despite the belief in inclusiveness, as of this writing, many groups in the Pagan culture seem to be relatively homogenous. Some individuals think that Paganism should focus on people of European decent. A few delineate ancestry more specifically as individuals from Celtic origins — ignoring the long history of witchcraft and folk religions in Eastern Europe, Italy, Russia, Africa, and elsewhere. However, most believe that Paganism should bring together all who self-identify as Pagan regardless of their ancestral backgrounds.

Although Wicca's roots were easily transferred from English speaking lands, ancient Paganism was not merely British. Scholarly studies of the origins of Paganism are typically limited in scope, for instance, focusing on a specific religion or on Western European history. In general, they are controversial because they tend to be written by non-practitioners. However, the number of available books increases yearly[10]. Prior to the spread of

---

[10] The authors are not professional historians but offer the following books for those who wish to delve further into the history of Paganism. The titles include

Christianity, the forerunners of contemporary Paganism existed globally; they were practitioners in small remote villages, members of large societies, and citizens of state-based religions. They and their ancestors lived in countries all over the world. Consequently, it would be sad if Pagan culture did not continue to grow in diversity.

A number of books focus on topics related to diversity within Paganism[11]. An anthology written by and about people of color called *Shades of Faith*, edited by Crystal Blanton[12], has been well received. One recent anthology, *Bringing Race to the Table: Exploring Racism in the Pagan Community*, has led to beneficial and animated conversations about modern and historical racism, indigenous spirituality, and cultural appropriation — topics of concern to Pagans who want to help create a better future for everyone[13]. Slightly older books have grown in popularity due to the expanding awareness of the beliefs and practices of the African Diaspora and Afro-Caribbean Pagan religions. One of

---

Modern Paganism in World Cultures: Comparative Perspectives, Michael Strmiska, Editor (ABC-CLIO, 2005); *America's Alternative Religions*, Timothy Miller, Editor (State University of New York Press, 1995); and *The Earth, the Gods and the Soul: A History of Pagan Philosophy from the Iron Age to the 21st Century* by Brendan Myers (Moon Books, 2013). *Introducing Latino/a Theologies* by Miguel A. De LA Torre and Edwin David Aponte (Orbis Books, 2001) is a review of Latino/a beliefs; although the text includes non-Pagan religions, it is one of the few books available for Latino/a people. For the history and a summary of the religions that evolved from the fusion of Traditional African religions with indigenous practices, check out *Afro-Caribbean Religions: An Introduction to Their Historical, Cultural, and Sacred Traditions* by Nathaniel Samuel Murrell (Temple University Press, 2009). Of course, there are well-known classic texts. Originally printed in 1979, an excellent book for United States Paganism is *Drawing Down the Moon: Witches, Druids, Goddess-Worshippers, and Other Pagans in America* by Margot Adler (Penguin Books, 2006). Covering Wicca in Great Britain, *The Triumph of the Moon: A History of Modern Pagan Witchcraft* was written by Ronald Hutton (Oxford University Press, 1999).

[11] The authors do not speak for any of these sub-communities within Paganism and provide the suggested books as resources for interested readers; perhaps they will provide a basis for education and respectable discussions.

[12] Crystal Blanton, Editor. *Shades of Faith* (Megalithica Books, 2011).

[13] Blanton, Crystal, Taylor Ellwood, and Brandy Williams, Editors. *Bringing Race to the Table: Exploring Racism in the Pagan Community* (Megalithica Books, 2015).

those titles is Stephanie Rose Bird's *The Big Book of Soul*[14]. Another book, Luisah Teish's *Jambalaya* continues to be popular and currently ranks in the top twenty in sacred texts category on Amazon.com[15]. In addition, there are several Pagan organizations devoted to minority races or ethnicities, such as the African-American Wiccan Society, the Ausar Auset Society, which has chapters in many countries, and a recently established convention called Dawtas of the Moon.

Rather than ignoring the difficult issues rising from sexual and gender variations (as mainstream culture tends to do), Paganism confronts these issues. A recent publication was Yvonne Aburrow's *All Acts of Love and Pleasure*[16], which strives to motivate covens to include people with disabilities as well as those of various sexual orientations. Just published, Carolina Dean's *Secrets of a Sissy Boy*, provides spells based on a merger of Witchcraft, Christianity and Hoodoo, and it ranges from autobiography to self-help tips and from ancestor reverence to conjuring work[17]. Although published in 1997, a book that provides a starting point for exploring LGBTQ mythology and symbolism is *Cassell's Encyclopedia of Queer Myth, Symbol and Spirit: Gay, Lesbian, Bisexual and Transgendered Lore*[18]. Michael Thomas Ford's *The Path of the Green Man* is also not a new book, but the focus on Wicca for gay men keeps it on suggested reading lists[19]. Raven Kaldera's *Hermaphrodeities: The Transgender*

---

[14] Bird, Stephanie Rose. *The Big Book of Soul: The Ultimate Guide to the African American Spirit: Legends and Lore, Music and Mysticism and Recipes and Rituals* (Hampton Roads Publishing, 2010).

[15] Teish, Luisah. *Jambalaya: The Natural Woman's Book of Personal Charms and Practical Rituals* (HarperOne, 1988).

[16] Yvonne Aburrow. *All Acts of Love and Pleasure: Inclusive Wicca.* (Avalonia Press, 2014).

[17] Dean, Carolina. *Secrets of a Sissy Boy: A Gay Grimoire of Modern Magic for Men Who Love Men and the Hags Who Worship Them* (CreateSpace Independent Publishing Platform, 2016).

[18] Conner, Randy P. *Cassell's Encyclopedia of Queer Myth, Symbol and Spirit: Gay, Lesbian, Bisexual and Transgendered Lore* (Cassell, 1997).

[19] Ford, Michael Thomas. *The Path of the Green Man: Gay Men, Wicca and Living a Magical Life* (Citadel, 2005).

Spirituality Workbook[20] provides a manual for transsexual or transitioning Pagans.

Particularly when a community is not homogeneous, people must discuss boundaries and expectations, and learn how to cooperate and reach compromise. Perhaps more importantly, they must decide when negotiations and concessions are wrong. A recently published book tackles the difficult questions that can arise in Pagan society: *Pagan Consent Culture*, edited by Christine Hoff Kraemer and Yvonne Aburrow; the book offers arguments and perspectives from viewpoints as varied as Wicca, Druidry, Neoshamanism, autism, and feminism[21]. After disagreements about gender caused a public division at a national conference, the anthology *Gender and Transgender in Modern Paganism* was written to provide insight into misunderstandings, highlight challenges, and propose resolutions[22]. The willingness to discuss such topics and to improve interaction within the community provides evidence of a significant commitment to respectful inclusion.

In fact, Pagans value individuality in a variety of expressions. They accept and strive for a personal connection to the Divine, to a greater power, however they define that. "I can decide for myself" is the consistent identifier of what a Pagan practices and believes. This thought infuses, first and foremost, the various spiritual beliefs of all people that identify themselves as Pagans or Neopagans. Some Pagans are atheists or scientists, but they still find a home within this community. Whether they are interested in Folk Magic, Hoodoo, Wicca, Heathenry, Druidism, Kemetism, Lucumi, Voodoo, Shamanism, Earth traditions, various Native American beliefs, or ancestor reverence, Pagans believe that it is their right, perhaps even duty or obligation, to find their own way and decide for themselves.

Truly, Pagans will search for years until they find a suitable spiritual path, religion or spirituality. Many feel comfortable with

---

[20] Kaldera, Raven. *Hermaphrodeities: The Transgender Spirituality Workbook* (Asphodel Press, 2010).
[21] Kraemer, Christine Hoff and Yvonne Aburrow, Editors. *Pagan Consent Culture* (Asphodel Press, 2016).
[22] Pond, Gina, Sarah Thompson, et. al. *Gender And Transgender In Modern Paganism* (Circle of Cerridwen Press, 2012).

mixing various traditions to get the right fit for themselves. Some reconstruct ancient traditions by researching old writings. Recently individuals have created new practices incorporating, for example, chaos magic, Neoshamanism, modified Wicca, or genres that include vampirism, fairies, dragons, and werewolves to meet the needs of their shifting perspectives and the changing world.

Such acceptance of integration within spiritual paths can lead to obvious divergent attitudes. For example, drug usage can be accepted or rejected. Timothy Leary and others introduced the idea that mind-altering substances could enhance our spiritual lives. A number of Pagans accepted that viewpoint. Because of that, various drugs used by Shamans in indigenous cultures are generally well received, but numerous people reject all drugs. They favor altering perception through meditation or dietary changes. Within the Pagan community, freedom to self-express in all of these ways is acknowledged.

Often public rituals at Pagan festivals are designed to include common themes from various faiths. Pagans expect to be accepted, and this belief is what makes the community hold together, even when it appears to be a loose connection between groups or practitioners of different belief systems. The trust that Pagans feel, expecting and knowing that they are accepted, allows them the freedom to explore their own spirituality, as well as personal choices, and modes of self-expression. This carries over into other aspects of their lives. Countless Pagans believe the motto, "do as you will, harm no one," is the right way to live a life that is spiritually or magically driven.

Language

Language is the first and foremost identifier of a culture or subculture since it is necessary that everyone communicate with each other. In the United States, we have English as a primary language, but Pagans use certain words within this common language more frequently or with a more nuanced meaning. In addition, most people in the Pagan community have shared words to describe their beliefs, discuss spirits and deity, and explain their relationships with other people and to the planet.

For example, the word *energy* is used to describe the quality of a location, time or person; it encompasses more than a visual recall of these events. Energy is used to describe people's interaction with all that is going on around them, the way the situation makes them feel, and their reactions to what they can see, hear, smell, taste or touch. Commonly, the energy of an individual or situation is described with innumerable variations, such as serene, happy, sad, strong, creepy, dangerous, or focused. Most Pagans believe that a common focus is necessary for smooth and productive relationships, and specifically, shared energy is a requirement of good rituals or ceremonies.

Typically words such as priest and magician pop up in conversations, often with very different meanings from the ones used in mainstream culture. For instance, *priest* is a common term for a Pagan spiritual leader and the word *magician* is not limited to stagecraft or entertainment but refers to someone who studies specific metaphysical systems.

In addition, many Pagans learn words and phrases from ancient languages or use ceremonial terms taken from the country where that spiritual path developed. Listen to a gathering of Pagans and you will hear terms from many languages, such as athame, talisman, boline, karma, and chakra — and the term pagan itself comes from Latin.

Names

The concept of naming holds great importance within Pagan culture. Although some Pagans use their legal names, many consider taking a Pagan name as almost a rite of passage. Rather than a nickname based on the legal name, the chosen name can be a designation of beliefs or a statement of a spiritual goal. In fact, the name might be an act of liberation or an affirmation of commitment. Individuals might pick names to represent their ancestry, their connection to a certain aspect of nature, or their interest in a specific tradition. A number of practitioners acquire a name during a transition in their lives. Others may receive a name from a teacher or through an initiation. Some keep the name secret and reveal it only to their closest friends, but many use the names during rituals, magical practices, and coven events.

Even more people utilize one at public events. Certainly many Pagans also pick a name to maintain anonymity. While contemporary Pagans might not have the historical threat of imminent danger, modern news reports offer various reasons for use of a pseudonym to remain anonymous in certain situations. Public use of a specially chosen name can protect individuals from the impact that misunderstood religious beliefs and practices could have on employment or legal situations.

Art and Its Expressions

Typically, musicians are the first people hired for Pagan festivals or Pagan Pride Days. Songs have been written specifically for Pagans that include lyrics about nature, deities, Goddess themed chants, and even tongue-in-cheek tunes about Goth girls. A variety of musical expression is greatly appreciated and supported. At a Pagan festival, musicians might play acoustic or flamenco guitar, folk music, Irish and Celtic music, Brazilian music, jazz, or electronic music. There are troupes formed exclusively of drummers. All of these styles of music can happen at the same event.

Clothing is another indicator of culture. Pagan styles of dress can be expressive! The colors of choice for countless Pagans are black or purple. Many Pagans wear capes or robes with hoods for ceremonies and rituals. Influences of the diverse spiritual practices and personal traditions inspire apparel. Students of traditions of indigenous people wear leather, fur and animal parts. The New Age movement lends its expression through flowing shirts, pants and dresses. Many Pagans also like to go to reenactment events and are inspired by renaissance clothing complete with ruffles, corsets, and gathered skirts. Additional clothing choices come from other subcultures such as pirate outfits, steampunk, and Goth. Often, the selection of garments, color and adornment, including belts or hat style, will signify rank or initiation status. Although clothing can be worn just for fun, generally it is considered a way to show personal truth and beliefs.

Beyond clothing, Pagans accept body tattoos and piercings, admired not only for beauty, but also as a way to capture or release energy. Since body adornment is important to most

Pagans, jewelry is crafted in magical shapes such as pentacles, circles, mythical creatures or Celtic imagery. Frequently people wear stones that have special spiritual significance. Jewelry can adorn not just the body but also the head. It can be worn as a crown or circlet to designate initiation into various Wiccan or other traditions. Pagans express their creativity with jewelry that decorates the face, neck, hands, arms, nipples — literally anywhere that someone can figure out a way to create enhancements to fit the area of the body.

Many Pagans have an affinity with the arts in one form or another. They act, draw, paint, craft, garden and farm, write, dance, sing, and play musical instruments. Some have revived traditional crafts or trades such as drum making, hand crafted pottery, or blacksmithing. Many practice the art of healing through herbalism, aromatherapy, massage, or ritual. Through self-employment, they offer their unique talents in the community. If they are not artists in these ways, Pagans support artists within their communities emotionally and financially, buying artwork, using tarot cards designed by Pagans, going to concerts, and reading blogs, magazines and books written by other Pagans. We write novels that include references to Pagan beliefs or focus on characters that include Wiccans, magicians, and magical beings or creatures such as the Fey, vampires and werewolves. We write about each other. Within the reclamation traditions, Pagans write how-to manuals for practitioners of these practices; we write books for others on the theory, philosophy, and rituals of our various paths. In addition, authors continue to research and write about Pagan community and culture.

As a subculture we have been the subject of documentaries and news stories; have started our own publications; have created blogs and websites; and have even founded publishing companies. In recent years, there has been a trend with Pagans exploring the use of video or film to tell a story. There have been some movies released that were adapted from personal writings or from novels they have written. Jane Hash created her documentary *Plain Jane the Shockumentary* about her life as a Pagan with special needs. It has been well received, even in the mainstream culture. Currently the novel *The Fifth Sacred Thing* by Starhawk is working on funding for a movie version, hopefully acquired from the Pagan community.

Food

As humans we love to get together and socialize and share food. When Pagans gather for ceremony or ritual or "just because," a potluck is common. Sharing food ranges from feasts scheduled for hundreds of people to small ritualized gatherings like blots. They include mead tasting events, tea room nights or "let's all bring a dessert and hang out" visits. Although most Pagans seem to be carnivores who appreciate a good steak, food choices vary greatly. Many individuals prepare dishes similar to what their ancestors ate or food from the country associated with their deity. Quite a few Pagans become vegetarians or even vegans as a health choice, a political statement or as a way to raise or improve their energy. Those vegetarians hope the diet will help them progress spiritually and become better at certain practices such as yoga or meditation.

In addition to the ubiquitous potluck meal following a ritual, food can actually be a key ingredient in various ceremonies. Groups enjoy communal opportunities to make bread or color eggs. In fact, a number of cultural events and sacred rituals revolve around food. They include eating of foods associated with specific deities, the sacred sharing of special foods, and ceremonies focusing on gratitude for the gifts of the Earth. Many celebrations incorporate seasonal food as part of the ritual. For instance, in the US (depending on climate), Spring rituals could focus on blessing seeds. Autumn ceremonies concentrate on the harvest and could incorporate apples; Summer rites might include strawberries. Obviously, climatic differences (and the reversal of seasons in other hemispheres) affect the local food and drink available for sacred uses. From milk at Imbolc ceremonies to cider at Autumn Equinox, from the Yule Wassail to celebratory mead, beverages are important too. In fact, no Heathen blot would be possible without an appropriate beverage. During Sabbat rituals, Wiccan covens share "cakes and ale," which may actually be a plate of cookies or loaf of bread and a cup of juice or wine. Whether simple or fancy, offerings of food and beverages are given to divine beings, gods and ancestors.

Gatherings

> Social interaction is such a big part of being human.
>
> - Shaina Golden

Pagans love to spend time with other Pagans. Frequently they mention that gathering with other Pagans is like finding the family that they dreamed about as a child. Whether a festival is held outdoors or indoors, attendees go to meet other like-minded people. Whether or not others follow what we believe, we do rituals together, share information, and dance and drum — at night when possible. We celebrate important life events such as births, unions, coming of age, elderhood, and death rituals. Festivals that cater to the Neopagan movement have sprung up all over the world. One of the longest-running yearly events in the United States, Starwood, a festival started in the early Eighties (by the Chameleon Club, which morphed into ACE, the Association for Consciousness Exploration), still holds to its basic format as a diverse place to explore the forefront of human consciousness. Various festivals cater to members of specific traditions. Many individuals go to festivals alone, but others bring their whole coven or family together to connect with the larger circle of the community of Pagans. In addition, numerous churches have been formed around our spiritual beliefs as a way to have a consistent spiritual family to share with and depend on.

Fun and Games

Many gamers are part of the Pagan culture and join with one another to play many different games. Games played at Renaissance festivals or Scottish competitions have crossed into Pagan society. Caber tossing (throwing a log) or stone carry (also called stone walk) are very popular as well as less strenuous activities such as kite flying or attempting to break records for how many bodies you can paint in a day. There is a market for Pagan tourism with companies offering tours to sacred sites and the holy places of our ancestors, often with the chance to do ritual there. Many Pagans dream of "going home" to the land of their Gods.

Death and Remembrance

In recent years, it has become possible for Pagans to be buried with symbols of their traditions on their gravesites. That success came from a complicated fight begun in 1997 by Rev. Pete Pathfinder Davis, Archpriest of the Aquarian Tabernacle Church (ATC) who requested the pentacle be included on the United States Veterans Affairs approved list of religious decorations for gravestones. In the years that followed, additional requests were filed on behalf of actively serving and deceased Wiccans by the Isis Invicta Military Mission (part of the Temple of Isis), the Nomadic Chantry of the Gramarye, and Circle Sanctuary. Americans United for Separation of Church and State filed a lawsuit on behalf of Circle Sanctuary and finally won in 2007. Additionally, in 2007 the American Civil Liberties Union (ACLU) settled a lawsuit against US Veterans Affairs on behalf of Aquarian Tabernacle Church, Correllian Nativist Church International, and several individuals including a WWII veteran.

In the last decade, in response to these lawsuits, the United States Department of Veterans Affairs added the pentacle, awen, and Thor's hammer to the official list of religious symbols for use on government-furnished headstones. Consequently, US State and Federal veteran cemeteries, including Arlington National Cemetery, now offer these Pagan symbols as choices on grave markers. In addition, they allow other non-Christian symbols such as the medicine wheel, infinity symbol, and the landing eagle.

At death, a number of Pagans have asked friends to take their ashes to festival sites and place them in the sacred bonfire. Recently, festival locations such as the Brushwood Folklore Center have designated an area for ancestor reverence. These repositories for the ashes of our Pagan brothers and sisters mean that individuals can be remembered in the space where they gathered with their community. We have come into our own as a distinct community: not only can we live, play, and work together, but we can now rest and remember together.

Connections

Despite the diverse expressions within the community, it should be obvious that a Pagan culture exists. Pagans identify each other through their shared symbols and values. For instance, a necklace such as a pentacle or triple spiral worn discretely on the job would be recognized by another Pagan. Additionally, they recognize each other's energy.

Joy's story:

> When I traveled to Africa, we came from all over to one airport to take the flight to Africa. In the airport, we found each other. I asked the people in our group, "Did you know each other?" They answered, "No, we did what you did: we just walked up to each other." After a while the whole group was together.

৪০৫৪

The Pagan culture is the people that follow the Old Ways and the Old Gods in ways that are not mainstream in our regular culture today; we're a counter-culture, not accepted by mainstream, but our numbers are much bigger than they [mainstream] realize. It's an encompassing culture: it's in our clothing, in our jewelry, the ways we live, the fact that we recycle, the way we care for the land. The way we care for ourselves and our children — everything in our lives is flavored by our culture. The plants we choose. The way we decorate our homes, even in the way we view the world. We see magic everywhere! We live the magical life. I know I see the world in a different way than my Christian friends do. I feel sad for people that don't see the magic in the world as I do. It has a profound effect on my day-to-day happiness. To be involved with nature even though you are in the city: to watch the sky, the wildlife, the weather. So many people in mainstream culture seem to be removed from it all. I am always the one in the grocery store parking lot pointing out the rainbow to strangers passing by, pointing out the first star, or the full moon. I get more than my share of strange looks as well as my share of smiles. I hope those people notice for themselves the next time.

~ Tina Frick (Freya Hlin Vrana)

Pagan customs come from more than one particular spiritual path, but our community is greater than a particular organization or coven. It is a growing and developing society of people who merge modern beliefs with ancient principles.

> I have finally come to embrace the idea of Big Tent Paganism. I struggled with that for a long time. I thought that Paganism was becoming so watered-down as to be meaningless. I had to let go of the idea that Paganism was a religion — and that was a very difficult thing for me. Neopaganism is a cultural movement. One of free thought and individual expression. Within this movement there are Neopagan religions. Some are polytheistic, some are pantheistic, some are animistic, and some are purely philosophical. But there is a broader culture beyond that. A culture of acceptance, tolerance, open-mindedness, creativity, and a love for the Earth. We are the inheritors of the hippie movement, and that's okay. I went through a period when I wasn't okay with that. I thought the "true Paganism" was a thing that existed, and that all of these cultural elements unrelated to spirituality were a distraction. I am okay with it now. And I am happy to identify as part of the Pagan subculture.
>
> - Fred Johnston

Yes, we Pagans have a culture and we share it in community. The uniqueness and variety of our philosophies generate strength. In many ways, the attitude of acceptance allows greater diversity in functions and roles within our population.

Challenges of Our Community

Now, as the Pagan movement starts its second century, it begins to work through different issues. It has moved through the beginning stages of development, that is, it has progressed from the exuberance of creation, through the paranoia of rejection (and associated fear of consequences), and into the spotlight. Even though many individuals remain in the broom closet, the traditions under the Pagan umbrella have been recognized as valid religions. Just this year, the US Department of Defense expanded its list of recognized religions. Although Wicca has been recognized by US Courts since the Eighties, US armed forces now includes religious designations for Shaman, Pagan, Humanist, Druid, Native American, Heathen, Asatru, Troth, Magick, and Spiritualist. It has expanded categories for Wicca to specify Seax Wicca, Dianic Wicca, and Sacred Well Congregation. Although many traditions are missing from the military's list, it represents a huge change and an increase in acceptance in the last forty years.

Military acceptance means that more people will be open about their beliefs. As these traditions become more recognized, a greater percentage of the US population will adopt the beliefs. How will Paganism and its followers handle that publicity — and the resulting misinformation and notoriety? Our Elders have the wisdom to help us move bravely and honestly into the future.

In fact, numerous people gravitate to the Pagan groups because they recognize that their chosen lifestyle and/or their spiritual viewpoints are marginalized in the dominant culture. In addition, many new members arrive at Paganism in an attempt to heal soul sickness and recover from the effects of mainstream religion. As more people enter our community, room is created for them.

However, the considerable number of newcomers that need to be welcomed into the community brings challenges; new individuals arrive with their own attitudes and assumptions about Paganism. This, too, contributes to the evolution of this exceptional culture. Pagans are serious about defining uniqueness. Even so, as connections form foundations within Pagan society, space is created for everyone to be accepted or, at the minimum, tolerated without bias.

Despite the strength arising from that attitude, our freedom-loving beliefs challenge us when we face questions that arise naturally from communal events and larger group interactions. Pagans can have contradictory feelings especially when longing for a tribe conflicts with the need to protect personal identification. In addition, there is a tribal yearning for the experience of a cohesive and collective group, which can be overshadowed by an individual's desire to create internal strength or to focus on a small group at the expense of the entire community. Differences between subgroups, and possessiveness towards beliefs, can produce detachment from the larger community. Many leaders have recognized this and have created events to bring everyone together, such as Pagan Pride Days, and similar gatherings to strengthen the forward movement and, yes, the survival of this culture as a whole. There is a desire to celebrate each individual's unique contributions to the greater community, and yet, as we function independently in short-term communities, we struggle to set up the ideas, the people, or the support we need to grow within our common culture.

When we feel this contradiction, we look for Elders to guide us. As we search for the support we need to develop, both individually and collectively, once again we ask Elders for advice. When we struggle to hold our Pagan beliefs in spite of mainstream society, we turn to them. Since they carry information, knowledge, and love from one generation to the next, they can help us to function at our best levels of being. Elders help us to gain competency, function at our optimum, and then carry that essence courageously into the dominant culture. With their guidance, we can become wise people, develop into careful leaders, and act as positive forces within our community.

Many Pagans identify the wise and knowledgeable individual within their own group as an Elder. Although a Wiccan coven, for example, might have their own Elder, they may not recognize those from other groups. This can occur when people identify only with a small subgroup and reject the concept that they are a part of a larger community of shared cultural values.

As Paganism has expanded and developed over time, another challenge surfaced: age. Our Elders are getting older. The turning of the years has not treated many of them kindly. Quite a few have been hindered by debilitating illnesses. Each year the number of Elders in attendance at Pagan festivals and outdoor events goes down because they no longer have the assistance of others or cannot physically handle the difficulties of participating. Additionally, many of the significant individuals of the past have passed on. Their deaths have impacted the groups they founded or headed as well as many who respected and admired them.

> The first wave of our founders is passing, though it is not past yet. Nevertheless, if the work is to continue we need those who are 20+ and 30+ now to step up for 20 years of solid organizing. There's no help for it — this is different from the work of one's spiritual path, more like a combination of politics and drudgery. Nevertheless, if we are to establish social institutions to support modern Paganism, that's what will be required.
>
> - Ian Corrigan

As a community, we can join together to support the Elders, preserve their teachings, and learn all we can from them. As Ian Corrigan said, the future will require social institutions. As Pagans, we need to find a way to maintain as much of the Elders' wisdom and craft, concepts and philosophies as we can. First, we must be able to find the Elders, establish interactions, then study, and eventually transmit the teachings to the next generations.

Perhaps the most obvious challenge to Paganism is one that is also an issue in mainstream society. How do we go about defining an Elder? Given the limitations of the dominant culture, how do we define this important person for our Pagan culture? How do we take only the best from the dominant culture? What can we use to identify leaders or distinguish wise and knowledgeable people? We need their help us to achieve the goal of learning, sharing, and preserving our traditions and beliefs. One way is to develop ideas, and maybe even consensus, on who carries the wisdom that can help us move forward through life's challenges. This book is meant to be a guide that will allow us to answer these questions.

What is an Elder?

Authors from novelists to self-help gurus have discussed the concept of Elders. Philosophers, anthropologists, psychologists, and sociologists debate generational roles. All of them have considered the significance of Elders in maintaining the continuity of community. Since our varied populations and cultures agree upon the necessity of interactions with Elders in our society, the nebulous concept of eldership should be defined. Specifically, how does the diverse Pagan community define an Elder? What are their roles within our community?

> I appreciate the title of Elder, but there is a growing concern as to what that title entails. I know someone who is a generational witch, has a huge following under this person, but has not done anything for the community. Although this person is an Elder in their group, no one else knows this person. I know another generational witch who has always kept solitary. Again, although in advanced age that should equal the wisdom of an Elder, there have been no actions to show the title is deserved.
>
> - Anna Calhoun

As a society, we use the term Elder in conversations and presume that the listener knows what we mean by the term. Anthropologists, psychologists, historians, and sociologists scatter the term throughout their writings, and it is likely that they mean incredibly different classifications. In fact, everyone assumes we understand the definition of Elder. But do we really?

> I don't find the term *Elder* meaningful. It's thrown around in spiritualist circles as if it's coherent, but I've seen no reason to think it means anything other than perhaps 'people with white hair.' Given that that group contains both Nobel laureates and purveyors of ignorance, I don't find it useful.
>
> - Collin Meyer

So, what is the difference between a "person with white hair" and an Elder? How can we find a useful description? More specifically what are the characteristics that cause others to recognize an individual as an Elder? Is an Elder defined by age, gender, occupation or by something else? Most importantly, how does the Pagan community define an Elder? Do Pagans accept the same definitions as mainstream society?

If age is the key, what year is the magical one that turns an adult into an Elder? Carl Jung declared that a person had to be 35 years old in order to be a good therapist — an advanced age in a society that expected individuals to be working adults by the age of sixteen. Generally, Native American cultures believe that an Elder must be 50 or 60 years old. In the past, that may have been because few people lived that long. In fact, life expectancy on US reservations is still much lower than that of the general population.

> In Guatemala, you are considered an Elder at 52.
> - Rocio Darlene Arriaga

In describing the beliefs of the Dagara people of Africa, Joy explained, "They say a person has to be solid before they become an Elder; to them, becoming solid requires initiation, training, and the experience of a lifetime." In the US, retirement is typically linked to a worker obtaining 65 years of age. Although retirement signals a time of movement away from work-life, it is often viewed as a withdrawal from active life rather than a rite of passage into a new role. Certainly, the age of elderhood varies from society to society.

As portrayed in mainstream media, US culture characteristically values youth over age. Worldwide, society offers contradictory messages about older people. Indeed, cultures might define Elder in a different way for a man or a woman.

Globally the status of the elderly is a problem, especially in regard to older women. Specifically, a society's established attitude about customary gender roles can impact its view of Elders, and in particular, acceptance of women as leaders. Since women tend to live longer than men, this distinction can lead to huge sociopolitical differences in treatment of the aged. It certainly helps determine who fits the category of Elder. In many cultures, and in a number of religions, the subordination of women is based on their femininity, their womanhood; in other words, subordination is related to the roles they fulfill in society. In those cultures, we find that the rank of Elder depends not only on age but also on gender. In a few cultures, a woman's gender actually changes as she ages; she is no longer considered female, but has the same ranking as a man. This usually happens after menopause. Those who answered our questionnaires agreed with the global custom of equating *Elder* to age even when they had difficulty pinpointing the necessary age.

[An Elder] is a person of an older age than myself.
- Lisa Owen

Ultimately an Elder has years on you.
- Sarenth Odinsson

An Elder (Sage/male or Crone/female) no longer has dependent children in their care and is near the half-century mark (50 years).
- Penny Goody

Using the term *Crone*, some people considered menopause to be an indicator of Elder status. Certainly, many Croning rituals have been based on a woman's completion of menopause. However, Donna Henes disagreed and wrote a book because she did not believe that women wanted to or should move directly from Motherhood to Crone[23]. She created a fourth stage called the Queen, effectively pushing eldership into a later time of life.

We have outgrown our tenure as Maidens and as Mothers, yet old age no longer follows immediately after menopause.
- Donna Henes, *The Queen of My Self*[24]

---

[23] Donna Henes, *The Queen of My Self: Stepping Into Sovereignty in Midlife* (Monarch Press, 2004).

[24] Donna Henes, "On Finding Myself Middle Aged with No Role Model I Could Relate to Because I am Not a Crone" from *The Queen of My Self* (2005). Retrieved February 2, 2014, from http://www.thequeenofmyself.com/a-queen1a.shtml.

Regarding the astrology of elders, some really want to become a crone too early. It's not appropriate to do a croning ceremony until after a woman has had her second Saturn return, around age 56-58. Age 60 is better, as by then Saturn will have moved into the next zodiac sign and completed the return cycle. Same for men who want to be Elders. Age does count, because the whole thing about a crone is the accumulated wisdom of a lifetime. I've heard from women who feel that they can become a crone because they've had a hysterectomy or are done with menopause or because they can best relate to the crone archetype, or whatever. A crone is a female representative of Saturn-Cronos-Father Time. So that second Saturn return is the key, but it can happen at slightly different ages since its orbit is slightly irregular.

- Elizabeth Hazel

Thus, we found that age does influence both mainstream and Pagan considerations of Elder; however, in Pagan classifications, gender was less important. Even though some groups use titles that differentiate individuals by gender, Pagan culture is not comfortable with the sexism that may be accepted as a worldview in other communities. Certainly, alternative communities span a broad spectrum with seemingly inconsistent cultural roles, but in general, Pagans reject the subjugation or subordination of women. That attitude is likely derived from their acceptance of Mother Goddess or other divine female beings. In fact, a number of Pagan groups have consciously eliminated mainstream cultural gender mores.

Still, to the Pagan community (and perhaps to mainstream society as well), an Elder is not simply a person who has lived many decades or survived to very old age. The term *Elder* — as opposed to terms such as *elderly* or *aged* — is only assigned to an individual who is judged to be an expert in life skills or spiritual work. In fact, when describing Elders, numerous respondents linked age, experience and knowledge and expected them to share that expertise with others.

I do not define an Elder by age alone but by their maturity coupled with their knowledge and work.

- Anna Calhoun

Elders have long-life experiences, and set an example by their behavior.

- Penny Goody

An Elder, in general, is a person who, through both study and life experience, demonstrates the ability to live in a manner congruent with the beliefs of their chosen path.

- Karen Thoms

[An Elder is] someone who has experience in their own tradition, in life, and is able to truly mentor someone looking for those experiences.

- "J"

Years involved with spirituality. What have they contributed to community (service/teaching/ knowledge)? An experienced leader. Life experience.

- Bernadette Montana

Those who have applied their accumulated knowledge successfully in their life experience, and as a result of this wisdom, have reached a deep understanding of life are the true Elders.

- Bona Dea Lyonesse

An Elder is a person who has been in their chosen religion for at least 20 years and has lived their life, experienced life, long enough so that religion has become part of who they are, how they view others, how they view the world, and how they view themselves. A lot of this has to do with feeling — it's a feeling so it is hard to put it into words. Quite often Elders know their religion well enough that they've struck out and started seeking other religions and added that to their religion. Their knowledge base is very large.

- Tina Frick (Freya Hlin Vrana)

An Elder is an individual that has years of experience and practice what they believe is in their faith. An Elder should have gone through several rites of passage in their tradition. That gives me the confidence to work with them.

- Peaceful Rivers Rainbow Warrior White Wolf

I define an Elder as someone who has a balance between knowledge, experience and wisdom. It is one thing for someone to have knowledge and experience but they are nothing without the wisdom to understand that on occasion you need to go against what training and tradition state. Wisdom is important, but it cannot stand alone either. Wisdom shifts and changes, based on the experiences encountered and how knowledge is applied or not. So Elders are these wonderful individuals that have this balance of the three: knowledge, experience and wisdom.

- Mary Hudson

Joy's story:

I prefer that my Elders have more life experience than I do, i.e. they have lived longer. Since I am now older, I have learned to appreciate others' personal wisdom, whether they were spiritual studies or life studies and skills. I value their ability to be willing to share what they know and their desire to be helpful in teaching and conveying their knowledge. I find myself being aware of the age that they are as they share their knowledge and opinions. I can see how the gifts of each phase of their life are influencing their advice. I find myself looking for the heart of the teachings without the bias of their own age perspective. Sometimes I feel that this gets in the way and does not allow me to have enough appreciation for the work that "younger" Elders have accomplished. I believe a person becomes an Elder when they are in their late fifties or early sixties, but most importantly when their heart embraces all that came before them, including themselves and their own experiences, so they can embrace all those that come after them. They have a sense of time that seems very fluid and all encompassing.

Lifestyle and Elders

As a descriptor, the word *experience* adds many levels of meaning to our definition of *Elder*. Experience infers knowledge gained over time, not just in working through extraordinary situations but also through handling daily life. An Elder can live an ordinary life; in fact, ordinary life is important. Even a routine life teaches great lessons to those destined to be Elders. Despite living a life that most would view as commonplace, the person who becomes an Elder lives that life in a special way.

> Age gives so much beauty through a loving heart.
> - Sheree Johnson

> Age alone or length of practice does not, to me, define an Elder. I have doubt that people who have not ever provided for themselves or their family are Elders as the struggle for home and hearth are intrinsic learning experiences towards becoming an Elder.
> - Karen Thoms

Elders may work at professions in a masterful way; they may dedicate themselves to a chosen craft or to practicing a spiritual path for a lifetime. The Elder looks at life from a different perspective. Regardless of the differences, through the experience of the highs and lows of living, an Elder gains wisdom and knowledge.

> I really don't know how someone becomes an Elder but I imagine it takes a lot of dedication and time to develop the title. From what I gather an Elder is someone who is highly gifted with the power to help other people in ways ordinary people ... cannot help, they use spiritual mediums to help create a balance in people's lives.
> - Alejandra Licea

> I have had many teachers, some of them were considered charismatic. Charisma by itself does not an elder make, I discovered. Neither does 'book-learning.' Those who have applied their accumulated knowledge successfully

in their life experience and as a result of this wisdom, have reached a deep understanding of life are the true Elders. There is total commitment to the path they are called to, but they are not fanatics. Fanaticism implies a degree of internal fear, and true elders are recognizable by their peaceful confidence. Their auras seem to radiate light like beacons in the night to those who seek. They are most often of advanced age, primarily because it takes a while to collect life experience and to determine which knowledge is worth keeping.

- Bona Dea Lyonesse

I see how they behave and know them by their actions. They have the ability to teach and are connected to higher spiritual awareness. They recognize their ability and know they have something to offer. I don't pay attention to their words. I watch what they do. That is how I know them. That is how I know if they are good elders. They "walk their talk." There are Elders that are very young in Australia, India and Africa because of how they act and behave and because of the knowledge they come into this incarnation with. Elders listen and respond appropriately to situations.

- Peaceful Rivers Rainbow Warrior White Wolf

The ability to respond appropriately to situations can include counseling, healing therapies and healing practices. Sometimes an Elder must be willing to make judgments about behavior within a community, educate the members in proper behavior and mediate between people.

It is the role of the Elders to make things work out in a positive way for the community.

- Michael Banutu-Gomez,
*Africa: We Owe it to Our Ancestors,
Our Children, and Ourselves*[25]

---

[25] Michael Banutu-Gomez, *Africa: We Owe it to Our Ancestors, Our Children, and Ourselves* (University Press of America, 2005) 14.

Healing work is also a vital part of being a spiritual Elder. Not necessarily in the physical sense of healing disease or injury, but facilitating the healing of the mind and spirit also. ... True spiritual Elders understand and accept that they are merely guides and vessels for the energies needed for the individual to self-heal.

- Bona Dea Lyonesse

I believe that in their Spiritual world and in the mundane world they should have similar roles. [My Elder] Sweet Medicine was a good example of this. She was a psychologist in the mundane world. Others used their ministerial skills to deal with people.

- Peaceful Rivers Rainbow Warrior White Wolf

As a result of their life experiences, Elders have a broader perspective, and they understand the bigger picture. They can guide someone through the larger picture that students are not able to perceive. As a result of this, Elders, at least in the Pagan community, are defined as individuals who are old enough to have extended experience in life. They have a great deal of knowledge in their specialized areas. Often they work at jobs that permit them to utilize their knowledge. Additionally, Elders can be defined in more than one way, and they can be involved in more than one community. In short, Elders are people recognized as carrying on traditions, whether those traditions come from culture, family, society, art, trade or religion and spirituality.

Cultural Roles of Elders

There is a very wise saying in North American indigenous cultures: "for the seven generations." It refers to the belief that we influence the future for the next seven generations. The point is that no important decision should be made without considering the impact on the seven generations to follow ours. However — and perhaps more importantly — the statement means that no actions should be taken that would knowingly hurt the link between generations. The connection includes the generations that are younger as well as older ones.

Within the Ifa traditions from West Africa, there is a reciprocal relationship between the members of the Ile: the Elders in this tradition have the responsibility to teach by words and by example, and the younger members are expected to help them and treat older members in respectful ways. In addition, Elders may be expected to clarify problems between the members of the Ile and offer solutions. They are capable of maintaining a continually evolving tradition, culture and community. For example, Ifa Elders understand the binary divination system that explains the creation of the world and our relationship to all of creation.

> Elders have the courage to lead by example, to encourage others to be their best. Elder experiences demonstrate both what not to waste time on, and show the results of their belief and lifestyle choices. They have earned respect.
>
> - Penny Goody

In general, in the Pagan community, we refer to Elders as individuals who are older, knowledgeable, and more experienced or of higher status. Although "senior citizens" are defined by the expectations of mainstream society, each Pagan group views the purposes of Elders differently. Often the social role of an Elder grows out of their cultural tradition. Eldership can be divided into various functions that are delineated by roles within a family, a community, a trade, or a religion.

Family Elders

As in past times, modern families gather for celebrations of life, for consolation, and for holidays. Some of these ceremonies mark rites of passages from one phase of life to another: births, weddings, and funerals. Family gatherings connect the individual to the relatives, the community, and to the world around them. It is much easier for children to develop into mature and healthy adults when they have a variety of experiences that also include intergenerational interactions.

> If you associate enough with older people who enjoy their lives, who are not stored away in any golden ghetto, you will gain a sense of continuity and of the possibility for a full life.
>
> - Margaret Mead[26]

> As much of what I learned about magic, herbs, and mythology was from my own family, I do consider those teachers to be my Elders!
>
> - Karen Thoms

Historically, the common thread in any culture has been the fact that the oldest living generation teaches the younger ones. Only recently, have small nuclear families become the norm. Since WWII, the custom has developed for parents and children to live in homes without other relatives; for the first time older generations were not in the house or living in close proximity. In the past, convention viewed Elders not just as members of the household but also as important members of society. Historically, the family Elder would be a grandparent or another individual of that generation, but that was not always the case. The Elder reveals a distinctive viewpoint and passes on family beliefs,

---

[26] Laurie Edwards-Tate, "Weekly column in the Washington Times Communities by Laurie Edwards-Tate" *At Your Home Familycare* (originally "Anthropologist Margaret Mead addresses today's aging issues") (posted February 3, 2012). Retrieved January 6, 2018 from http://atyourhomefamilycare.com/washington-times-communities/anthropologist-margaret-mead-addresses-todays-aging-issues/.

history, and traditions. All of that training occurs through forming a relationship with an Elder.

Joy's story:

> My Mom was an awesome lady. She was raised Catholic, but became really interested in Metaphysics and took me to classes with her. This occurred primarily because she had a gift herself for communicating with spirits and she had me, who was always seeing something that was spirit related. She also took me to my first Psychic/Medium. He became my first teacher and taught me to read and develop my psychic and mediumship abilities.
>
> When I was in my twenties I wanted to plant a garden. By the time I read all that I could about gardening, seeds, planting depth and fertilizer, I was totally confused and unsure that I would even be able to grow anything at all. I told my Mom that maybe I would not plant the garden since it would surely fail. She looked at me straight in the face and said, "Just throw the seeds in the ground and water them. Everything strives to grow and live. It will be fine." I think about that every time I am worried about someone or something. She gave me my first lesson about being in the world. Everything wants to live.

Although planned activities can be the reason used for the family visit, even when there is no special reason, amazing things can happen. For instance, "we're here to help Auntie with her yard" could mean the parents would be mowing and weeding while the teenager helps Auntie inside. The tasks given to the teen might be simple; however, the right Elder can turn fetching ingredients, stirring, and washing dishes into a special time when Auntie shows the teenager how to cook a traditional dish for the family's dinner. The Elder has free time to listen to the child and to share company and communications.

While children learn to cooperate and be helpful, they recognize that they are capable of doing something new, have valuable service to offer the family, and can become skilled at something that their parents or friends may not know how to do. When they are together, whether playing or actively completing tasks, they develop a mutually beneficial relationship. While the child helps the older person, the interaction between them can give the younger one balance and a sense of belonging within the family. As a result of that placement, the child is more likely to grow up confident and well-adjusted.

Lillith's Story:

Every child should have a special Elder: one person who is unhurried and unstinting in the time they spend together. For me, that special person was my grandfather. Throughout my childhood, my grandfather had been the one person in my family who seemed to understand me. We shared music and stories, laughter and strolls. I remember meandering walks through the neighborhood. His leisurely pace matched my short legs. It was a relief that I didn't have to scurry to keep up with him.

On our walks, we talked about things only a granddaughter and a grandfather could discuss. We talked about school, trees, music, and my parents. How the environment worked and why we should respect nature. Although he wasn't demonstrative, he managed to reveal immense feelings in a smile and a touch on the shoulder. Eloquently he captured my attention with tales imaginative and classical; teachings were scattered throughout the stories. Descriptions of an old strange culture combined with accounts of the history of faraway places. Around them, he sprinkled creative tales.

My imagination filled in every missing detail with wonder. I envisioned that faraway country through his words. People were different there: as they performed their daily tasks, women wore aprons, and the men sang as they worked. Everyone wore hats. Dragons protected the homeland. They hid in caves, but sometimes they chose to befriend a special person, maybe even a good little girl. (Maybe me? Please, oh please.) Perched in the trees, birds talked to each other, and then flew about the sky sharing weather tips and warning of thunderstorms. If we listened carefully, they would even chat with us.

The history of that land was full of legendary events. Long ago, determined men built a wall to keep out the invaders; they would fire arrows at anyone who tried to climb over the stones. It worked for a long, long time — there was a song about that. Back then the women were as fierce as the men, and they ardently protected their families. One famous woman managed to defeat a Roman legion — there was a song about that too. After things quieted down, I imagined they tucked their children into bed at night and sang them to sleep just as Grandpa did sometimes with me.

In my head, it was all mixed up together; the fantastic tales out of prehistory mingled with conversations about his childhood and bits of plant lore. Most of it was muddled. Yet, his teaching stories were so much more fun than the lectures I heard from my parents! I recall his imaginative talks when I was a three-year old and when I was a teen. During narratives, Grandpa managed to explain complicated ideas. Through stories, he expressed standards of valuable characteristics: gratitude, frugality, loyalty, and generosity. On those walks, he passed onto me a love of nature. It was a simple appreciation ranging from the enjoyment of birds happily flitting around a birdbath or a kitten chasing a moth to the awesome view of lofty mountains covered in trees and capped with feathery clouds.

I wish I could remember all of those conversations. Although I don't recall many of them, I know his stories helped form my values. A healthy child needs to know that he or she exists in the world surrounded by family, supported by ancestors, centered in the place where he or she lives, and in harmony with nature. My grandfather gave me important bricks in that foundation. Instinctively I know that my time with him contributed to my identity in the world. Even as a child, I knew our time together was exceptional.

Due to the shifting nature of society, the role of family Elder has changed over time. Despite that, interactions with family Elders remain important.

I think older people know much more about change than young people. What children have to learn is how to live in a changing world. These children that are born now think the world was made the way it is today — complete with transistors. They need someone who gives them some kind of perspective — someone who can convince them that you could be born in one world, grow up in another, and grow old in a third.

- Margaret Mead[27]

Indeed, interactions with family Elders provide stability and a sense of resilience. Based on their experiences, they view life differently. In fact, how they explain the world makes them exceptional. Despite contemporary social changes, they continue to be valuable members of the family, offering a long-term assessment of life.

My father started out as an engineer, decided that was not his thing, and became a stock broker. He went to Xavier University and got his MBA when I was in elementary school. In 1976, when my mom had a stroke, her roommate in the hospital had Guillain-Barré that she had gotten from the Swine Flu shot. This was in 1976, when they had the suit against the government for the Swine Flu shots. So my parents got involved in that lawsuit. My mother had the Swine Flu shot two weeks before her stroke — it had nothing to do with her stroke, but it got my dad interested in law. So he went to get his paralegal degree and then later went to law school. We were forever asking him "What are you going to do when you grow up, Daddy?" Or, alternatively, "So when are you going to medical school because it's the only thing you haven't done yet."

---

[27] Laurie Edwards-Tate, "Weekly column in the Washington Times Communities by Laurie Edwards-Tate" *At Your Home Familycare* (originally "Anthropologist Margaret Mead addresses today's aging issues") (posted February 3, 2012). Retrieved January 6, 2018 from http://atyourhomefamilycare.com/washington-times-communities/anthropologist-margaret-mead-addresses-todays-aging-issues/.

When he died, he donated his body to medical school. He got there anyway. So that is my story. He taught me: you're not done until you're dead and even then, you can go to medical school. Never give up on your dream.

- Euphrates

Community Elders

With the number of blended families in our society, Elders have taken on additional roles. A few grandparents raise their grandchildren with no parental involvement. Others baby-sit while the parents work. However, a great many families have limited contact with their older relatives. Despite the mainstream's touting of nuclear families (often expressed as "traditional" for political and religious norms), that definition of family is not how most of us live.

In other words, we have developed functioning family units in a wide range of definitions, and we need to support the family patterns we have created. However, homogenization of culture has moved us away from the ethnic devotions, spiritual practices, and familial traditions of our ancestors (such as going to the cemetery to clean graves of relatives) even though we continue to need those traditions for individual and family emotional health as well as cultural endurance. Because of that, a lot of families search outside of the family unit to find Elders. They tend to look for them in their chosen communities.

[An Elder is] someone who has lived, experienced living, taken notes, shared their experiences and provided a teaching or leadership role within a larger community.

- Ladyelle

Others in community come to them with serious life questions.

- "J"

For a person to be regarded as a community Elder, I believe that they should be able to demonstrate skill from a spiritual standpoint within their chosen specialty (specialties) and should be able to put those skills to practical use building a life, home, and nurturing relationships. An Elder should also be available to their community in some fashion for assistance in spiritual and life crises.

- Karen Thoms

In addition to the role of counselor, many of our contributors believed that a community Elder should hold a more enlightened viewpoint than the typical person.

As a person who gives back to those that [come] after them. It might be through teaching or it might be through activism, but in either case they are giving of themselves and all that they bring with them. It could be a matter of quiet knowledge, or understanding that sometimes it is okay to color outside the lines without fear of being reprimanded. The Elder is still the person we turn to in difficult times to help us understand what is happening and how to work our way through the darkness – both internally and externally.

- Mary Hudson

An Elder is a person who has offered their knowledge and shared in their experience to benefit others and the community as a whole. An Elder has moved beyond petty incidents and has the knowledge and respect of their peers, their craft, and their community.

- Anna Calhoun

We Pagans may expect more from our community than mundane people. Sometimes it seems we think we're more evolved — if you prefer, more spiritually enlightened or educated — and so we shouldn't have any interpersonal difficulties. And so, when we fail at achieving continual ongoing positive relationships, things really blow up. There are ongoing ripples whenever things blow up because we aren't good at clearing up difficulties — just like mainstream people, we're not educated in how to communicate and work through problems.

This society, both the larger mainstream society and the Pagan or Neopagan subculture, has been teaching the idea of "walk away" as a way to solve all problems — or worse, take a little purple pill and pretend that it solves things. To truly participate in a community means that you cannot simply walk away from an uncomfortable situation. Community is not always pleasant. Sometimes others have opinions you would rather not hear.

> Everyone says we should be able to take care of ourselves. To accept a teacher or an elder is accepting they are more capable of doing something better than you. Just like in life: we don't expect ourselves to be our own therapist or doctor. People feel like they should be fine — they feel shame from having a problem. They don't trust others; they don't rely on them. They are always told they are not enough: so they can't accept that they have a problem. But in a healthy community, everyone is accepted as they are and is supported by others. When people are not willing to accept they have problems, they fight against their problems because they feel powerless. They don't want others in the community to know they have problems. Eventually they have to give up the idea they have to do it themselves, and reach out to a person that can help them.
>
> - Shaina Golden

The role of the Elder of the community is often a difficult one, especially when friction breaks out in the group. Often the Elder is the one that must suggest compromise or mediation. The Elder has to be willing take the stance that is needed to move the people towards proper actions. They need to promote communication and behaviors that are necessary to heal the group, even when those actions might not be acceptable to every individual in the group. Perhaps the focus should be on enjoying the discovery of why a community exists, who is there, and why — instead of making judgment about how individuals are doing something they don't like.

After decades walking this planet, interacting with countless people in numerous situations, we know that people in general can be lazy, stubborn, compliant, hard-working, stingy, compassionate, kind — in short, they can fit into every category. And at a particular time in life, any individual has done so. An

Elder has learned that people can hurt others, and they know that people can hurt the Elder's feelings too. However, the Elder has realized it is best to cry or rage in private, and then be willing to walk back because Spirit requires it, because it is good for the family or community, and because it is the right thing to do.

> The Elder will also be the one to stand up to the bully and tell that person to sit down. Elders have a distinct and sacred duty to protect the standards and mores of the community. Particularly in community ... Elders will be seen as tribal leaders with the authority to decide between right and wrong and to make appropriate judgments. Elders should not see their role as protecting peace at all costs. Elders need to guard against enabling bad actors in the community and need to sometimes engage in tough love, much as a parent must with a child that has turned to crime and addiction cannot continue to [provide] opportunities for the child to continue to harm self and others.
>
> - Karen Thoms

Elected Elders or Founders

As a society, we are comfortable with the Elder who founds an organization or is elected to a permanent or temporary position as an officer of a congregation or group. Both mainstream and alternative religions accept the hierarchy of leadership. In addition, civil, political, and social organizations elect leaders. This is also true in Pagan organizations.

> While my definition of Elder does include founders of religions/traditions and the like, an Elder is someone who has years on you in the religion, tradition, etc. that you are part of.
>
> - Sarenth Odinsson

Many Reclamation Traditions, such as Eastern European Wicca, Druidry, and Norse spirituality, are founded by a person or a group of people in order to define and recreate as closely as possible the heart of those beliefs and the rituals of those traditions. As founders, they maintain a position of Elder status within that community even if they do not hold an official office or title.

When local Pagan Pride events and festivals are ongoing, the people who originate them are recognized as the Elders of the event and are afforded respect. Examples of these founders would be Selena Fox who started Pagan Spirit Gathering, and Heather Killen who created Earth Warriors. Globally, there are many other events associated with various Pagan traditions.

Elders in the Arts and Occupations

In many occupations, our society has transitioned away from apprenticeship and towards higher education based on classroom learning. Despite that, the US Department of Labor recognizes twelve broad employment apprenticeship areas[28]. Actually, quite a few employment areas have longstanding requirements for sponsorship and certification through a training program with a formal apprenticeship. Because of that, Elders continue to be recognized in industries that maintain apprenticeship-based training.

> Someone who has been involved in something for only five years is someone I would have a conversation with. But that level of experience would not make them qualified to teach. Sure, they can teach you something, but they are not qualified to be a teacher. For example, a Tradesman starts out as an Apprentice, then becomes a Journeyman, and then becomes a Master. While an Apprentice could teach you how to swing a hammer, they can't teach you how to build a house. A Master is the Elder.
>
> - Cameron

A similar hierarchy exists in various artistic occupations, such as conductor, choir master or director. In fact, when a particular individual rises to the level of Elder, an organization sometimes recognizes the person with an award for "lifetime achievement."

---

[28] US Department of Labor registers apprenticeships from a diverse range of jobs; a few of them are seaman, carpenter, dental assistant, electrician, fire medic, and pipefitter.

This type of award is not due to one particular production but to decades of experience. Even without an award, widespread acknowledgement of recognition is not needed because certain people stand out. They rise to the level of Elder.

> Eugene [Lion] taught me how to become sensitive to subtle energies. The prism with which I viewed the world changed because I began to understand how human energy behaves: consciously, unconsciously, subconsciously, cause and effect, a unique way of understanding how life energies interact. How smaller patterns intersect with grander ones. How to consciously create an "art experience" that people would value as being authentic, cathartic and genuinely moving. This is akin to ritual that succeeds in elevating its participants to higher spiritual awareness and insight.
>
> - Ladyelle

Within Pagan culture, the aesthetics found in an "art experience," to use Ladyelle's term, is recognized in many areas. Certain crafts established within the Neopagan subculture are not prevalent in mainstream society. However, Pagans admire and value historical techniques, for instance, those used in metal working or in designing period costumes. In those areas, art often overlaps with the apprenticeship system. Pagan culture abounds with such individuals. From blacksmiths and metal workers to potters, seamstresses and tailors, hand-crafted items are esteemed. Artisans, artists, and crafters enjoy status. Not only does the Pagan community treasure the work of painters and crafters of spiritual items but also the work of musicians, bards, and poets.

Spiritual Elders

Perhaps the most important role in any spiritual community is that of spiritual Elder. In fact, their roles gain important status in smaller religious communities. If someone has practiced the same tradition for 35 years, that person would be a spiritual Elder. By maintaining the traditions they acquire personal wisdom. Because they understand the symbolism and meanings within their customs, they can interpret them through myth, metaphors, and language.

> The Elders in my life are touchstones. I believe that is a huge role that they play in the Pagan religion. To learn from what they say, as well as learning from bouncing your ideas off them, I feel is a huge part of the role they play in our culture.
>
> - Tina Frick (Freya Hlin Vrana)

Spiritual Elders are willing to share their knowledge to keep the teachings and traditions alive, to make sure they are done correctly as support to the community or support to the individual.

> The Elder's cultural role is to guide the newer people and answer questions whenever possible. The Elder can assist people to have experiences that lead to growth or understanding. Ideally, an Elder is the Grandmother or Grandfather figure who is there to give people a boost when they need it and an eye of disapproval when they've earned it.
>
> - Karen Thoms

Keepers of Shrines and Temples

As keepers of shrines and temples, Elders have the important roles of being custodians of traditional songs, sacred stories, and history. This can include researching and teaching a foreign or ancient language, performing important chants or playing associated musical instruments.

Within the majority of Christian denominations, religious buildings are often maintained through a centralized governing structure. Although member donations and dues help support the church and its leaders, a substantial portion of the sustaining funds come from a larger body. That is, each local church denomination receives a stipend from the larger governing body of that denomination. For instance, local Catholic parishes receive donations from the members of the church, but the church also receives funds from the diocese. The diocese reports to the archdiocese and also receives money from the higher level of the church. In turn, the archdiocese is accountable to the higher body of the church. A similar hierarchy exists in the larger Christian denominations such as United Methodist, Evangelical Lutheran, Southern Baptist or Episcopal Church branches.

Although religious organizations in mainstream culture are part of a federation, only a few Pagan communities maintain such public spaces. Large venues such as the Isis Oasis Retreat Center managed by the Temple of Isis in California or Circle Sanctuary's nature preserve in Wisconsin are wonderful exceptions — but Pagans must admit they are the exceptions. The majority of temples depend on personal incomes, volunteers and donations. Even fairly well-known temples subsist on donations and volunteerism such as the Sekhmet Temple in Nevada, officially known at the Temple of Goddess Spirituality Dedicated to Sekhmet. It has existed for 23 years with the majority of financial support being provided by the founder and one other donor[29].

While there are national Pagan organizations that own and conserve land and preserve buildings, Pagans acknowledge the idea that individuals can and should create their own shrines, altars and sacred spaces. In Paganism, consecrated structures rarely receive money from a larger organization. A unique fact is the number of Pagan shrines, temples, and groves in private ownership. In other words, many dedicated sites are owned and maintained by a single person or a small private group. An enormous number of Priests, Priestesses, and other spiritual leaders set aside part of their houses or yards as grottos, sanctuaries or ritual areas.

In addition to maintaining the songs, language, sacred stories, and history of their traditions, many Elders create and conserve these spaces. They dedicate and maintain sacred fires; they may provide property for sweat lodges, offer support for ceremonial space, and maintain permanent groves. They provide a place for others to worship or come to receive healing or education. In short, they are caretakers of both the intellectual and physical aspects of their traditions.

By doing so, they provide an outward representation of the spiritual culture of the tradition. Additionally, their work stabilizes spiritual practices, anchor the energy in a location, and help maintain balance on Earth. Through designated shrines,

---

[29] More information about the Temple of Goddess Spirituality Dedicated to Sekhmet and ways to donate to its continuance can be found on the website: http://www.sekhmettemple.com (accessed 2/11/2017).

distinct structures, and sacred places, they pass down the wisdom they learned from their teachers to future generations.

Frequently, individual Pagans participate in covens and other groups to learn how to build and sanctify their own altars. In addition, they study and work with Elders to understand how to handle sacred objects and take care of dedicated shrines. As caretakers of sacred objects, Elders are responsible for the tools of the lineage and for carrying the sacred bundles and pipes. In order to pass down the wisdom of the tradition, they teach how to make and maintain tools. They provide knowledge of the sacred objects and teach others the proper rituals. In addition, Elders communicate information about the relationships inherent in those sacred objects, and disclose how to pass them on.

Through teachings, stories, and ceremonies, Elders share knowledge with others. They teach how to perform rites in the temples, the proper steps for consecration of shrines, and how to be protected while working with the powers in the sacred places. Through their work, they provide a connection between the community and the divine aspects of the tradition. In addition, they train others to find and nurture that connection.

Continuity of Culture

No culture exists for long without Elders. The health of the community depends upon an interaction between generations in which those with more experience share with those who are less experienced. Elders want to explain things, to teach, to comfort, to share stories, communicate information, and offer the lessons of a lifetime to others.

> The role of elders in a culture is to keep the old stories and knowledge alive and to pass them on, but I believe that is only part of their purpose. They also are entrusted to progress the tribe/clan/family by evolving the old ways to create wisdom for the future. They are the 'bridge' so to speak, between the old and the new. They have established connections and alliances with the world (both seen and unseen) around them and they teach those skills to others.
>
> - Bona Dea Lyonesse

Joy's story:

> My spiritual practice, Regla de Ocha, has a very well
> defined culture within the spiritual teachings and
> practices of the tradition. Many of the "New Elders,"
> those that do a lot of borrowing from similar traditions,
> are becoming more popular, partly due to a loss of more
> traditional Elder teachings and partly because they feel
> they have gleaned the best out of these paths as they
> apply to our modern culture. I have concern about this
> practice. I am seeing some of the essence behind the
> teachings being less important than the technology of the
> practice. The "how to do it" seems more important than
> a deeper understanding of "why we do it." I believe an
> Elder is capable of understanding the true essence of the
> teachings that have been carried by the ancestors for a
> long time. I believe an Elder's job is to make sure the
> truth, the heart of the teachings continue to live and are
> not lost to modern culture practices.

In addition to the roles already mentioned, Elders help people
grow and evolve. Culture is integrative. Because of that fusion,
new viewpoints disseminate from community forerunners into
mainstream society. In addition, culture is adaptive. Elders can
help with all of that.

Truly, an Elder can offer an experience of transformation to
others; it does not matter if you meditate with them or make
cookies together, the change can occur. This is the difference
between Elders and others: you can watch a teacher — in fact our
society completely accepts this method of learning. You cannot do
that with an Elder. If you passively sit and observe, you sleep-
walk through the experience, ignoring the life interaction
happening. As an observer and not a participant, you are not
engaging in life. Merely watching the older person squanders the
opportunity because you are focused only on the thoughts in your
own head.

Pagan Teachers, Leaders and Elders

During the research leading to this book, we discovered several areas of confusion in those we interviewed. Instead of answering our questions, several people asked us questions. Is a teacher the same as an Elder? What about a person who influenced someone greatly in a short time? Could that person be an Elder too? How should we treat Elders from another community? If one group has recognized an Elder, should people outside of that association have the same attitude? Can teachers at workshops or festivals be Elders? Are all spiritual leaders the same as Elders? Must an individual be a spiritual leader to be considered an Elder? In this chapter, we will consider these questions.

Perhaps we can blame some of the confusion on the overlap of roles filled by teachers, leaders (especially spiritual leaders), and Elders. Based on definitions of each title, teachers or leaders can be Elders, and certainly, Elders can be spiritual or religious leaders as well as teachers. For instance, the Dalai Lama is not only the spiritual Elder of Tibetan Buddhism and a well-known teacher of Buddhism, but also the publicly declared political leader of Tibet (although he has lived in exile since 1959). However, most Elders do not function in all three roles.

If you ask anyone to name a few qualities of an excellent leader, a celebrated teacher, or an impressive Elder, characteristics might be the same. A short list of desired traits would probably include honesty, integrity, and dedication. However, after those core characteristics, the list of desired qualities varies greatly. For instance, people might state that a spiritual leader should be confident; however, many of the best leaders, teachers, and Elders are actually modest, quiet, and humble. An individual might view an Elder with an unpretentious demeanor and decide that the individual lacked confidence and might even judge the person as unknowledgeable. However, in many traditions, proper behavior does not include assertive behavior and so putting oneself forward might be viewed as improper egotistical bragging. The truth is that some truly remarkable Elders are not charismatic or charming. Perhaps it is exactly those unassuming traits that give some spiritual leaders the ability to connect with the amazing powers of the universe.

Teachers and Elders

During our interviews, the most prevalent questions were those comparing teachers and Elders. Should any teacher be considered an Elder?

> Yes, teachers are Elders — they have more experiences than I do.
>
> - "J".

That attitude was not unanimous; some stated that only noteworthy teachers would develop into Elders. Others completely separated the two.

> [Are all teachers Elders?] Not necessarily. I learn from many different things: nature, spirit, animals, children and Elders. You can't look just one place for learning. The whole world around you is your teacher.
> - Tina Frick (Freya Hlin Vrana)

In addition, a few of the teachers who bring us important lessons may not maintain a high level of integrity or commitment. In fact, they might not even be considered Elders.

> When the time is right, the teacher appears. This remains true for me — but I also know that the lessons learned are not ... always the ones the teacher intends to impart. I welcome new people into my life as they arrive: some I feel I can learn from directly, others I learn through their examples set.
> - Kurt Hohmann

Many people agreed that teachers could be Elders, but some decided the individual might only be an Elder in one area. This limitation was common. Others brought a wide range of viewpoints.

> I do consider several of my teachers Elders.
> - Anna Calhoun

Some people are very good teachers, but don't have the skill set or experience in life to be where I would consider them an Elder. I define 'my' Elders as a person with significantly more experience in a tradition or with a practice in which I participate.

- Karen Thoms

Do I consider my teachers my Elders? The answer to that is yes and no. I consider all of my Elders teachers, I learn from them every time that we interact whether that be intentional teaching or through example and observations. However, I don't consider all of my teachers Elders. Some of the greatest teachers that I have had, giving life's greatest lessons, have been centered on what I don't want to be. I have learned invaluable lessons from individuals who are unhappy, lack wisdom and foresight, and generally made everyone around them miserable. Those I don't consider Elders, but still important teachers.

- Mary Hudson

Lillith's story:

From an early age, I studied with many different teachers in various traditions. I was searching for a person who lived close to the source, whether that was the source of knowledge, power, energy or the Divine Source itself. Back then, I continued to look for a different sort of teacher: a master. Now I know that I wanted to find an Elder.

Elders, even ones who don't call themselves by that title, have an almost indefinable quality that makes them more than a teacher. They feel responsible for what they teach and how the person will use the knowledge. Although an Elder can be a terrific teacher, the Elder's focus is not just about information. They view teaching as more than passing along knowledge. Elders teach more than rote steps; they teach responsibility for your own actions.

There is a difference between book knowledge and real experience, between facts and wisdom. Individuals with limited experience can be excellent teachers, but they would not be Elders. Elders don't just collect information. Because they share teachings based on long-term experience, they ask questions in order to check the learner's reality. Some Elders want their students to surpass them, but not every teacher feels that way. However, Elders consider the bigger picture. They know their example lives on, and they concern themselves with the evolution of their pupils. Through those they educate, through those who come after them, their teachings will shape people and events, as the Native Americans say, for Seven Generations.

Leaders and Elders

In most organizations, including Pagan groups, leadership is equated with power, including the ability to deny or confirm resources to someone else. Certainly we can easily understand how this works in a job: the leader influences pay, etc. The same is true of Pagan groups and individuals who network with them. Pagan leaders spread attitudes and expectations along with their conversation and teachings. This authority extends to countless Pagans who want to be solitary. Although they move from one experience to another, lack of official membership does not negate influence. For instance, some Pagan leaders and Elders speak out during challenging times. This might include the need to set boundaries when someone drunkenly interrupts ceremony or educating the community about expectations about proper conduct. Not all leaders step up. Still, countless people have been attracted to certain Pagan path because of the teachings of an Elder or a leader.

Both leaders and Elders view the health of their communities as important; both would be available to assist with resolving conflicts or mediating disagreements within the group. However, not all leaders can be viewed as Elders, and some Elders have no interest in being organizational leaders. In fact, Elders from an indigenous tradition repeatedly reject the idea that they are spiritual leaders. The vast majority of Elders rarely obtain widespread recognition. In many situations, their contributions are unknown to the rest of the greater Pagan community. Even non-indigenous Elders can often be unrecognized outside of small assemblies who work with them.

Without doubt, famous Elders lead organizations, covens, and other spiritual groups. Despite a few prominent and well-known Elders, fame does not suitably define an Elder although it may describe a Pagan Leader. For example, a young person may write a book that develops popularity. Due to the publication, the author might be considered a leader by the Pagan community, but many (perhaps the majority) would not accept a young person as an Elder. On the other hand, many Pagans would consider Starhawk to be both a leader and Elder.

What sets apart an Elder from a leader? Leaders, especially those that continually work with a specific group, tend to view their smaller community first. They look at their own group in light of its interactions with the larger Pagan community. Elders, especially the best Elders, look at the individual and see how that person fits into the community, what abilities the person brings and what the person needs from the community. The Elder also considers how the community impacts the individual.

> A friend of mine said, "When a bunch of us are trying to decide what to have for dinner, and everyone says, "I'll have whatever everyone else decides," the first one to get fed up with that says, 'okay, let's order pizza,' that's the leader. That's all it takes. They don't even know it, they didn't try to lead, they just don't have the patience to wait for someone else to do it." I think leadership is most often determined by the followers. Who are they willing to follow? If they're willing to follow an idiot, then that's who will lead. If, like me, they really aren't interested in leading, they can be followed anyway.
>
> - Mowglellan

Certainly, many leaders work diligently at their work; however, Elders often view the community and its members in a distinctive way. Because Elders connect to and maintain sacred space on a regular basis, whether public or private, they obtain an awareness of guideposts. They can see where an individual needs to focus and what is interfering with the individual's process. They can sift through ego and personality to achieve a goal. When Elders are versed in a specific practice, their insights can distinguish a reality around a tradition separate from what students make up in their heads. All of those traits might give the Elder a goal that differs from the Leader's or even the group's objectives.

To an Elder, just because you have tools doesn't mean you have to use them — or should. It might not be beneficial or safe to use them. For example, an Elder might question the safety of an accepted practice or the preparedness of individual to participate in certain actions. In that situation, Elders would be willing to spur a group or individual away from hazardous practices; however, they would be just as likely to urge people away from complacency and towards advanced development. An Elder doesn't just say, "Do it this way;" an Elder makes you responsible for what you are doing.

Becoming an Elder

Most would agree that developing into an Elder takes a long time, probably a lifetime. Our contributors fit into three categories: those who purposefully trained for Eldership, those who became Elders through unusual circumstances, and those who declined the role. Several respondents absolutely rejected the idea of becoming an Elder.

> Do you know what would make me an elder? Putting me in the ground, that will be the day. And then it won't matter.
> - Peaceful Rivers Rainbow Warrior White Wolf

Despite personal reservations about Eldership, quite a few situations direct people into a leadership role. Various traditions include training towards priesthood; in these systems, positions tend to be hierarchical, and titles are conferred after initiations. In many organizations, standing is based either on those initiations (and the ensuing changes that they bring) or through a testing of knowledge and experience. Because certain traditions include a path to Eldership, some individuals begin training for the role from the beginning of their spiritual practices.

As they grew older, a few respondents mentioned the realization that they needed to prepare for Elderhood. To them, becoming an Elder was a conscious transition, arising from their educational and spiritual journeys and based on awareness that they were entering that phase of life. Because of that belief, they choose to shift their studies to fields that would assist them in developing into a good Elder.

> I am an Elder in training. I can't call myself that [an Elder] because I am still learning.
> - Rocio Darlene Arriaga

> This whole discussion is so fraught with cultural baggage and interpretation. I remember an episode many years ago. I was playing the part of Odysseus in a production at CCM and one of the younger actors who

had watched me practicing Tai Chi during warm-ups asked me if I was a "Master." The question shocked me and left me very flustered. I had not considered it. Having been asked, I gave it some thought and decided that I was not, but that I did want to become one. I'm still working on it.

- Kenn Day

At 57 ½, I have been consciously transitioning to cronehood for about the last 7 years, thinking that by 60 I need to be ready. With that in mind, I have been trying to build on my experiences as maiden and mother, to broaden my capacity for service and to deepen my understanding of how things work. My goal is to attain enough grace and commitment to become an Elder if I should be so fortunate as to be called. Currently, I am studying with Kathleen and Breighton Dawe in Shepardstown, WV, and their Sophia Course in Conscious Co-Creation. Part of that training is a willingness to stand, serve, and protect using all the tools at hand. Sustainable development will require a tradition of spiritual generosity, respecting of different beliefs but with willingness to offer support to all creatures. This distils to: "Seek not to justify, but to find justice."

- Ladyelle

Perhaps the most commonly known path to Elderhood exists in Wiccan communities. Typically, members of the group move through levels of initiation, which focus on different teachings. Together with years of involvement, that instruction will lead to individuals who are able to create their own coven. In addition, they can return to their own communities as an Elder.

To become a high priest/ess one must move up through the ranks from neophyte to third degree. The first degree was initiation, the second degree was gaining title, and third degree was ordination as high clergy. An experienced priest and priestess under Lady Circe initiated me and later elevated me to third degree, but the Lady Circe herself gave me my second degree...

74

Three years later, after much hard work, I received my third degree ordination. I branched out on my own and founded Circle of the Sacred Grove. I spent the next year proving myself as a teacher of the tradition. Then, seven years and some months after my first day as a neophyte, the Lady Circe and the other Elders honored my contributions to the tradition by making me a fellow Elder in a very moving, affirming, ritual of light.

As an Elder High Priestess, I am still learning and always hope to be. I gain much from the students' questions and I am enthralled with their creative reasoning. When I respond, sometimes I hear Lady Circe's words come out of my mouth and sometimes it's the Goddess speaking. My students and I listen together.

- Bona Dea Lyonesse

I am well over the half-century mark, have given good counsel to many, raised children and grandchildren — none of whom live with me. I still set an example at fire circles and teach sacred dance when called to do so.

During my weeklong Crone challenge I came to accept the title, after much soul searching and physical-mental-spiritual transformations. Now I have not only the wisdom of being thankful and full of gratitude daily, but I also assist and encourage others to be thankful. Now I happily accept their words of "Thank you" with a sincere "You are welcome!!"

- Penny Goody

Just as people grow into the role of Elder through purposeful training and study, some individuals do not realize that life experiences have been preparing them for that position. After they were thrust into Eldership through group consensus, they acknowledged the task and tried to live up to it.

The reluctant hero of many legends does not intentionally choose the course that they are destined to follow. Being an Elder is not easy or always convenient, nor does the title bestow respect automatically. I would not have chosen to become the dancing Crone that I am, and I am grateful that Fate stepped in and gave me this challenge.

- Penny Goody

Many years ago I was sitting in my office when a student, non-traditional, walked in. We had met at a small Pagan gathering a couple of months earlier and they had a request: would I consider being the advisor for a student Pagan group registered at the chapel? This student had been working with the Lutheran chaplain to get Pagans recognized, as it had become evident based on the amount of students looking for such a group that something needed to happen. I asked what my duties would be and I was told all I had to do was sign the paperwork. Well, that wasn't exactly true as I came to find out. I stuck with it because the students needed to find community someplace and they needed to learn, from elders and from each other, that they were part of a larger community and not alone[30].

Since that time it has developed and now I am a full Chaplain at the University with all the responsibilities that go with that title. I do love my work with the students, but it isn't just the students; it is with everyone that is involved. I have developed and changed with this role. I'm careful to listen and careful to speak and my own Elder's words always echo in my head — words have power; speak wisely because you can't take the words back once spoken. The responsibility of influence is great, and I always try to make sure that what I am doing both through example and through instruction is the best that I can give.

- Mary Hudson

---

[30] This paragraph was previously published in Ward, Terence P. "Pagan Chaplain's Voice for Change is Heard by Global Conference" *The Wild Hunt* on April 27, 2016. Retrieved May 7, 2016, from http://wildhunt.org/2016/04/pagan-chaplains-voice-for-change-is-heard-by-global-conference.html#sthash.F1LSOwgt.dpuf. Used with permission.

Since Pagan practitioners can be spread out over large areas, they may have difficulty finding each other, and this can lead to limited contact with older practitioners. Once they do connect, they might recognize the need for an Elder. Therefore, they go searching for one. In that situation, a group might even appoint one.

Lillith's story:

"It is a family event," the young man said, "and we would like you to be there." As an older person, I was surprised to be asked to meet them for breakfast. Over the years I had done readings at a coffee shop, I had met quite a few of the young people. They had a loosely affiliated community of people in their twenties organized into groups they called clans. In the past, I had enjoyed lively conversations with them.

When the meal was winding down, the de-facto leader of the clans tapped his knife on the glass. Ding, ding, ding. "Is everyone cool with this?" I had no idea what he meant. Around the table, people nodded.

"Cool," he turned to me. "We've asked you here — well, we've talked about it and we'd like you to be our Elder."

Frankly, I was astonished. Thoughts tumbled around in my head. *I'm not ready for this … I'm not old enough … I don't know enough.* Truthfully, I had little confidence in their decision. *Maybe I misunderstand what they want.* Trying to pinpoint what they really meant, I asked questions.

Their responses were easily summarized: they wanted an Elder. Since the community needed an Elder, they had spent time talking to a number of older people. All of the months of seemingly random conversations had ended with this discussion.

Finally, I asked the most important question, "Why me?"

"We like you, and you know a lot. There's no one else we trust. We want you as our Elder. Will you do it?"

How could I reject that request? I would do my best, and we would learn along the way, together. And that's what we did.

A number of people who function as ministers in the Pagan community were uncomfortable with being viewed as an Elder; frequently, they left the idea unconsidered until confronted with the option. Many of those who acted as leaders were not pleased with receiving the title. However, because of their service and work in ministerial roles, others began to designate them as such.

> I guess I kind of struggle with that term in regard to me, but I have to say yes, at least in regards to this area where I teach. I lead a rather large coven, teach a lot of workshops, do a lot of counseling, help a lot of solitary practitioners with their studies. I share my life experiences with this community. I also facilitate open sabbat and esbats and ceremonies, contribute to a lot of Pagan periodicals and put on an "open to all" Pagan festival (Beltane) every May. The experience is wonderful, fulfilling and tiring.
>
> - Bernadette Montana

> I am the Pagan Chaplain at Syracuse University and as much as I do not consider myself in any regard an Elder, this role thrusts that upon me.
> I am the Elder to the students that I guide and mentor at the University — that is how they see me, and I have to accept that. However, with that comes a great responsibility to live up to what I understood my own Elders to be. I kind of live in this in-between world where I still look to those I consider Elders for guidance and wisdom and accept that I am the Elder for the students who look to me for the same thing.
>
> – Mary Hudson

Many people don't think of becoming an Elder as a goal. However, because of their accumulation of education and experience, they grew into the role. In conversations with their own Elders, a few people mentioned that they were surprised when they moved into that phase of life. Even when their Elders did not plan to be promoted to Elderhood, it was thrust upon them. Although they did not choice that path, they did have a personal choice: whether or not to accept the role.

> I don't believe Teacher started the spiritual path thinking she would be an Elder. I think we are aware that we will age and grow older, we will become an Elder having wisdom from life experiences. But we never really intentionally go into a spiritual study to accomplish an Elder status. It seems as if this position is obtained quite by accident. My desire to know more about the mysteries, humanity and the understanding of the connections to spirit world will someday take me to spiritual elder within a community.
>
> - Lisa Owen

For some, others in their community view them as Elders, but that title feels elusive and unsettling. It doesn't feel right. Because they don't have clarity, they doubt their preparedness. They invest time in waiting for an event to bring cohesiveness to their inner acceptance and knowing. Sometimes sacred beings, divine ones or elevated spirits intervene to affirm that their status has changed.

Joy's story:

> Yes, I do think I am an Elder, but not necessarily because I meet the standards of my own beliefs or fit someone else's criteria. I believe I am an Elder because of the changes that I have experienced around my reality after studying with an Elder and then moving forward in life from that point.
>
> When I was in my 40's, I was able to study with Native American Elders. I was fortunate to become part of a women's group that met every month on the full moon. Many of the women in that circle had studied with a prominent Native Elder that was a Sun Dance Chief. He came through occasionally to pour Lodge.
>
> One of the women in the group was taught how to pour a lodge for woman, as this Elder did not want to

lead any mixed lodges. As quickly as I have stated her new role in the community is how abruptly this all happened. He reviewed fire tending, which she already was doing, taught her some songs, explained the doors and the rounds and told her to take care of the women.

I was always grateful to be in a lodge that she was responsible for. They were always well tended, sacred, and very much needed. I learned to tend the Fire and she became my first Elder. Her name was Marge [McCabe].

One day I was in a Lodge and I heard very clearly, "You are a woman that pours water." I did not really understand what that meant so I asked Marge what she thought.

She said "Oh good. You can pour the Lodges, and I will be the Fire Tender. I am too old to pour Lodge; it is hard on my body. I will teach you what you need to know."

I wish I could say that I protested or that I did not feel ready, but that was not my reaction. I was excited at the prospect of learning something new and being able to do more in the community. At the time I did not realize the weight of the responsibility.

The truth is, without Marge always watching, correcting, teaching, and supporting me, I would not have been able to carry on the tradition in a good way. Her knowledge and wisdom and the strength of her commitment was the cornerstone of my learning. Her connection to the Fire and to the Lodge gave me a firm foundation to move forward, not only in Lodge, but in all areas of my spiritual and personal life.

Sometimes I would feel like I was an Elder. There was so much responsibility on me, and so much need in the community that I thought for sure I must be an Elder by now. I told Marge how I felt and asked her opinion. She paused for a long while and said, "You are practicing to be an Elder." I was a little disappointed, but since she had a good 15 years on me, I figured she must know what she was talking about.

Then the dreams started. It was always the same. I was being pushed along a road and carried within a crowd of my ancestors and spirit helpers as they were going home to the Earth, the ground, and the mysterious ancestral dead. I was totally terrified. I was protesting while I was dreaming, "No, not yet, I am not that old, not ready to be done, definitely not ready to die." Waking up was always a huge relief. I thought, maybe the dream was from hanging out with someone that was older than me, or it was something about Lodge I didn't understand — or anything else but being carried to the shoulders of the dead deep in the ground and living there with them.

As the years went by I had the dreams less frequently, but they were still just as intense. It seemed that every year I would get a little closer to those dead. I never got there though, only closer. I just figured one day I would understand what it all meant. I was not afraid anymore.

When I was 61, I had the dream again. I was being pushed and carried within the crowd of my ancestors and spirit helpers and it was a celebration! We were all skipping and dancing and laughing and singing on the road. Before I knew it, I was standing on the shoulders of those ancestors deep in the ground, the mysterious dead-that-know-everything-that-came-before. It was quiet and peaceful there, and I had the sense that my new home on Earth was a place of soft ground, fertility, and cycles of becoming. The ancestors that had supported and carried me along the road said, "Listen to the words of these primal ones and share what they tell you with the living." When I realized that sharing the words of the ancient ones meant that I was responsible for the dissemination of the heart of the teachings to the people, I knew then that I was truly an Elder.

A number of those we contacted expressed mixed feelings about being an Elder. However, even when they hesitated to use the title, all of the Elders spoke about the rewards of doing the work.

The question if I like being an Elder seems odd. No, I don't. Don't get me wrong I love working with the students, and I love what I do in the community, but the responsibility of being on display 24/7/365 can be very daunting. The knowledge that I can change the course of someone's belief through a simple conversation, or that I am the one to talk to during a life crisis, is a weight of enormous proportion. I take it very seriously and work hard to help all that I can. But I also know that I am not the keeper of all knowledge. I have to tell people that I don't have all the answers, but like my own Elder I will stick by their side while we discover all we can together. The students teach me all the time, and that, I think, has become the greatest part of being their Elder.

- Mary Hudson

[Do I like being an Elder?] Yes and no. It is not easy being an administrator for such an eclectic group. But I DO know this: people may not remember me, my words, or even what I did — what they remember is how I made them feel. Life is too short not to help my friends, family and strangers achieve their dreams and to become their best.

- Penny Goody

As these stories show, a variety of experiences and valuable life lessons lead to Eldership. An Elder fulfills a role delineated by age, experience, personal preparation, and willingness. It is a role that includes recognition by others. Some Elders come by the position naturally, brought there by dedication or perception. Others seem to have a knack for helping others and doing the right things at the right times. A few are recruited. Good Elders rise up to the top and can be recognized for their abilities.

Recognition of Elders in the Greater Pagan Community

People tend to default to a definition of Elder based on their participation in a specific group. However, the Pagan world is bigger than one tradition; there are many loosely associated spiritual assemblies. At festivals, Pagan Pride events, and public celebrations, Pagans interact with others who follow a variety of spiritual practices that may not be their own. According to our interviews, quite a few were unsure how to figure out who the Elders are at those events. As previously analyzed, Elders have qualities that can be recognized. Despite variations in beliefs and customs, it seems reasonable that we can distinguish an apparent level of experience and knowledge.

> For a person to be regarded as a community Elder, I believe that they should be able to demonstrate skill from a spiritual standpoint within their chosen specialty (specialties) and should be able to put those skills to practical use building a life, home, and nurturing relationships. An Elder should also be available to their community in some fashion for assistance in spiritual and life crises.
>
> - Karen Thoms

> An Elder is a person who has offered their knowledge and shared in their experience to benefit others and the community as a whole. An Elder has moved beyond petty incidents and has the knowledge and respect of their peers, their craft, and their community.
>
> - Anna Calhoun

> The title [Elder] indicates a person of respect, wisdom and authority.
>
> - Penny Goody

Regardless of their tradition or group affiliation, Elders who achieve those abilities should be acknowledged and treated with respect. Many contributors mentioned important contacts with an Elder at a short-term event. Although the interaction was brief, perhaps during a ritual or at one festival, the Elder had a great influence. Therefore, it is good to acknowledge the role the Elder played in our development. Can an individual work with an Elder for a period of time, stop studying with the Elder, and still consider that person an Elder? Our contributors thought so.

> Some people I have had as teachers I regard as my Elder even though our association was not long.
>
> - Karen Thoms

When you participate in another group's rituals, you may not recognize the leader of the ritual as your Elder (or even as an Elder). However, the person who is responsible for carrying out the ritual is the head of that rite, and for the duration of the ceremony, the ritual leaders should be treated as Elders. The persons leading the ritual may not continue to be your Elders after the event, but it is important that they are given the courtesy afforded the title during the rite.

Therefore, a guest at a ritual or an attendee at a workshop should default to courteous interactions. If an individual is unsure about approaching the Elder, watch other people to see how they approach and speak to the Elder. In any case, begin with politely introducing yourself. If you have a question about the event, do not assume that the Elder will have time to talk to you. If the Elder is too busy, be respectful and look for someone else to talk to and answer your questions.

Pagans value the concept of respect for human beings (and other life forms); therefore, we should begin our interactions with respectful behavior toward anyone who might be an Elder. As an example, we might acknowledge the oldest person at a Pagan event as such, and treat that individual with the appropriate respect. Once we observe their exchanges with others or listen to their teachings, we can decide if we want to accept them as a personal Elder. Time and experience will show whether or not they live up to the designation.

The problems that arise at a temporary community, such as at a festival, are both greater and fewer than the problems that come from an intentional or long-term community. Similar issues can arise when people gather only for ceremonial events. Often problems occur in a community because the people want different things; complications grow when no one truly discusses what they want. If no one talks about expectations, the group cannot agree on them. We don't mean whether people will eat meals together or who will stand in which quarter; we mean matters like how we should handle a disagreement or how we should communicate a dispute to each other. It's learning how — and why — we should manage the difficulties. It's so easy to walk away from a conflict or let it go when we only have a week to be together. It's much harder when we practice together regularly or live on the land together, especially when those people are our beloveds as well as our neighbors. Everyone has had the experience of knowing when something isn't working. The question is whether you deal with it. Will you try to solve the problem in person or will you walk away? We have to learn to talk interactively, proactively, and honestly from the heart.

That honest communication begins with learning to show consideration not only for our personal Elders but also for other people's Elders. In our society, we can easily travel to distant locations to study. Relationships can be lost when we move to a new address or no longer travel to the same festivals. That mobility means that we can form new links with different groups and choose to drop past associations. However, this type of action contradicts an accepted belief in Elders as providers of continuity. Pagans of many different paths acknowledge the importance of Elders in maintaining traditions, teaching, and counseling. Therefore, Pagans often recognize and acknowledge past Elders, even ones that have been left behind. The Pagan belief in honoring and respecting Elders as holders of wisdom is an excellent practice, one that should continue in the Pagan community and expand into the dominant culture.

Establishing Respectful Relationships

A number of contributors told us that they were not sure how to treat an Elder that practiced a different spiritual system. In fact, several people we interviewed asked us to include advice about establishing appropriate contact with unfamiliar Elders. Many individuals mentioned their difficulty understanding interactions with Elders who they did not actively associate with. Solitaries with no recognized Elder or Pagans that followed a non-hierarchical spirituality were particularly confused about social or ritual expectations.

Lillith's story:

> I work in several traditions and most of those include respect of Elders as a part of the tradition. As students we admire our Elders, and we understand that they are important to us, to our culture, to our own growth, and for the knowledge they impart. We show that importance by offering them respect.

Although Elders want to be respected, this can be difficult to identify for both the Elder and the student. Personal respect is important, but it may be fluid and depend on circumstances. It may need to be discussed and agreed upon. Respect within the context of a tradition can be more rigidly expressed. Certain situations (such as a ritual) call for a higher level of courtesy. It is also important to establish clear boundaries at the beginning of the relationship. This will take some time and a lot of conversation.

We begin to establish relationships by learning how to be respectful to the Elders that we are interested in communicating with. There are some simple guidelines we can follow when we first meet Elders from various traditions that will convey signs of respect. Acknowledge Elders you don't know; treat them respectfully and be willing to help them. Be aware of the Elder's cultural standards. For example, some traditional Elders do not accept nudity in their tradition and would be insulted if you approached them that way.

Cultural norms for that tradition can dictate behavior towards an Elder.

- Bona Dea Lyonesse

After finding Elders, perhaps the most difficult part of connecting with them is how to approach them to ask them to share their teachings with you. For some, this can be a fairly simple process. You may meet them through a mutual friend, or at a workshop or a festival, or even find someone on line. If they are approachable, it is just a matter of asking them if they take students, and the first hurdle is resolved. For people who are interested in studying with an indigenous Elder or participating in a lineage tradition such as Sorcery, Lucumi Orisha worship or Shamanism, this can be its own challenge.

It can be especially difficult to approach a Medicine person or traditional storyteller. Sometimes the spiritual Elder will not speak to a newcomer even if asked a direct question. In fact, they might not allow the new person to ask a question. The behavior might be a test to see if the individual knows how to act; a way to find out if the newcomer can remain respectful, quiet, and patient. Can that person wait until the proper time to talk?

In certain traditions, waiting to be invited into a conversation is expected. If you have not been introduced, you may find it difficult to participate in discussions with Elders. Joy experienced this first hand.

Joy's story:

I was at the Seneca reservation when a group from the Rosebud reservation stopped by for a visit. In the evening a circle formed outside with the Rosebud and Seneca singers. I really wanted to pull my chair into the circle, but I felt like it was an intrusion and not the right thing to do. So I just listened for a long time while I was sitting about 7 feet outside the circle. After about an hour I started to drift off from my eavesdropping and was looking at the beautiful night sky. When I focused back on the circle there was a space open in front of me. I thought maybe someone had left and was trying to figure out who it was, when an Elder looked back toward me and motioned for me to join the circle. When I was settled in my place, they asked me what I had learned from their conversation. I felt so blessed to be included and did my best to be respectful during all conversations.

Sometimes the Elder has an assistant or apprentice who talks about behavioral expectations. That person would be a great resource to find out how to interact with them. In other settings, the event organizer, meeting facilitator or host might know the best way to interact with the Elder.

When you approach Mother Meerra, you don't look in her eyes. She is sitting and you sit on the floor and you put your hands on her feet. You have to keep your head down. She puts her hands on your temples. When she takes her hands away, you are allowed to look at her, but you are not allowed to speak. When I looked in her eyes, it was like looking into the universe.

- Rocio Darlene Arriaga

Many cultures have specific ritualized greetings. Often, these can be certain words we use to acknowledge the Elder's status in the community. The following examples are common titles used when speaking to or about an Elder. The easiest one to remember that will work effectively in most Westernized cultures or in traditions such as Hoodoo or folk curing traditions would be the titles of Sir or Ma'am. This is an accepted norm to show respect especially with the older generations. This simple sign of respect also allows the Elder to say, "You can call me _____," and that may be the easiest way to find out the name or title they wish you to use.

Other possibilities in many traditions are simple words such as Mother and Father or Grandmother and Grandfather although sometimes those words are translated into another language. The title can be related to certain Native American traditions or simply an honorific others applied to the Elder for a long time. These names could have a spiritual significance or just be a term of endearment that they prefer. It is important for the student to find out how the names are being used and what meaning they convey.

Special terms of address for older siblings or cousin, family friends, uncles and aunts may exist within the tradition. It may be important to know not only how to address your Elder but also their Elders and their family members. The use of titles to denote relationships is also true within assemblies such as covens, groves, circles, temples or Pagan churches. In Heathenry, the labels *kith* and *kin* are widely used to respectfully designate family and chosen enduring relations. Many Wiccan groups (and related practices) refer to the Elders as High Priestess or High Priest. These designations show the rank of the people that are in charge; they help new people to understand associations among individuals that are in varying places in their initiatory process. Modern Pagans have also adopted more traditional titles for their clergy such as Reverend.

In the Orisha traditions, such as Lucumi or Ifa, the Elders are referred to as Godmother, Godfather or in Spanish speaking circles as Madrina or Padrino. They may also be referred to by their initiated names or titles such as Iyalosha (Mother of the Orisha), Babalosha (Father of the Orisha) or Babalawo (Father of the Mysteries) which could add some confusion to knowing which greeting to use. Non-initiated students in these groups refer to each other as Brother and Sister, helping to cement the personal bonds that are formed in these communities. If you aren't sure, it is appropriate to ask people the correct way to address specific individuals.

Within various cultures there are also specific gestures and motions that are used to convey a certain level of respect. Examples of these would be bowing, saluting, or even hugging. Touching the ground or lying on the ground may be appropriate in the African Diasporic religions. Sometimes priests in these traditions are also greeted by standing in front of them with arms crossed and asking for a blessing. The fivefold kiss, although not as common as it used to be, may be appropriate in many Wiccan rituals, but more customary greetings are "Blessed be" or "Merry meet." In Hinduism bowing and touching the feet of the Elder is considered respectful. Saying "Namaste" with hands held palm together is a traditional greeting in Asia that has spread worldwide with the influence of Eastern religions, philosophies and practices. Some Pagan communities have adopted the practice.

> Treat your Elder with respect. I treat people the way I want to be treated: with honesty, compassion, graciously, and with a positive manner. Each Elder is approached differently. If I don't know how to approach them in their tradition, I ask somebody, "How do I approach them? Do I bow? Do I hug? I don't want to be disrespectful."
>
> - Rocio Darlene Arriaga

In long standing relationships with Elders, especially those that live close by, a strong sense of community, even family ties, will develop from the relationship. When people bond with Elders, the connections can last a lifetime.

> I always treated him with warmth and high regard, like a family member. We remained in touch for 37 years until his passing at the age of 80 (in 2013). We always had a lot of love and respect for each other.
>
> - Ladyelle

> Your Elders should be treated with honor and respect whenever they are welcomed into your home. Your table should provide for their taste or health, even if it's a smaller preparation just for them. You don't need to agree with your Elder to honor them, but you must refrain from hurtful, spiteful, or arbitrary unpleasantness regarding any issue now or in the past. Although these are good rules for all people enjoining your hospitality, your Elder should be offered the best of everything you have.
>
> - Karen Thoms

The same considerations also apply to Elders' treatment of their students. Remember, respect goes both ways. Elders should offer equal consideration and respect to their students and the students' families and friends. Mutual respect will help with development of trust.

I was able to trust Joy with my troubles, and I felt she wouldn't judge me or my faults.

- Alejandra Licea

I treat Lilith [Dorsey] with the respect I would give my mom and a most respected teacher; I think I treat her with more respect than most other people.

- Tehron Gillis

Once the relationship between student and Elder has begun, it is essential to maintain a high level of respect in all future interactions. Respect is not static: it may develop (or shrink) over time, but it continues as a necessary component of communications with Elders.

Entrance: Meeting Your Elder

In our interviews, we discovered two recurring but contradictory viewpoints. First, there is a belief that the Elder will arrive in the individual's life in a synchronistic way or with little effort. Second, because the Pagan community has few Elders or the Elders are difficult to find, people must travel a good distance away from home and extend a great deal of effort to meet them. Respondents' comments express that polarity well.

What causes people to select an individual to be their Elder? What draws them together? Although many individuals choose an Elder intellectually, people frequently mentioned an instant connection or knowing when they met. From our research, we found that synchronicity played a part in their search: no matter how far they traveled, regardless of the length of their journey, they seemed to be led somehow towards the person.

> She found me. When I first became a professional reader, she came to me to have a reading and we became fast friends and [developed a] teacher/student relationship.
> - Lisa Owen

> This was more like we were chosen for each other. I trusted Craig [Parsons-Kerins] and still do and would never hesitate to ask him anything or do what I could for him if need be. We just clicked. I love to be around intelligent people and he is highly intelligent and that is part of what first engaged the two of us. How the rest of it happened, I really don't know! I think in one way this is just the way it was supposed to be.
> - Mary Hudson

> When I first started learning from the Lady Circe, I had no aspirations to be a priestess, even though her coven trained Wiccan clergy. I just knew she could teach me what I needed to know to satisfy my soul.
> - Bona Dea Lyonesse

Many people were lucky to find their Elders near home, sometimes in a store or through acquaintances. A few discovered an Elder when applying for a new job. Often the individual discovered an Elder on vacation, at a ritual, or workshop. In fact, Elders appeared in people's lives in a variety of ways. Yet, the introductory meeting was not always as anticipated.

I met Tara Wolf at a gym that I was working at. I was wearing my pentacle necklace that day and she came up to me and said, "Blessed be!" The rest is history!!

Janet [Farrar] and Gavin [Bone]: we met thru a wonderful Priestess named Courtney [who] was making travel arrangements for Janet and Gavin and setting up places for them to teach. My store "Brid's Closet" was one of the stores she had in mind. I've been studying with them ever since. I had been working with their "philosophy" and read their books for many years before I had the chance to actually know them personally.

With Wind Daughter, I had a friend who was already studying with her and introduced me to her. I am part Taino/Arawak and wanted to explore my native roots.

With Isaac [Bonewits] I was a part of his "Black Dirt" druid list for a few years. He contacted me in regard to checking out my store. He and his lovely lady Phaedra [Bonewits] came up, looked at the store, had dinner, and [we] got to know one another. He and Phae have been a part of Brid's Closet ever since (until his death a few years ago).

- Bernadette Montana

I auditioned for a play called *The Execution of Jean Paul Marat Under the Direction of the Marquis de Sade*. It was set inside an insane asylum during the Napoleonic Wars. Eugene Lion was the director. I was 19 or 20 years old, but had already been studying acting and performing for ten years; he was 43 or so and had started at about the same age.

I was ready to spend more time studying with Eugene because I had already evaluated my local options in theatre, and Eugene was the only artist I had met by that point in my life who was willing to explore what the metaphysics of theatre was all about. Since I had been raised as Roman Catholic but had already rejected parts of that experience and was deeply interested in the ritual of theatre, perhaps as a substitute, I was looking for ways in which the theatre experience could be made to feel more "sacred."

- Ladyelle

Many people meet Elders at classes, a festival or ritual event. Actually, this was the most commonly reported method of finding an Elder. Quite a few people mentioned they felt admiration and esteem for the Elder when they participated in a ritual or class. Here are a few of the numerous responses from people who encountered an Elder that way, as well as why they continued the relationships.

My primary experience with Joy was seeing her work in a Misa at Sirius Rising. It was a very enlightening experience for me because I had never been involved in a ceremony like that. After watching the whole process I was in awe from what had gone on during the ceremony and my respect for Joy grew not only as a person but as a teacher.

- Alejandra Licea

I met her [Teresa] in a class held at the Psychic Eye Bookstore. I liked her immediately. Soon after, I invited her and the group of people we sat with in the class to my home.

- Tina Frick (Freya Hlin Vrana)

Attending lectures, enrolling in the School [of Wicca] and traveling to other coven's Sabbats where the Frosts were visiting. After several meetings we connected as friends as well as student/teacher.

- Penny Goody

We met at her class on Voodoo and Afro-Caribbean Paganism at a Pagan event. She talked, I listened. She made me laugh while making [me] learn and grow. She seemed sane, and she and I have a way of talking that I have not experienced with anyone else. She was the one other person of color in this community that seemed to get where I was coming from.

- Tehron Gillis,
speaking of his Elder Lilith Dorsey

I met him [Craig Parsons-Kerins] through a group in New York. It was a coven that I was considering joining and ended up not. He was a member of that group and we continued our friendship after I ended my association with the group. He and I entered into our teaching relationship, and our friendship, and that changed how I viewed the world. I could almost say that he introduced me to me.

- Mary Hudson

We met at a Mensa party back in the early 80's. ... The party was at the home of an old high school chum of mine. His parents had bought a house for him down in Clifton when he started his second year at University, and he would throw weekly parties at what was referred to as the Black Hole. When I arrived at the party I ran into an inebriated acquaintance who told me that there was someone upstairs I would have to meet. He said that she was an Israeli who worked for Mossad.

There is a little background necessary here. For the past few months, a series of poseurs had been showing up ... I was somewhat Zionist at the time, so being told that someone was claiming to be a member of Mossad, the Israeli Intelligence service, made my blood boil.

I stalked up the stairs with every intention of calling out this latest fake. When I stepped into the room, I saw a woman sitting on the floor chatting with a couple of the regulars. She was dressed in olive drab coveralls and wore those government issue black framed glasses that Elvis Costello made so popular back then. Her hair was black and in a short bowl cut with straight bangs, and her skin looked very tanned. On top of all that, she was smoking a corncob pipe! I sat down and listened to the conversation and was quite impressed with her Israeli accent. Very believable, I thought.

When the others wondered off, leaving me alone with her, I introduced myself and then said, "So, I understand you're with Mossad..." You have to understand that NO ONE in Israel would even consider saying that they worked for Intelligence — they don't even talk about what Army unit they are in — I figured that this was a clear indication that she was a fake. But when I saw her go very pale with anger beneath her tan in response to my offensively inappropriate comment, I knew at once that she had never said any such thing and that she was indeed the real thing: an authentic Israeli. I back-peddled quickly, saying that I had been misinformed, and asked to start over. We have been fast friends ever since.

- Kenn Day,
speaking of his Elder Elisheva Nesher

Whether people meet at classes, festivals or in stores, they recognize that they require interaction with an Elder; it is essential to their growth. In many cases, there seems to be a connection. Without that bond, the person might not follow-up on the moment of meeting.

You meet somebody, and you want to be next to them and you don't know why. It must be a past life thing. They feel warm and fuzzy.

- Roci Darlene Arriaga

A few people are lucky enough to be reminded of the need to connect with the Elder through repeated meetings.

Personally, Isaac [Bonewits] has been a part of my life in one way or another for most of it. I met Isaac's ideas as a 16-year-old occultist, when I purchased the first edition of *Real Magic* while on a hitchhiking jaunt. ... I met Isaac in 1984, when he attended the first Winterstar

Symposium in central Ohio. … that year he made his first direct announcement of the formation of ADF[31]. Over the years Isaac and I became friends and, I might hope, even colleagues. In the small-things-that-make-life-cool department, I consider this one of the honors of my life. As a chum, Isaac was clever, generous, a fine raconteur, a supporter of homemade music, and an open-hearted guy, interested in new people. He was flexible and adaptive with his ideas, and our many chats and debates about mythography and ritual, magical theory, and Pagan culture changed and shaped both of our ideas.

- Ian Corrigan

I had heard of Lady Circe when I was a teenager. She was rumored to be the Witch Queen and was often spoken of in hushed tones. I actually saw her for the first time around 1970. A couple of my college friends and I visited her small shop in Toledo. She looked very mysterious and rather intimidating. I felt a tug on my belly, something pulling me in closer. I had a feeling I would be seeing her again. I didn't understand for years that the tugging was the pull of my destiny. I spoke with her for the first time many years later through my art agent who had set up a meeting for my work to be promoted in a local store. … My agent introduced us, and the Lady Circe said, yes, she had met me before. I was stunned that she remembered me! I hadn't actually talked to her when I had first seen her, but she had had a laugh at my expense that day several years ago.

When I walked into her store with my friends that afternoon, I was awestruck by both the accouterments of the shop and by the legends of the Toledo Witch Queen. As I walked around the store, I wondered where she was. There was a short, dark hallway off to one side and I peered down it, then jumped with a startled yelp as I saw my own reflection in a full-length mirror at the end of the hall. I heard a chuckle and turned to see her

---

[31] ADF stands for Ár nDraíocht Féin: A Druid Fellowship.

standing right behind me. I jumped again! We all purchased a few items, but I wouldn't look up or speak. I was well out of my comfort zone.

Lady Circe's shop started selling my art and I became more comfortable around her. After some time had passed, I heard she was taking students. ... I remembered that strange pulling sensation when I first encountered her.

- Bona Dea Lyonesse

At the beginning of this chapter, we mentioned the second belief in the Pagan community. That is, the belief that Elders are hard to find and can only be found by searching or traveling. Some recounted stories of their quests for an Elder. However, a few do not ever find an Elder.

Sadly, when I was coming up there were no elders to model. I endured poor leadership in order to gather material but had no real teachers... That is why I mentor today — no one should have to do it alone, and certainly having someone to help along the way in our service saves one from many mistakes!

- Deanne Quarrie-Bendis

Certainly, the lack of an Elder in a person's home area has caused numerous people to journey far from their homes. Many times they traveled after reading copiously on a topic. At other times, the pursuit was more meandering. Occasionally the search lasted decades.

Lillith's story:

When I was 20-something, I looked for a teacher to give me answers, to explain the use of power, offer tools and practices, and lead me to supernatural experiences. I wanted someone to make things easier so I could understand the big questions, such as how this planet was supposed to work. After a number of years, I realized that no teacher could learn my lessons for me. Actually, I realized that I didn't want someone to give me answers other than in broad terms. I wanted someone to show me how I could learn to control power, learn to use tools. More importantly, I wanted to learn how to discover answers. In addition, I wanted someone who could show me that the search for those answers was worthwhile, that it could lead to a good lifetime, a great journey during this lifetime.

Many times, reputation drew me to someone; often I met a person at a spiritual gathering who would say, "You should go meet him, you would like him" or "She knows a lot about Native American ritual." And so, I would go. I participated in observances with Hindus, a few ceremonial magicians, and countless Native Americans. I wandered from place to place, but I always returned to nature-based teachings, to healing work, and to indigenous rituals. Sometimes I was there for only an afternoon and other times I studied for years.

After a while, I grew tired of the multitude of confusing messages from teachers. I wanted to learn from Elders. In other words, I wanted to learn from people who were direct sources. I wanted to learn directly from the Elders without having the teachings interpreted by middle men. I yearned to meet those people. Specifically, I wanted to be close to those individuals who had stepped beyond rote responses, rites that just went through the motions, and memorized prayers. I wanted to participate in rituals with individuals who were truly connected to the Source, who walked the Tao — it would be obvious that Divine Ones were answering them. I was driven to experience that. By being around them, I knew I could learn something that no book could ever teach.

In fact, I wanted them to tell me their stories: how they got to that level, how they suffered and overcame life's difficulties, what they did when times were hard. Not because I wanted to walk the same path that they walked, although I loved when that happened, but so I could see why they were different from others. I wanted a glimpse of how they had maintained the spark — the sense of truth or the divine connection — that sustained them when others turned into broken, sad, people who had lost their way. (By that time in my life, I had seen a lot of broken people.)

And so, I prayed. I prayed for a teacher who was directly connected with Spirit. I prayed for an Elder that I could learn from, who would teach me what I needed to learn. Soon after that, I was offered two amazing chances. First, I received an invitation to participate in a weekend with Beautiful Painted Arrow, an Elder to the Tewa and Ute peoples. Shortly thereafter, I was accepted as a student of an Elder in the Mexican healing and dreaming traditions. I traveled to meet with them, often driving by myself for hours or flying alone cross-country. But it was worth the effort.

A few individuals realize that the correct teacher is not located nearby or easy to find. Those seekers must leave their homes to look for their Elders. Often meeting an Elder means stepping outside of the commonplace and leaving the familiar to try something new.

[I met my Elders] by making myself available to them in their geographical location or a geographical location that they were going to be at. And pushing myself outside my little comfort zone in an attempt to gain that wisdom.

- Jase Peck

In order to find an Elder, some people literally move to a different state. Since they had to go find them, the encounters become very valuable.

I went to the reservation to learn about sweat lodge. Since I was one-quarter Indian, I got agency housing. I lived next door to my elders [Iron Moccasin and Ervin Cook]. All those people taught me what I do today. ... I made a four year commitment to learn about the lodge. In one year, I was pouring sweat and speaking Dakota.

- Gene Rowand

I worked for American Airlines in Texas and became friends with a "white boy" that was adopted by Native American parents. I was the opposite, an "Indian" adopted by a Caucasian family. He took me out to the farm that Sweet Medicine owned. I went there and lived in a tent. There was a two-story building on the property and when the weather was cold I moved into a room and paid rent. The rent went toward the land.

- Peaceful Rivers Rainbow Warrior White Wolf

But how do people know when the Elder is present? People report that they recognize the Elder through their feelings at the meeting. They sense that the Elder is the obvious one to speak with or the one that knows. In fact, the Elder draws their attention. Whether they are quiet or loud — one extreme or the other was reported — Elders are noticeable because of the parts they maintain in the entire experience. An indefinable quality states "I am here; it's time to pay attention."

Through an amazing set of circumstances, I had flown to California to study with Merilyn Tunneshende. She had arranged to meet three of us in the lobby of a hotel. Although the other two travelers were staying at that hotel, I did not have the money to do so. After the adventure of driving in California, I parked the rental car and walked to the hotel. When I entered the lobby — a grand old hotel lobby full of large leather furniture and chandeliers hanging from an ornate ceiling — I chose a couch that would work best for my short legs. Then I noticed two people seated together opposite me. We quickly realized we were there for the same reason. Although they talked quietly together, I sat silently, with my back to the main entrance, waiting, eyes roving over the architectural ornamentation. The size of the lobby swallowed up any sounds, leaving only hushed murmurs from the front desk.

Suddenly a presence entered the lobby. I felt a field of golden energy, warm and cool at the same time. I knew it was Merilyn. Immediately, I said, "She's here."

The other two travelers asked, "How do you know?"

But I had already turned to see her striding into the building. Our eyes met. She smiled and nodded in recognition. And my world shifted. She was a slim woman surrounded by an enormous effervescent field of vibrant golden energy. How could anyone be the focal point of all of that energy? Why didn't the other two travelers recognize that energy? And then, I wanted to know how I could do what she had done. How could I tap into the source to build that amazing abundant energy in my life?

Since my time of studying with Merilyn, and her controversial passage from public life, a number of people have attempted to belittle her teachings and negate her story. To them I state: I saw no touch of illness in her; she was lucid, rational, vital, strong, inspiring, active and powerful. Do you know what is truly amazing? Decades have passed since that first recognition event, and I have never met anyone whose energy field filled up a building as hers did. No shaman, priest, mage, indigenous healer — I have met no one else with that aura.

- Shadow Walker

Perhaps Stormcrow 's story of meeting a "Magic Man" at a festival is the most memorable.

The air was heavy with moisture and energy was at a standstill... The nights had become so cold that the dancers did not want to go to the fire. Earlier in the week, there was a night when the drummers huddled together under a tarp, and the dancers danced in the rain to keep warm. There was hope in the rhythms and everyone prayed for sunshine. Now it was Friday night, and everybody at the festival was sick of the rain. They wanted to celebrate the new moon with drums and dance, but people were cold to the bone from rain every night of the week. The drummers wanted to drum, but did not want to take their drums out in the rain. This night had a crisp chill in the air.

I decided to take Bullman's invitation and hang out in his area. ... Now, Bullman was special in many ways. I found over the years he was consistent in his ritual of giving his magic juice blend to the warrior drummers and dancers that stay up all night. Bullman and his friends would wake up in the morning and come out to walk around the fire with the jug to pass it around to the survivors of the night. They would join the energy by taking antlers and hitting them together. The sound was amazing. They had a few pairs of antlers around the circle, and when they passed each other, they would hit one another's antlers.

... Bullman's fire would be very positive because I could burn away some old energy and get to know some new people. I prepared well. I brought some wine to share and wore a purple velvet jump suit that was extremely warm. ... When I showed up, I was welcomed with open arms. Bullman was extremely sweet and offered me a chair. Bullman was ingenious and had three chairs together with umbrellas above them. ...There were a couple friends of his there. The fire was burning and the conversations with the people passing by were very moving.

Now, it was not until the night progressed past midnight that the energy started to shift. The laughter was heavy, and we warriors had a couple of drinks, but no one crossed the threshold of too much alcohol. The laughter was so great that it pulled people into our little circle. Bullman and I realized we had a matching sense of humor. This was wonderful, and we laughed as we shared who we were and our stories. ... Now, throughout the night there had been people coming over to join our laughter for a few moments; then they would get up and leave. So the energy was moving all night. ... As we were all chilled ... another person came over and joined our fire. This person was not just anyone, this was a very magical being.

This man was from Africa and he was tall — well, tall compared to me. He sat down and joined us in our circle. He said he ... hoped to hang out there for a few. Bullman extended his hospitality, offered drinks, and we all were on alert in an unexplainable way because the man had a presence. We all felt it. He was a magic man.

He and I talked throughout the evening. I was delighted to hear he loved drumming as much as me. He heard my story about how I fell in love with the djembe drum and all it represented. I shared how I lost my daughter and walked in a very dark place and did not want to come back. When I heard the drums, it pulled me back and helped me want to be here again. I started living again and wanted to give back what the drums did for me. I had been on a focused path for years to learn the djembe drum. He listened and told me there were many different paths for the djembe drum. He went into detail on how spirit has a way to bring people together with tools. This magical man told us how he was a djembe player as well, and he taught drums. At this point of the night, I still had no idea who he was, but I was enjoying his company. I treated him as I treat everyone, although I might have been shyer if I had known who he really was.

The magic man told us that back in Africa they were celebrating a very special ritual. On that very night we were all sitting down together, in his home country in Africa, all of the people gathered for the rising of a star. This only happens every 60-80 years, and he really wanted to be there. He shared how people of science had just learned of this star, and his people had been celebrating this for centuries. There had been great debate over its existence, but his people knew. This was a very special occasion. He shared how people there danced and drummed together like we were doing at the festival. He felt very at home at the festival. He said he missed his home but was happy to be here to share his story and great knowledge.

When he told the story, he was very serious about what this meant for his people. The star gave his people hope. As he was telling the story ... Bullman and I were intently listening ... this gentleman took us on a dreamwalk: I could see his country and his people.

When he was finished telling us the story about how people gathered for this celebration and joined together from all over, he told us it was much like our gathering because people from different clans came together. At this festival [in Africa], about 800-1,000 people (maybe more) came from all over the country. Some people went every year, and others were invited by a friends or family. The difference was that people only gathered for the star every 60-80 years ... I don't remember exactly how many years before the star shows up, but I know what I learned from him. The spoken word and storytelling time is sacred. The African talked about how tradition is moved through stories, and every time the story is told, it is like a living entity. It is much like an African song played through the djembe drum. As the songs are taught to other people the song is extended, like a story being told as it is being played.

The more I talked [about] drumming with this gentleman, the more I realized this was no fool. This man had deep knowledge and I loved listening to him talk. Now, at this point I thought the night would end, but to my surprise I was stunned by what he had said to me. Before he left, he asked me something that I did not expect. He looked at me straight in my eyes and asked me how I did it. I looked at him and was curious exactly what he meant. Although inside I knew, I needed to hear it, and he said it.

He said, "How do you navigate through this spiritual world here, and walk both worlds at the same time so easy." He explained how much he struggles here in America with the spirit world. He said, "People expect you to be on time and they are very unaware of the forces around them."

I laughed because I did not know what to say, but I told him my truth. I spoke to him of my journey of childhood and how I got here. He then looked at me and exclaimed how that dreamwalk experience was the first time he was able to do that here in America. Back in Africa these vision talks are common because people were much clearer. He was convinced that I had been to Africa, but the truth was, I had not (and still have not). One day I hope to go to Africa and experience drumming on that side of the world.

As for the rest of the journey, it was a fabulous drumming experience in the morning. I was so charged that I went out in my clothes and drummed in the rain and woke up many people. Now I thought I made people mad, but instead I received a poem from a woman... The woman stopped the drumming to speak this poem out loud so all the drummers and dancers could hear. She read it with passion, and she looked as if we all had awakened her. She was so happy to hear the drums because nobody had been drumming through the night because it rained so hard.

The next day was sunny. Before I finish, I must share that this gentleman was no ordinary person, this was Babatunde Olatunji. I did not realize this fact until the next morning when I saw him on stage teaching. I looked at the schedule and yes, it read there at that time. I saw this beautiful sister standing up dancing to his drum, and she said, "I just love Babatunde Olatunji." She told me how she was always afraid to express herself as a big woman, and he helped her feel beautiful again. She shared how he helped everybody dance. He lifted people's soul, and said that no matter who you are the heartbeat was within all of us and the heartbeat was your drum. He spoke some more from stage, and as I listened, I had a tear in my eye. I never felt more blessed to have sat next to a legend, a saint, a drummer.

- Stormcrow

The poem given to Stormcrow illustrates the exceptional experience everyone had that day.

Gift from a Drummer
Anonymous Author

Drop by drop the water wore the granite down.
Never Ceasing, even to find me, to deny me my crown.
Weary and down trodden, my heart darkened with fears.
Only one place left to hide a mind saturated with tears.
That as when a long-ago child of dreams,
Returned to me with my lost strength, sewing loves seams.
The Goddess returned to me all the tears
from her vaults in the sky.
Quenching my trust revealing a new threat drawing nigh.
I was drowning and my spirit felt numb.
Still though the dark night came the clarion call of a drum.
I held my breath and listened through each pregnant pause.
Yet the beat never stopped, each thrum gave me new cause.
Then in the midst of the sodden new day,
My face found a smile 'fore the drums called me to play.

In addition, Stormcrow 's story offers insight about the excellent character of a true Elder. Despite his fame, Babatunde Olatunji was humble enough to meet new people with respect and kindness. He listened to the stranger's story. Although he was not shy of asking questions, he did not need to prove his wisdom. Still, he was generous enough to share his time, energy, and knowledge with those he had just met. He did not view life as idyllic, yet he believed that simple interactions could be sacred moments.

The poem illustrates how one Elder can influence an individual or a group. Babatunde Olatunji reenergized Stormcrow and through her drumming, she spread that vitality to others. Exhausted people were renewed through the teachings of the Elder — although no one else knew that the Elder had planted the energetic seed.

Stormcrow mentioned that everyone at the fire recognized the stranger as special. As she wrote, they knew he was a magic man. Shadow Walker 's story also indicated an unusual quality, a set of characteristics that are difficult to explain. The best Elders encompass excellence. Their perceptible quality is not simply charisma or an elevated energy level. It is the intermeshed combination of a lifetime of work — not just working on a tradition but also working on the self — which creates a unique combination of characteristics. Elders with those characteristics are not perfection personified; however, they have more awareness of both the good and the bad in other people. They recognize what is important as they help us move towards the future.

How Elders Teach

Teaching — the word is loaded with meanings. In mainstream culture, children sit unmoving in classrooms while the instructor lectures, randomly asking questions. When an individual chooses to study in a Pagan tradition with an Elder, similar passive learning options may be found, but the majority expect active interaction. Their styles cover a range of methods from meditation to intense collaborations and from formalized individual plans to spontaneous associations. In addition, Elders, especially Pagan ones, demand that people learn how to determine the best course of action.

> From the start Yvonne [Frost] encouraged me to 'get over myself' and get up and sing and especially to lead The Dance.
>
> > - Penny Goody

> He would construct physical exercises, like one he called "Body Chess" to explore what it felt like when several actors moved in a delineated, restricted space. He would then ask us to apply that to the staging of a play, our movement within the space and our awareness of each other at a deeper level than is customary in theatre. The other artists were selected by Eugene and were also capable of deeper participation and seeking such answers.
>
> > - Ladyelle

> Joy taught me by hands-on interaction and explaining why certain things are done during ceremonies and why things happen in life. … I helped her through a few ceremonies and blessings and throughout each experience I learned and felt things I had never felt before.
>
> > - Alejandra Licea

> She always had a task for me to do. It started in simple way by doing journeys or meditation, then cooking,

painting or driving her. Then she would ask me questions and investigate what I had been doing and where I was going next. All that seemed to tell her something but she never told me what that was clearly.

- Lisa Owen

The next day, we went to the river with Grandfather Bear. It was very cold and sunny. We were going to get a blessing in the river's water. Grandfather Bear told us that in the Ute tradition, it is a cleansing and works like a sweat. We dunked ourselves under the water. It was cold! When we came out of the cold river water, Grandfather Bear had us stand in a line. We were all wrapped in blankets or towels. Grandfather Bear went to his chair to sit down and proceeded to look at everyone behind those sunglasses (he always wore those sunglasses).

He looked at everyone in line, moving his head left to right, and then spoke these words, "Which one of you will follow me?"

People started leaving the line and started running towards him. I could not just run up to him. My daughter kept looking at me and saying "come on let's go."

I didn't want to go. I kept standing there, looking at everyone to the right and left of me, as they all ran to Grandfather Bear. I told my daughter, "No not me, not you." I didn't want to go. Eventually my daughter ran up to him with one of the other little girls. There was this woman who kept telling them, "Let's go! Let's go!"

I was left there, standing alone, the only one left where we had been all standing in a line. I was alone. I felt really small and everyone was looking at me. I decided to stand up straight, looking to the right and left of me, I even looked behind me knowing no one else was in line, and I was shaking. I knew that Grandfather Bear was looking at me through his sunglasses.

He proceeded to ask me "Why don't you want to follow me?"

I said, "If you walk off a cliff or jump off a bridge, I am not going to follow you. You are just a man, I mean you are a medicine man, and I don't mean to be disrespectful of you, but that is no reason to follow you off the cliff or bridge."

He laughed, and said, "That is good." ... Later I realized that he had taught me I was strong, and that I should always speak the truth even when I stand alone, even when there is no one there to back me up. He made me realize I am not a follower; I am a leader.

- Rocio Darlene Arriaga

I considered her [Lady Circe] my spiritual mother, and she thought of me as one of her daughters. She teased me often about the fact that she thought I was too polite, too nervous, too worried all the time. When she was frustrated with me, she patted my head and sighed, "Oh, you poor dumb child!" It was the verbal hug that refocused me.

- Bona Dea Lyonesse

In our age of mobility, people can easily travel long distances to meet with an Elder. Flexibility in movement means that people can develop relationships with Elders who live far away. Due to the opportunity of long-distance mentorship, that separation has transformed contemporary Elder-mentor relationships. Historically, apprenticeships were established with tutors living nearby. In fact, in earlier times, a student might have moved into the Elder's compound to work in a formal internship.

Today, connections of convenience have influenced all relationships. As mediated interactions grow in popularity, contemporary communications with Elders include telephone and Skype, email, social media, text messages, and sharing of photographs. Both Joy and Lillith depend on pictures to verify that a student has properly set up an altar. In addition, online classes have grown more popular.

There is much reading and practice involved with the School's courses, and Yvonne [Frost] was always willing and able to discuss at length all the assignments.

- Penny Goody,
regarding the Church and School of Wicca,
an online correspondence school.

111

Since he lived 5 hours away from me, most of our conversations were on the phone or through emails and other means. We would come together about once every six weeks to do intense work. But he was always there for me whenever I needed anything.

He did give me one book to read and do the lessons as I could. ... It is a book I reread on occasion ...That book, though, was the only "formal" written word that I was given. How Craig [Parsons-Kerins] taught me worked in my case.

- Mary Hudson

Sometimes she [Galina Krasskova] teaches in a style that reminds me of student/tutor and others in master/apprentice. Given the constraints of time and space on us, a lot of these lessons are written, or written after I've performed them. I tend to do a lot of reporting and reflective writing, and ... we've started incorporating Skype. ... This is so she has a good understanding of what I am doing and also a good way for me to mark my progress.

She makes use of primary sources, books on philosophy and religion, and asks tough questions that make me think. ... She has also had me develop regular devotional practice, such as praying at my ancestor altar at least once a week. ...The format changes according to the work that needs doing and the lessons needing to be learned.

- Sarenth Odinsson

While numerous Elders use mainstream methods and technology, many still focus on an oral tradition. In such traditions, learners are expected to listen, cooperate, and incorporate observations into the body of knowledge. They expect students to work, to make mistakes, learn by accomplishing tasks — and perhaps to fail and do it all over again. In fact, comprehension is not always immediate.

Sometimes it took years to understand.

- Eli Thorn

This was oral teaching; everything was given to me by word of mouth. It wasn't until he was satisfied (and I don't know how he judged that) I had learned what I needed to that he would go on to the next topic. While I was in the midst of it all it seemed random but looking back I see the progression and the flow of what he did. Whether it was intentional or not it had a logical method based on what I had been given prior, and understood, the next lesson was presented, and the cycle began again.

- Mary Hudson

It is a commitment to a certain amount of time, certain number of moons doing ceremony, a commitment to doing things a certain way as I developed my own style.

- Jase Peck

I had to write down all my dreams, journal everything, learn the path, the rituals and the ceremonies. She wanted me back on the path of my lineage.

- Peaceful Rivers Rainbow Warrior White Wolf

I would check in with her every week for the first four years of our relationship or see her often throughout the month. Most of the time, we would spend a weekend doing work together.

- Lisa Owen

Elders' personalities range from reticent to charismatic and enthusiastic. Some ask a multitude of questions while others teach through silence. They may speak with animation or explain through quiet words and tranquility. Others provide space for the students to proceed at their own rate of progress.

Elisheva's teaching style seems to be based on her experience in the Israeli military and Kibbutzim, which is very different from anything here in the states. It is a kind of unspoken mentoring that supports the positive growth as long as it seems possible.

- Kenn Day

The format was verbal and experiential and assisting to obtain some of the deeper wisdom. "Is this making sense?" "Do you understand this?" Even sometimes asking me to repeat back my understandings of what was taught. "Do you understand what this is for?"

- Jase Peck

Quite a few Elders teach by example, and a number do not spend much time in explanations. A few teach valuable lessons without talking at all. They teach in many ways.

Grandfather Bear was a Ute medicine man who created beautiful artwork. A quiet man, he always wore sunglasses, even if it wasn't sunny out. I met him at a weekend retreat (with Joseph). I didn't know anyone there. ... I was really quiet and had to muster up strength to talk to anyone. We did a sweat lodge and after the lodge, Grandfather Bear had a giveaway blanket. Everyone was supposed to walk around and take whatever called to them. There was this sad looking plant on the blanket. Everyone passed it because it looked like it was dying. I just knew I was supposed to take care of it, so I picked the plant.

Grandfather Bear asked me if I knew what it was. I said no. He told me, "It's a tobacco plant. You take care of it. It is a male and female plant."

Others were taking beautiful crystals off the blanket. I took this beautiful plant that needed love. It was a lesson for me: I was learning to take care of a sacred herb. I was learning how to take care of a sacred living thing, which included myself.

- Rocio Darlene Arriaga

Teacher was dreamer, receiving information and prophecy through the dream world. Over some years she had received teachings from her people ... After our initial meeting, over the next few months, we spent time sharing shamanic journeys together, talking and building a friendship. I came to look to her as a sister, an

Elder and more. We spent lots of time playing music and traveling into the upper worlds and middle worlds.

She had a room that was bare walls and we would do all our journeys in this room. ... we explored ... and brought information ... so the healing could come ... and my lessons could happen. As we built this relationship in the room, we documented our vision by painting them on the walls, bringing the information to the third dimension space.

- Lisa Owen

He taught by example. He taught in silence.

- Rocio Darlene Arriaga

Lillith's story:

Stern people directed us down a wide path. It led through the woods and down a gentle slope towards an unusual structure that peeked out from behind the hill. The building looked like no other I had ever seen. It rose out of the hill, emerging from the land in the same way the trees grew around it. At the end of the path, a wide entrance led into the domed structure. There was no door to shut out the elemental aspects of nature: just a space outlined by wooden beams.

As I walked through the opening, I noticed wide wooden beams continued to delineate the architecture. They radiated out from the center of the ceiling in widening spokes that bent downwards until they reached the ground. As I walked underneath the dome, my feet made a slight crunching sound. Sunlight shown through the opening and reflected on countless rocks and crystals embedded into the ceiling and walls. In the relative dimness of the interior, chairs were arranged in semi-circular rows outward from the entrance.

No one seemed to be in charge; nobody offered directions. Carefully I walked across the gritty floor to pick out a chair. Around me people noisily talked to each other. As I looked curiously at the unusual structure, I

115

tried to settle comfortably into the vibrant energy of the chamber.

Suddenly, something changed. Automatically I looked towards the doorway, trying to figure out what had happened. A quiet man caught my eyes; he sat near the opening in a space demarcated by sunshine. Without movement, he existed, just as the rocks did, in a space of patience. Immobile, he was the epitome of the phrase "all the time in the world." He wore a bandanna covering his graying hair and pulled low onto his forehead.

Recognition dawned: this was Beautiful Painted Arrow, the Elder. Without fanfare, he had arrived. No one had announced him, and no one had seen him enter. Although he was recognized as an Elder by multiple indigenous nations, he sat quietly waiting for the students to notice.

Very slowly, people became aware of him. When it was time to begin, more individuals noticed. Gradually the room grew quieter until eventually we sat in silence. Still, he waited longer — one minute, two, and three — slowing down time for all of us. Only then, he shifted slightly, settling his back into the chair. A moment more passed before he began to speak in a soft musical voice. Without haste, he talked. Soon it was obvious that he was an educated and knowledgeable man. He interspersed his native language with explanations in Spanish and English, and his quiet words wove a spell.

As I leaned forward to catch his words, I realized that the Elder had taken us out of our normal world; we had entered a special place. Now we existed in an extraordinary time without clocks. In fact, we sat in a space where the movement of the sun and the shifting of breezes measured the day. Moments were established by the cadence of words moving in and out with our own breaths.

The Elder had created a condition where we could be present, conscious of our actions in the current instant and in the ones that followed without awareness of what we did. We were immersed in the now, surrounded by rocks, guided by his quiet voice. Thus, he taught us the power of silence and stillness — and humbleness.

Elders, especially those from traditions based on covens, village life or indigenous cultures, can be reticent or even unfriendly when they meet new people. Actually, several respondents talked about confusion due to cultural differences. Students needed to learn about cultural attitudes and behavior, and how to discover accepted behavior within the tradition. Although respondents followed various traditions, many mentioned that their Elders set rules of behavior.

> Some Elders spoke with a spiritual urgency and wanted to impart their wisdom. As long as they were still walking the earth they wanted to share that wisdom. Some Elders were very closed mouthed until you understood how to ask for their wisdom in their traditions.
> We as North Americans do not understand that there is a particular way to ask for the wisdom, and we have to work that question out first. We do not know: what do I need to do first in order to ask a question about this?
> - Jase Peck

> Proper etiquette was of vital importance to the Lady Circe. She taught us early on that the outside world would judge Wicca by our appearance and actions. If we were to be her priest/esses, then we must be above reproach. She required us to dress appropriately, which meant clean, well-tended clothes, black for class, and proper black, unadorned robes for ritual. We were to make our own robes by hand. We wore black both to honor our ancestors in all things and to equalize everyone in class and ritual. There was no room for egos or distractions. We must carry ourselves with dignity at all times, obey the laws of the land, and above all, show respect to our Elders.
> - Bona Dea Lyonesse

As these anecdotes show, some Elders speak eloquently, while others rarely talk. A few communicate bluntly or use humor to highlight a lesson.

> At the Frosts' next speaking engagement, there was, as usual, some grumbling and pontificating by others giving their own lectures at this conference. During the discourse Yvonne paused and interjected, "If we have not said something that offends you, please raise your hand and we'll try to get to you before we finish." With a chuckle everyone stopped taking their selves so seriously and began enjoying the many facets of our Pagan culture. Yvonne taught me to disagree with, but not disrespect, their views.
>
> - Penny Goody

> Iron Moccasin was ancient like waxed paper, and sugar would melt in his mouth, he was so sweet. One time, I went to Iron Moccasin with a problem. Iron Moccasin said, "When you have a bucket of shit, it's always going to be a bucket of shit until you dump the shit out."
>
> - Gene Rowand

A few of the finest Elders might offer humorous lessons and Heyoka Teachings, that is, they teach through contrary or comical behavior. Perplexing and disconcerting, a Heyoka's complex behavior appears reminiscent of the Fool archetype and is just as difficult to pin down. However, even though the Fool card in the Tarot deck has many conflicting definitions, you know when you pull it.

Joy's story:

> When I first met my Elder, he would find ways to test me to discover what skills I already had and could access. He took me to an antique store. I noticed that he walked around for a long time looking and touching many pieces of furniture. I thought he just liked what he saw and was considering buying a new piece for his home. Unexpectedly, he told me to go over and put my hand on the top of a side table and tell him if I noticed

anything about it. I went over and touched the table and immediately developed a severe pain in my chest and started gasping for breath. I just froze. He ran over to me and pulled my hand off the table. Very casually, he told me that he was so happy I could receive that impression from the furniture and feel that the man had a heart attack as he had leaned on the table. I was angry at him and stormed out of the store.

It turned out to be a more valuable lesson than I was aware of at the time.

I learned that my psychic senses were always active, and I needed to pay attention to the constant input I was receiving. I was pretty good at reading objects and spaces, so he moved our lessons on to other things.

Certainly, Elders mentor their pupils in ritual times, but significant learning happens during participation in everyday activities. In fact, ordinary events can turn into substantial training grounds.

Much of her teaching is acquired in conversation (at least for me).

- Anna Calhoun

Yvonne is always taking notes in shorthand. We often discussed these encryptions at a later time, as friends and confidants.

- Penny Goody

[Learning is] usually through casual conversations that transform personal or popular stories into profound parables.

- Tehron Gillis

Since sharing of knowledge is not limited to involvement in ceremonial events or formal workshops, relationship with Elders evolves into learning.

Lady Circe was an excellent cook and often prepared the main dish for the feasts. The most memorable lessons were learned while she was cooking. She would usually invite us to have tea and we would sit around her dining room table and ask her questions and listen to her stories. Those were truly the golden moments. I loved her.

- Bona Dea Lyonesse

Truthfully, Elders teach even when we are tired of the lessons — especially when we don't know there needs to be a lesson. They feel responsible for people in their communities and may introduce themselves to others through precise lessons.

I was working in my metaphysical store. Late in the day a woman from India came in. I was showing her around. She was looking at some jewelry and there was a pendent of Kali Ma that she looked at.

I said, "Oh, that's Kali Ma; she's an interesting Goddess. As a matter of fact, I'm Wiccan, and I hang out with Druids who like to do a Kali Ma chant."

She said, "What's a Druid?"

"It's a Pagan religion — we're considered Pagans — it's Celtic."

"It's Celtic, but you do a chant to Kali Ma? What's the chant?"

Her eyes got as round as saucers as I did the chant for her: "Dark Mother ..."

She said, "And then what do you do?"

I was confused.

She said, "You've called Kali Ma and brought her there, then what do you do?

I said, "Well, I guess we usually do another chant."

She asked, "To Kali Ma?"

I said, "No, to one of the other Goddesses."

She looked shocked, put her finger up and wagged it back and forth at me, and said: "Silly Pagans, you have called the Mother of the World, you have called the Destroyer of the World. You now stand before her and you do another chant? To someone else?"

Throwing her hands up in the air, she began speaking rapidly in Hindi as she walked out of the store.

Lesson learned.

- Tina Frick (Freya Hlin Vrana)

Elders can walk in, upset our worldview, and then walk back out of our lives. They can arrive in our lives when we most need one or they can be an elusive as springtime after a long winter. Just as humanity is a diverse population, Elders vary; they can be stern, humble, charismatic, personable, approachable or aloof. In addition, they can be serious or humorous, formal or casual in their interactions. What they always do is teach. And their teaching styles vary as much as their personalities.

> Demonstrating, talking, querying, repetition. Physical exercises. Tantrums with designers. Sharing of deep satisfaction when moments went "right." Obsessive use of a stopwatch.
> I was embarked on a journey of exploration requiring new methods, a willingness to risk, and unfamiliar landscapes, within the context of "putting on a play."
> - Ladyelle,
> explaining Eugene Lion's teaching style.

Elders may teach through personal interactions, homework assignments, books or hands-on activities. They work one-on-one with pupils and through long-distance methods. During their mentoring, they expect others to think, pray, and mediate. They might ask individuals to puzzle over questions or they might demand answers. Sometimes they speak the loudest when they remain silent. Without doubt, Elders train by example and by explanation. Through a desire to share their tradition, they lecture on the rules and guidelines for learning the path, work alongside those they mentor, and require hands-on training. They communicate in many ways so that their teachings cover all aspects of daily life. They instruct not only during times set aside for ceremony or special occasions, but also to provide a foundation that will assist the person in finding the way through any situation. Most significantly, Elders share in order to do something very important: to change people's lives.

Student Designations and Roles

A number of the contributors to this book worked with Elders in a position defined as "student." Students needed to succeed in particular tasks, attain definite levels of competence, and achieve an ability to perform practices with an amount of precision or meticulousness. In addition to expectations about learning, students had responsibilities and duties. Duties might be related to a particular task, for instance, praying during Sundance or creating a ritual object, or they might focus on certain learning requirements, such as memorizing information about certain herbs.

I had attended several lectures by the Frosts before enrolling in the School of Wicca. I followed their School of Wicca course, practiced The Craft for a year and a day, and went through the rite of initiation upon completion of the Essential Witchcraft course in 1990. Initiation was not simple: I made tools and faced many challenges along the way. Now I have a working knowledge of Celtic Witchcraft.

- Penny Goody

I was her student. I needed to attend circle every full and new moon. I needed to help plan spiritual outings for the coven, find classes and speakers to go hear. Find festivals and drum circles. I was responsible for the water used in circle and standing with the west, for the candles used for the west. And for any watery type altarpiece, seashells, sand, driftwood — sometimes I would bring seawater in a beautiful old fishbowl I had.

- Tina Frick (Freya Hlin Vrana)

I was officially a student; it was known that I would help with my teacher's needs, making sure there was enough food for the gatherings, cooking, cleaning and offerings to the ancestors. I spent many hours with her talking and learning from her about journey work.

- Lisa Owen

Certain Elders precisely define the student's roles and responsibilities. Sarenth Odinsson's Elder created a document that listed specific expectations:

> When I was officially designated as a student we actually both signed a contract, and some of the duties included helping her if she needed it. If she needs help at a convention we both attend, I am to help her as needed. In general, my responsibilities to her and to our lineage are respect, dedication, and hard work. This applies to my studies, our relationship, and so on. As a student this affords me spiritual protection underneath her, and the ability to call on her for help and divination if I need it. It is a relationship born in and sustained by Gebo, gift for a gift, between us.
>
> - Sarenth Odinsson

Others did not have a contractual agreement (whether spoken or written). Even when not clearly defined, the majority of Elders shared their expectations as situations arose. Students' experiences involved many missteps, mistakes, and misunderstandings. In a good number of Elder relationships, especially when there were cultural or language differences, a great deal of communication was required to clear up misinterpretations and miscommunications.

> Yes, I was [a student], but not necessarily in a conventional manner. It meant that I needed to learn how to be who I am and understand how I fit in the world. It meant that I needed to accept and change with the energetic and intellectual changes that were continually coming my way. It also meant that I was accountable to my Elder, my teacher, in what I did and how I used what he taught me. I had to work, and I had to practice, and I had to explain. I also had to learn to clean up messes and apologize when things I did went wrong or when others were hurt by my actions. I had to make things right. It meant that I wasn't spoon fed information, but I was required to do things on my own and to research and study and come back with questions

AND answers in order to progress. I had to travel to the Otherworld and the Underworld and introduce myself formally to whomever I encountered. I had to learn what was safe, what was harmful and how to work beyond the constraints of fear. I had to accept me in my new role, first of priestess and then High Priestess and all that it entailed for those that came after me.

It may seem like a rant, but it is not. To ask what responsibilities or duties I had is directly tied to what being a student meant and more than that, what it didn't mean or entail. I didn't get books to follow; I had direction and instruction given orally. I wrote down what I thought was important and key and then worked from that. It meant that I was tossed completely into a world of oral tradition where being a bard (teller of stories and singer of glories) was just as important as the role of anyone else. Words became my greatest friend and worst enemy at the same time for spoken words were the only thing I had to go on. I could ask questions, all the questions I wanted. But I had to understand what I was to do and then had to relate it back to help discover the lessons that I was given.

- Mary Hudson

Festivals and spiritual gatherings were introduced to me by the Frosts in the late 1980's. I was challenged to be in service to our community during these events. As the phenomenon of drumming and dancing developed, I took it upon myself to become a "bonfire mom." It became apparent that there was a need to coordinate the wood busters, fire tenders, drum leaders and sacred dancers in a safe environment. When folks feel safe they can travel upon their path freely — knowing that there will be water to drink, level ground for dancing, and a protected place to put down their drum.

- Penny Goody

Others we interviewed did not accept the term "student" for their relationship with their Elders. Actually, a number of respondents were not concerned with receiving a title. For instance, Eli Thorn did not consider the labels important: "If an Elder is true, it is not necessary to designate teacher or student." In describing experiences with Elders, respondents differentiated formal situations when they were recognized as students from informal meetings.

> I have not been officially designated as a student. I gain knowledge from many Elders yet focus much of my appreciation upon Daemon Wilburn who has guided me on several occasions.
>
> - Anna Calhoun

> Under Tara Wolf and Wind Daughter — yes. I was considered a student. Much of this work was one-on-one (with Tara) and workshops as a part of a group (Wind Daughter). Isaac [Bonewits] worked at my store and we had lots of time to talk and learn from one another. We spoke often of The Craft and his experiences with spirituality thru all his many years. He also taught workshops and classes at my store.
>
> - Bernadette Montana

A review of different traditions quickly illustrated that the designations used by Elders are not consistent. Although the Elder's system might recognize various levels of interaction, learning is not limited to the classification of a student. Often the discrepancies emerged from differences in language, cultural assumptions, and religious terminology. Differentiations and distinctions can complicate understanding, especially with those who are new to the practice. In particular, the diversity can cause confusion to those outside who are trying to comprehend a particular belief system.

Lillith's story:

> Many times, I was considered a student, a status that required learning specific rituals, giving assistance to others, being willing to help the Elder, and similar expectations of behavior. However, depending upon the tradition, the titles given varied. Within the healing and

shamanic traditions, my spiritual Elders treated me as a student, but they did not use that term. Indeed, they called me by a variety of terms such as warrior, seer, healer, or dreamer. One even called me a witch — and he meant it positively — although the title confused me at the time.

After the Elders initiated me to a particular level, the titles they used and their expectations of me changed because of the initiation. One indigenous Elder passed me through several initiations. I could list other titles, but they would be confusing when translated.

However, it wasn't the specific label that was important; it was acceptance by the Elder that mattered to me. That acceptance granted the privilege of being present. That is, acceptance as a student, regardless of a title or lack of one, was literally confirmation that I had permission to participate and learn.

In our research, we found that the social links between student and teacher complicated and confused the concepts of Elder. Maybe some of the issues between Elder and student have occurred because relationships have gotten more personal and less formalized. Despite that, countless Elder-Student relationships have evolved out of casual interactions. Based on informal meetings, a number of individuals requested teaching from an Elder. Still, sometimes even after several meetings, things did not go smoothly because the Elder might have decided to test the individual's determination and perseverance. Becoming a student, they told us, brought challenges.

Lady Circe's shop started selling my art, and I became more comfortable around her. After some time had passed, I heard she was taking students. I told her I wanted to learn from her. To my shock and dismay, she said no! She didn't think it was for me. I waited and thought about it, and a few days later, I asked again. She said no, again! I thought about this for a whole week and decided I was meant to be there and I was meant to be her student. I remembered that strange pulling sensation when I first encountered her.

I went back to her shop and told her what I had decided, and she said yes, we would give it a try, but she still wasn't sure about me. Her demeanor had changed. Now she was stern. I didn't care. I had searched for my spiritual home my whole life and I felt I was right where I was supposed to be.

- Bona Dea Lyonesse

As the answers show, people work with Elders in many different ways; so too, there are many ways that Elders teach others. Not all Elders designate followers as students. In fact, in some cultures and traditions, a learner does not progress to "student" or "apprentice" until many years have passed. Other practices offer titles more quickly. In actuality, each Elder determines the categories they use for those they mentor. They establish an ongoing interaction based on the needs and responsibilities of both the Elder and the learners.

Any cast member working with a director that is new to them is designated a student because they have to learn how to work under that director. They explore a new theatre piece, create a character, fit within the director's vision, find ways to reach the audience energetically, with authenticity. It is similar to becoming part of a coven because the end goal is to create a kind of magick known as "theatre magick."

- Ladyelle

In other words, in each situation, individuals learn through involvement with the Elder. They acquire skill and knowledge through cooperating and collaborating with Elders and their practices, and most importantly, through actually doing the work.

Naming

Elders bestow many types of names. Within the Pagan community, they include magical names, ceremonial or sacred names, names relating to roles in a specific ceremony, names that link the individual to mystical practices, and names that acknowledge an initiation. In subtle or obvious ways, a name identifies the recipient's path. Receiving a special name is a practice that is not limited to alternative spiritual practices; in a few mainstream religions, such as Catholicism, an additional name is given during confirmation. However, in the Pagan community, the custom of receiving a magical or initiatory name has a long and diverse past.

Historically, the practice may have protected the participants. Even in contemporary times, many people feel the need to use a different name in public. Yet, such a viewpoint is limited since it ignores the wide range of reasons for naming. It can provide a new beginning that can be ritualistic or private. For instance, a new one can be given during a dedication ritual, initiation or recognition ceremony or privately through the Elder's personal blessing. Thus, it can fulfill more than one function. It can acknowledge an individual's training and achievements, denote a new beginning, and boost people along their spiritual paths. The name might be shared in private or within a coven. However, it may be kept totally secret, only known by the Elder who gives it and the one who receives it. In fact, some spiritual names may never be spoken in public.

Elders who give names work in many different traditions. In a coven, the role of naming would belong to the High Priestess or High Priest. Within Druidry, the Archdruid often takes that task. In groups based on indigenous cultures, the community Elder provides the sacred name. In hierarchical traditions, the person in charge of training apprentices might offer a naming.

The individual receiving the name might also be required to participate in specific proceedings. This could include a traditional vision quest, a period of fasting, fulfillment of a challenge or other ritualized undertakings. A few traditions offer a new designation (or even add to a name) upon achievement of a specific level of training or completion of initiation rites.

Not only does naming provide kinship within the group, but it also identifies individuals within their chosen spiritual and cultural traditions. That is, the name rises out of the spirituality being studied. As a result, it strengthens the connection to certain deities, to an ancient or reconstructed culture, and perhaps to a religious lineage. It solidifies the potentiality of the spiritual path for that individual. In the best circumstances, the name enhances and supports the receiver's development.

Even lack of naming can provide guidance for the younger person. Sometimes, as in the following story, the Elder predicts that one will be given later when the individual is ready to receive it.

I joined the American Indian Scouting Association. ... There was a workshop given and people were divided into groups. Each group had an elder to oversee and a mediator to guide the discussion. The subject was "how the Europeans influx influenced the native culture." I was the moderator of a group and an Elder named Arnie Neptune from the Abenaki tribe ... was the Elder. The non-native leaders had much discussion, bringing up things like medicine, textiles, books, Christianity, different foods etc. ... I finally ... asked the group: "What about chicken pox? ...the different foods ... caused numerous diseases ... the forced integration of Christianity ... forcing the children to be schooled and taken from their parents at a young age — generations could no longer communicate the traditions. Wasn't that the true legacy left by the Europeans? Wasn't the reason we were all at this conference to re-teach our children these things?"

Mr. Neptune ... told everyone: "The discussion group is done. We will meet with the larger group to discuss our findings at the appointed time." .... He stared at me a long time... well, he didn't stare AT me, he stared over my shoulder ....

Finally he asked, "Would you like to go outside and sit down for a while?"

I said, "Yes." We walked silently to a shade tree and sat on the grass.

He cleared his throat and began to speak. Staring off into the horizon, he asked "Why did you ask those people those things?"

I said, while I too stared off into the distance, "It seemed a shame for those people to have traveled so far to not learn anything of value."

He asked, "How do you know those things?"

I responded, "I have friends who felt comfortable enough with me to tell me about Haskel School in Oklahoma. ..."

He cleared his throat again and shook off whatever was weighing on him. He turned to me and smiled and asked, "What is your native name?"

... I told him I had not asked for one. He asked why.

I said: "I believe that sometimes it is good to admire something for what it is, and not try to make it your own. The naming ceremony is something that is for natives alone. ... And a name was not offered by anyone in the native community."

He smiled and said, "Someday one will be offered ... and you should receive the honor with the dignity you showed today."

- Eli Thorn

Occasionally, an Elder believes the student needs to gain awareness of the impact of an existing name due to the embedded emotional and mental reactions. In other words, the Elder knows that the student must address the ramifications of unconscious feelings and reactions to the birth name. Therefore, to discover new understanding and appreciation for its influence, the individual receives the original name back. What an amazing gift from an Elder!

What was interesting was that he [Eugene Lion] insisting on me calling myself by my full, whole name, and making me explore whether/why I was happy or unhappy with it, as a form of self-knowledge and self-acceptance, I guess.

- Ladyelle

130

Naming rituals create a tribal feeling, a connection to an earlier time desired by many Pagans. Through the spiritual name, the Elder links the individual to the tradition, that is, to a continuum of those within the tradition, not only who lived before, but also those who live now, and those still to come. Regardless of the customs practiced by the Elder, naming is a blessing. Because of their life experiences and their intimate knowledge, especially when based on a lifelong practice of sacred traditions, it is a gift to receive a name from an Elder.

> It was a naming ceremony where I did a giveaway ceremony first, and then I was presented with my name (along with a secret): *Makwa Mekse Ekwa*: Bear Eagle Woman.
>
> - Lisa Owen,
speaking of her Anishinaabe Ojibwa teacher

In many Pagan groups, it is acceptable for a person to pick a magical or sacred name. Consequently, in those communities, the Elder allows the individual to progress through self-determined identification. Typically, such names are evocative of the person's chosen spirituality; they are picked because of an association with the group's customs or the individual's primary deities.

> I have taken the last name of Goody and have been known as Goody Goody now for many years. It is a reference to the courtesy title of Goodwife.
>
> - Penny Goody

After Penny's choice, her Elder, Yvonne Frost, accepted that name by introducing her as "Penny Goody, my friend." Through acceptance of the chosen name, the Elder strengthened Penny's ties both to current practitioners of her tradition and to historical women.

However, the Elder does not always agree with the chosen name. Even when the novice is permitted to pick a name, it may be rejected. Sometimes the reasons for dismissal become clear after the choosing.

> Lady Circe allowed her students to choose a sacred name, but she always had the final word on the matter.

> Sacred names are very important. When a sacred name is decided on, the chooser takes on much of the energy of that name, whether they like it or not. We were required to do research before presenting the name to her for approval. I felt particularly drawn to the Goddess Hecate and wanted to take that name. I received an emphatic no. "That name is way too strong and dark for you. You couldn't handle it. Pick a different name." Now, I have a willful streak in me and I was going to have my way. I did more research and discovered that according to ancient Roman mythology, the benevolent aspect of Hecate is the Bona Dea. She agreed that it fit me, and it has proven to be my true name.
>
> - Bona Dea Lyonesse

If the selected name is rejected, the individual has to choose to trust the Elder's judgment because it based on a more knowledgeable and objective viewpoint. In this situation despite her stubbornness, Bona Dea did pick a different name, one that her Elder accepted, and eventually, she realized the second name suited her perfectly.

Through their deeds, Elders affect others and provide a living continuum to the divine beings. For example, when an Elder opens a connection to an other-worldly encounter, the participants can experience the sacred realities or achieve altered states of awareness. With such actions, the Elders offer a new perspective on the functioning of the universe. Additionally, they can create safe and consecrated space in order to connect participants with inhabitants of sacred realities. Through amazing circumstances, a few fortunate individuals have received a magical name during a supernatural experience.

> Yes, I was named that first night, but it wasn't given by him. It was given by the Fey that came through in the ritual. I have to respectfully decline from giving that name, it is my true name, my magical name, and that is between me and those that gave it to me. That should explain the significance that it carries.
>
> - Mary Hudson

Although Mary Hudson's Elder did not directly name her, he activated the connection to the Fey, allowing them to participate in the ritual and offer a name. What an exciting experience! The Elder's familiarity and involvement with the Fey acted as the foundation, allowing him to introduce them to Mary, and through that interaction, to begin a personal association. Similarly, through a lifetime of practicing a tradition, an Elder can channel an elevated or divine being, permitting it to interact with the student.

Even when the naming occurs during less mystical circumstances, the receiver may not comprehend the situation or the name. In fact, often the name is perplexing or mysterious to the one receiving it. In those situations, not only the method of the naming but also the name itself becomes part of the Elder's teaching. Often, an individual needs time to connect with a new identity, and the Elder knows that awareness will develop over time.

> Yes, I got a big name. My name was *Peaceful Rivers Rainbow Warrior.* I had to discover for myself each aspect of the name, what it meant for myself and then work with it.
>
> - Peaceful Rivers Rainbow Warrior White Wolf

Lillith's story:

> The woman came to me asking for a naming. She appeared to have a good life: stable employment, a loving boyfriend and a nice house. So I was curious about her reasons for wanting a name. Was this now a fad?
>
> I asked, "Why do you want a new name?"
>
> "I need to make a change in my life. Something is missing spiritually too."
>
> Since that was a good motivation, I prayed to receive permission to search for a name for her. After I received consent, I was told to journey into sacred reality to discover the story of her soul, that is, the story her soul needed. I will share part of that experience.

Soon I was swimming in the ocean, floating effortlessly under a radiant sky. In the distance, palm trees grew out of an archipelago. Should I travel there? When I turned towards that island, I was swept up into a ripple of waves as swift creatures darted past. A few of them stopped, heads popping above the surface. Dolphins! One swam underneath me so that my hands linked onto the dolphin body. We were off, rushing through the water. Too quickly the delightful ride ended. As the dolphins left, I was deposited on the shore.

Returning to ordinary reality, I said, "Here is the story of your soul, the story of your naming."

She listened intently for a few seconds, but impatience soon moved across her face. "Did you get my name? What does this have to do with my name?"

"Yes, I received your name. I am telling you how your name was given because the information is important for your well-being."

Irritably, she demanded, "What is it? What is my name?"

Obviously, I was not going to be able to share the journey until I told her the name. "Your name is *Swims with Dolphins*."

"What?! What kind of name is that?!"

I was growing tired of trying to talk to this impatient young woman who would not take the time to listen. I said, "It is the name that your soul wants you to know. It is the name that was given in the sacred reality. It is the name you need so that you can move forward in your life and find what is missing in your spirituality. That is what you asked me to do."

She was quiet for a while. Silently I waited. Grudgingly she said, "It's a nice name. I just didn't expect that kind of name; it's a girl's name, a pretty name. I wanted something strong."

By her tone of voice, I knew she was disappointed. I realized that she really did not understand the name and why it was given. I knew the name was not simply a pretty name, but only time would bring that awareness to her.

A few years later, I saw her at a social event. She was effervescent, alive in a way she had not been before. I asked how she was doing. She was so excited that her answer came out in sound bites.

"I just came back — from vacation — the Caribbean — a cruise — we docked at a special place — I swam with dolphins! It was wonderful! The best day! My life is going great!"

"Wonderful!" I said, "I am glad for you." I paused and then continued, "Your name came true."

She looked at me stunned. Finally, she said, "It did."

Joy's story:

The Ganji Gathering was for people that wanted to join the Wolf Clan Teaching Lodge; you would go because you had decided you wanted to live as an example for others. Part of the process was receiving a name from Grandmother Twylah Nitsch. Twylah would go into the house with her students that were already in the Wolf Clan, and she would pray to receive names for the other people that had come for the weekend. When a person stepped forward to become part of the Wolf Clan, she would just know which name belonged to each one.

There was drumming, and people were dancing. I remember that I was dancing the whole time, feeling the pull of the community because it was a celebration. Normally I didn't dance, but I did there. When Twylah came out and spoke to me, welcoming me into the Wolf Clan, she named me *She Who Dances*. I mentioned to an Elder that I didn't know why she gave me that name. The Elder simply stated, "Sometimes we grow into the new name."

We all think that we know who we are. Then we find out it's something different. Later I started making drums and studying West African drumming and then dance. My world expanded in many ways. Then I went to Africa and was initiated. Receiving that name changed my life.

Within the Pagan community, an Elder performs an important function by bestowing a name or by accepting the one that has been chosen. Receiving a name from an Elder impacts the individual in countless ways. As we have seen through the contributor stories, people often have no idea what will happen after the naming, and they cannot foresee the changes it will bring. Without a doubt, the naming sets an individual in a specific place and time within the entire historical range of that tradition. By linking past, present, and future, it can anchor a person who was previously adrift. It can pinpoint potentialities, offer a spiritual direction, or bring necessary soul lessons. In addition, the naming can link an individual to a religious lineage or group as well as recognize a special relationship with a certain mystical element, power ally, or deity.

Testing

Within any relationship, understanding grows out of learning about each other. An interaction with an Elder also includes overcoming miscommunication, and frequently the learner realizes how to interact through trial and error, especially when it comes to asking questions.

> I asked her questions I had asked every other spiritual leader during my search for where I belonged. Most had either backed away or changed the subject because I was relentless and unsatisfied. She always looked me straight in the eye. She never backed down. Often she would counter with a question of her own to help me arrive at my own answers. Spirit and ritual, she taught me, were where the answers could be found. I trusted her.
> - Bona Dea Lyonesse

Often, the Elders will test the seeker; this is true of both the beginner and the more experienced apprentice. At the least, Elders challenge others to learn new things, and to view the world in different ways. As we found in our contributors, the testing occurred through questioning, conversation, assignments, expectations of behavior, active participation, and even challenges.

> My Elder has tested me in a number of ways, from pushing me to go back to basics and relearn everything, to the initiations I have gone through with her.
> - Sarenth Odinsson

> He would set telepathic tests and see if I picked up on them, would wait for me to report receiving one of his messages. He would write down on a piece of paper if he felt me messaging him (without a device), so that when I arrived, he would show me the paper of what I had been thinking.
> - Ladyelle

Yes, she did test me…it took a long time for her to trust me so it was always a test of truth with her and how much I could do for her…bringing and cooking food was a sign of respect.

- Lisa Owen

Many Elders expect successful completion of a previous lesson before moving forward into new assignments. A number of people reported that they were put into impromptu situations to see if they could demonstrate what they were supposed to have learned. This is customary.

He would give me new information, new tasks, new techniques of doing things and would ask how these particular activities went. He would tell me to integrate practices without telling me how to do so and then after the fact give commentary on what I had done. But as a formal test, no, nothing of that nature. I would ask so many questions on what certain things meant and why things happened the way they did and was I doing it right… I was certain that some time he would just tell me to be quiet, but he never did. So in one way you could say I tested his patience.

- Mary Hudson

She often called upon me at a moment's notice to assist in a public ritual or magical display. I came to be prepared for any circumstance — sort of like a good "scout!"

- Penny Goody

Tests? Maybe in having me do ritual, lead groups and/or teach others in their presence. I think that every time that you have a meaningful discussion with your elders, is a test of some kind — for both of us. They see what my ideas and thoughts are in regard to the lesson being taught. … I have learned that ALL experiences are tests in one form or the other.

- Bernadette Montana

Everything was a test. Showed us how to do things and she had students that also taught others. She taught by doing. She taught with stories. She taught building the lodge, setting up the fires, and learning the stories... She would tell us to do something. We would have to tell her how to do it and then do it correctly. She never got angry. She would ask, "Would it work better if we did it this way?" She got us to look at things a little bit differently than the way we were looking at it.

- Peaceful Rivers Rainbow Warrior White Wolf

Lillith's story:

My sensei required students to practice Tai Chi every day. Somehow, he knew if a student failed to do the exercises daily. He would tell that student, "You are stuck in your mind because your body does not remember." I was glad he didn't say it to me.

Joy's story:

Mr. William Molnar (also known as the Great Wizard Bill) was teaching me mediumship. He picked me up one day and asked if I would go check out an abandoned house with him. It was a big old Victorian house that had been converted into small apartments and sleeping rooms. We went upstairs, and he said, "Tell me if you notice anything up here."

I walked down the hall and I got a feeling about one of the rooms, so I said to Bill, "I think there is something going on in this room."

I stood in the doorway to check things out. There was an old beat-up filthy mattress on the floor. I scanned the room and my eyes kept going back to the mattress. I finally looked directly at the mattress, and I saw a dead woman on the mattress and blood everywhere. I "saw" a young man had killed the woman. I was overwhelmed and nauseated. I bolted down the stairs and out to the car.

"Why did you bring me here?" I asked.

He said, "I wanted to discover if you could see it or not." Then he showed me a newspaper clipping from the Seventies about the young woman that was murdered in the house. It described the exact scene I had experienced.

As these stories demonstrate, often the testing arrives in unexpected ways. In addition, Elder's lessons require dedication and endurance.

Lillith's story:

I felt fortunate to be learning from a well-known North American Native Elder, Beautiful Painted Arrow. However, it had been a long trip — more than eight hours in the car driving alone — and we had begun working early the next morning. In fact, I had been occupied non-stop day and night since arriving: sweat lodge, hours in prayer ceremonies, lectures, assignments, the requirement of learning and dissecting a new language with limited sleep and few meals. In addition to the necessity of dropping into visionary role at a moment's notice, I was required to assist in numerous healing sessions. It was physically and mentally exhausting. I loved it, but what an intense pace!

One morning he asked about the previous night-time assignment. I admitted, "I wasn't very successful."

He asked, "Why?"

I said, "I had a migraine." I suppose I expected that to suffice as an excuse.

His response? "Good, that means you're working."

Frequently you will be required to show dedication through hard work and patience. Perhaps you will be expected to come early and wait.

Joy's story:

I was invited to experience a traditional pipe ceremony. At the time my two youngest children were under five. I decided to go, but I had to bring my children. We were supposed to be there at 3:00 for the potluck. We ate, and finally, the Elder came at the end of the potluck. He didn't talk to anybody, but went into a different room with his traveling companions to eat. The house was packed. He came around 6 or 7:00. By 8 or 9:00, people started leaving because they were frustrated. About 10, my kids fell asleep under the dining room table. Around 11:00, he peeked out and said, "Just a little while longer."

Gradually more and more people left. Finally at 2:00 in the morning, there were three other people and me. He said, "Come in, we're going to do the pipe ceremony now." It was a moving and beautiful experience. After the ceremony, I woke my kids up, put them in the car, and drove home.

Testing by Elders can force us to step out of complacency, out of our comfort zones. Challenges can bring us to the brink of letting go of our egos. Some tests that we receive from Elders push us to change our places in the world and how we view our lives. Through adversity, we are compelled to deal with issues of concepts of life and death and the very essence of what we value in our existence.

It was a phone call I will never forget. Previously, I had been accepted as a student of Merilyn Tunneshende, and I was planning to spend a few days with my Elder. The voice on the phone asked, "Can you fly out early to have dinner?"

"I'd be thrilled to do that."

"Good."

After we scheduled the meeting time and place, I asked," Is there anything I should do to prepare for the weekend?"

The response was calm and terse. "Put your affairs in order."

I don't remember saying goodbye or hanging up although I must have done so. Her words had stunned me into silence. With them, the world stopped; it shrunk to one moment in time.

Eventually my awareness focused on my heartbeat. With my heartbeat, the world expanded outwards, past the confinement of the room, out of the building, beyond the sky and trees, past the planet, into the universe, through the depth and breadth of space into the void.

All afternoon, those five words echoed in my head. By bedtime, I had organized things as best I could: an envelope to be opened if I died containing legal documents concerning custody of my teenaged children and the insurance policy that would pay off the balance owed on the house and car. There were plenty of groceries in the house, and I had paid all of my bills.

In the days that followed, I meditated on that moment. *Put your affairs in order.* The words had arrived in my ear surrounded by meanings, yet they had shredded my expectations. I contemplated where I was in my life and analyzed where I wanted to be.

It was Merilyn's first teaching, succinctly delivered to me. If I truly chose this path, I could not turn back. I could no longer live blissfully unaware, focused on the past or the future. Instead, I could plan and decide, and then execute the plan with all my will, my mind, and courage. The lesson was encompassed by those words: *put your affairs in order.* Don't bring the past with you; start fresh. From that moment I had to be willing to change, to dare to become a different person.

- Shadow Walker

Advice for Students

When you begin your studies with Elders, they may ask you to stop doing your current spiritual practices even if they are similar to lessons you will be receiving. It is also possible that the Elder may feel that you need a fresh start. Be all right with that; you may really have to begin again. They will have reasons for this. For instance, you may need to review or relearn basic tools, techniques, and practices to create a good foundation for the lessons to be conveyed to you. They will also use this information to get a general idea of your spiritual knowledge and to determine if there are any gaps in your education. An awareness of where you are, what you know, and how you learn will help the Elder convey important teachings in a clear way without misunderstanding.

Joy's story:

> If people can present their feelings and thoughts from a place of honesty, communication becomes more fluid and flowing. If they are studying a certain tradition with me, then I want to be aware of what else they are doing and why and their beliefs concerning their other disciplines. This helps me to understand them better and gives me a clearer picture of their personal cosmology. For example, if they come to me to learn shamanism, I would like to know if they are intending to continue practicing chaos magic too.

Cultivate respect for the lessons and the teaching style. Let go of personal expectations, especially those that center on how the teachings should be presented. Often students insist that the training has to match their established worldview. Some people want the Elder to teach in a certain way. If the information does not follow what they are used to or match how they presently think, they may not continue the process and might reject the lessons.

It is important for students to immerse themselves into teachings since they will be a primary tool for growth. You might need to be more fluid in your attitude and more accepting of a different way of doing things in order to experience all aspects of the training: you to have make room. Do that by setting aside some autonomy in order to receive what the Elder is trying to give you. Be willing to let someone else guide your spiritual process.

Abstain from speculation about future titles and roles. Those beliefs may cause confusions and misunderstandings, and they certainly will hinder your progress. Do not presume you know where you are going.

There will be a rule — or many rules. Can you accept that? There are certain traditions that encompass a complicated spiritual order that may need to be presented in a precise way. The Elders have experienced learning the tradition in this way and know that it works by being taught in that order.

Many traditions need to be practiced in a certain way. Rules and protocols are protective and give an organized structure not only for teaching but also for solving problems should they arise. The teaching style and the framework are a legacy that allows them to endure. Trust in those long-standing practices. It is best for students to realize that they are now in service to the tradition and to the Elders that have taken them under their wings.

> We take learning for granted. It is only much later that we discover the significance of what we've learned and how better to apply it.
>
> - Ladyelle

Be driven to learn; don't just do it because you think it would be cool. Desperation makes for good learning. In fact, an excellent student wants to be engaged with the teacher and the process. Participate as much and as often as you can and make room for the tradition in your life. It is part of your path of being and for many will become a way of living.

> I had to show up to ceremony and classes to progress in my knowledge which began with getting my Lave Tet. Doing footwork, getting supplies and offerings, helping with the cleanup and set up, taking notes.
>
> - Tehron Gillis

Some students are motivated to find and create a relationship with an Elder, not only for knowledge but also for language for their own processes. Others are attracted to new ideas that complement their own. Whatever the initial fascination, the motivation changes because the teachings develop the person and lead to a clearer life path. What began as intellectual stimulation grows into a lifestyle.

It will be beneficial to work on developing trust. Trust that the Elder has the process you need and the teachings that will help you progress. Know and expect that even if you are confused at the beginning, eventually through the process of learning, the teachings will make sense to you. Trust that Elders have a bigger picture of how the information they have given you will begin to integrate. They can teach the same information you have heard before with a more nuanced meaning because they have more experience.

For some students, the giving of trust is an important part of this process and can have a more profound impact on the student than the actual teachings themselves. They have to believe in someone in order to learn to have faith in themselves and their own inner knowing. They will gain confidence themselves as they tackle their own trust issues and sometimes the feeling of "not being in control" of the process. The student has to have a certain amount of trust to evolve and strengthen abilities: you can't control the process when you don't know where you are going. The Elder may focus on things that are different from what you think is important. When that happens, accept that there is a reason.

Lillith's story:

> During a shamanic training session, my Elder had us working on visioning and journeying with sacred objects. In my journey, I walked through a forest and entered a building. After I traveled through series of rooms with wooden paneling, I climbed a staircase, passing a dirty litter box, and walked up several more floors. I recounted a detailed shamanic journey, and shared amazing (to me) details full of symbolism, staircases, and nature.
>
> When I finished, he asked me, "Why is the litter box

dirty? Why was it there?"

I replied, "I don't know."

He told me, "Go back and find out about the litter box." He did not comment on the wonderful story or the other aspects of my journey, he only asked about the litter box. Just as in ordinary reality, you have to take care of the dirty little chores in sacred reality too.

The Elder may be blunt. Actually, they often speak their minds. Sometimes they will say the obvious thing and talk about the proverbial elephant in the room. They may call people out on destructive behavior whether self-directed or toward others. Some may even say things like, "Don't do that."

Other Elders may ramble and tell a lot of stories, especially about themselves. Personally, we find that to be the best part of sitting with an Elder. Their personal stories tell us not only what they learned but also the context of the learning event. Assume they are telling the stories for a reason and enjoy the process of being present.

Spending time with an Elder is also a great opportunity to practice listening before talking. Listening is necessary to learning. Think of it as an active state. Pay attention not only to the words you hear, but also to what you see or feel. Often students don't realize there is more beyond what they perceive. For example, shamanic extraction is a complicated skill because the work is not only at the surface level. Be aware of what you know and don't know, and don't pretend to know something that you have never done. Becoming conscious of that tendency may take serious contemplation and honesty.

Realize the value of the space you are in. People tend to pick and choose when to concentrate in a conversation or focus during a ritual. What matters is being involved in the whole event or the entire exchange. It is good to practice taking your time and being in the flow.

Joy's story:

It was not just the job I was doing, but everything that was going on at the same time that was important. I watched what my Elders did beyond the mechanics of their movements. Why do they do that in a certain way?

What made it so effective and able to bring change? If I asked a question like that the Elder would look at me funny and say, "Because that is the way we build the fire so the sweat is good." It was really my job to figure out when things were working well, when it wasn't and figure out how to do my tasks in the best possible way every time. I became humble and happy to just carry my weight. After that, compliments seemed trivial. I was just grateful to be there and if I developed any wisdom at all my Elders were grateful too.

The proper way to talk is also important. For instance, questions need to be asked in a respectful way. In a Western classroom, although rude, the student might get away with asking, "Why should I do that?" That would be disrespectful in an indigenous setting. After establishing a relationship, one might be able to ask, "How should it be done?" But if you said, "Why should I?" that may lead to negative repercussions.

Be willing to learn how to ask clear questions. If you have the opportunity, focus on what you want to talk about beforehand. After the teaching is complete, take time to think of anything you might want to ask. The answer may not be simple, and the response may not only encompass the frame-work of your question.

Avoid saying "You have the information. Why can't you just tell me now?" In our technology age it is easy to treat people as a search engine or a library book. People are neither. The Elder might need time to pray about the situation, meditate or think about the best way to answer for that particular individual. Allow the Elder time to bring the teachings together, not necessarily in the way you may want them to come, but in the way that will work the best to convey the lessons.

One arrogant youth was S. He came over to me in the coffee shop, and said he wanted me to teach him about sorcery. I asked a bit jokingly, "When?"

He replied, "Right now. I have some time, about half-an-hour, before I have to leave."

Ignoring the fact that I had not accepted him as a student — nor had he found out if I had time to talk to him — I asked, "What do you want to learn?"

"Everything!"

Not only did S want me to teach him a complex spiritual and philosophical body of teachings, but he also wanted me to do that over one cup of coffee at a moment's notice. A bit sarcastically, I responded, "Everything? In a half-hour?"

When he nodded, I snapped, "You do realize that people can study Sorcery for years before they truly understand the concepts?"

He said, "Yes, well, it can't be that difficult. I'm smart."

Since I was annoyed, I said, "You want me to regurgitate twenty years of knowledge like a parrot. That's not how it should be taught. You must experience the teachings; you can't just learn facts."

He shrugged, "Just tell me the basics. That should take fifteen or twenty minutes."

"You want me to teach you the basics of sorcery in fifteen minutes?"

He said, "Yes."

Exasperated, I said, "Trying to learn so much in a short time will give you a headache."

His voice was arrogant and confident as he stated, "That's not going to happen. You can't give me a headache."

"Fine, I'll talk until you get a headache."

Of course, he viewed that statement as a challenge. I asked him the time, and I began talking. Although the topic is complex, S never asked a question. But, this session was not really about teaching him sorcery, so I kept talking. After about ten minutes, I paused to drink some coffee. Then I asked if he had a headache.

"No, I'm fine," he said.

Since his energy was starting to spin and flare randomly, I could tell he really wasn't okay — but he needed to learn to listen to suggestions of older and more experienced people. More importantly he needed to learn that his hubris would not protect his body from exhaustion. Although I doubted he would remember what I was saying, I began talking once again, quickly covering concepts.

After a few minutes, he put his hand up. "Stop, stop, all right, all right, I have a headache."

I nodded and quietly drank my coffee.

Finally, he couldn't stand the silence. He blurted, "How did you do that?"

"I didn't do it. The teachings did. Sorcery cannot be learned in a cram session. It's important to take your time and get to know how the energy affects you. To be safe, you need to move in partnership with your body and discover how it reacts to the lessons. You can't just assume you will be okay."

When he left to find some aspirin, he had more respect for the teachings. At least for a short time, he walked away with more awareness of his physical limitations. Perhaps he would be more careful in the future.

- Shadow Walker

If you decide to study with a particular Elder, you already know their qualifications; therefore, debating their training is disrespectful. Recognize the difference between asking them questions and questioning their education and experience. Elders have Elders and they give credit to them; they are part of a lineage. Questioning the credentials is questioning the entire lineage. Even if they do not speak of their Elders, it is not just about one person. Recognize that you are talking to someone who has personal wisdom plus the wisdom of those that came before.

Elders hold the vision. You can't argue with the person that carries the vision and preserves the foundational concepts within the tradition or organization. Give them time to develop the teachings and convey the meaning to you. Know that the knowledge gained and the experiences you have will become part of your understanding of the world.

Lillith's story:

A while ago, Spirit decided that I should start a church. In spite of my limited income, vague concepts, and incomplete awareness, I idealistically gathered together a group of intelligent individuals from various spiritual paths.

In that meeting several unexpected things happened. A dear friend who typically jumped on any spiritual bandwagon with enthusiasm stated that she didn't "know enough to be a part of this birthing." Perhaps she comprehended what I had not: that those who agreed to work on this association would become heads of a church. But the strangest thing to happen at that time was that everyone insisted that I had to function as Director: since it was my vision, of course I had to lead.

Time went by, and the organization grew into an interfaith church community. People in the organization continued to depend on me to hold the vision. They told me I should find the answers. Through the years, they expected me to have that responsibility, but agreement was not always forthcoming. Every so often when I said that a certain thing needed to happen in order to keep the vision alive, they said, "Who made you boss? Isn't this about consensus?" I admit to my frustration: after so many years of hearing you're the leader and having people ask me about the vision, now they were upset because I did the job they gave me.

Suppress your urge to be right or to be in charge. If you find yourself persisting in questioning the tradition, then perhaps the Elder is not the right one for you, and you need to move on and find another Elder or tradition. Sometimes that may involve some quiet time or mediation and prayer to get enough clarity on the best decision.

At times Elders will be disappointing or unclear in their expectations. They will fail in some way as all humans do. Be accepting of that and continue to move forward. Elders may not be without error, or even controversy, but they serve their communities and work to maintain the teachings and practices for those that come after them.

Just because you are an Elder does not mean you don't make mistakes. I make mistakes. Everyone makes mistakes. How else would one learn? To think that an Elder is far from making mistakes would be foolish.

- Rocio Darlene Arriaga

We shouldn't blame Elders for having flaws. Everything about a person teaches you something.

- Shaina Golden

Many Elders are aging adults. Be aware of physical limitations they may have that require adaptation. Show concern for their comfort and be aware of or sensitive to what they may need. Realize they may be hungry, tired, or hurting; for instance, at a festival, they may have been working for three days straight. Offer to lift, carry, move or bring food, water, first aid, or anything else they may need. It is good to realize that an Elder may have restrictions and deserves to be treated with consideration.

I have to say that I spent a bit more time making sure that I attended to their needs because I know that they were giving the extra time and availability to answer my questions. Driving onto the Hopi reservation with a Lumina filled with groceries to provide for the medicine man and his family — and that was for a simple afternoon of wisdom.

- Jase Peck

There is a protective space that is created when students make a commitment to Elders and defer to their wisdom while being mentored. Elders make a commitment to the process and growth of those they teach. They feel responsible for what they communicate and want the tradition to live on. Many are aware they are not only helping the ancestors that came before but also the next seven generations.

It is not necessary or helpful for students to share everything they know with the Elder. Students who focus on communicating their knowledge may complicate the relationship, dilute the teachings, and hinder their own comprehension. It is best for students to be grateful for the interchange and mindful that they have come to learn.

151

Joy's story:

> I was teaching a student of mine how to prepare a fire for a stone circle lodge. She was very connected to her good spirits, to the fire, and to the land. As I was trying to convey to her what we needed to do and why, she started to tell me things like "Well my spirits say it should be done this way" or "I feel like it would be better that way." She had never built a fire for the lodge before. I decided that what she really could benefit from as a teaching that day was to listen and try to understand why I chose to do it the way I was taught and guided. I gave her the task of not talking for the whole day, including the whole lodge ceremony that she would be fire tending. At the beginning of the day I watched her struggle to keep what she knew from falling out of her mouth. By the end of the day her whole demeanor had changed. She was observing, thinking and totally engaged in what was happening around her. When we were packing up to go home, she told me that she had learned so much, that there were small details that she might have overlooked if she was doing it by herself, and that it was one of the best experiences she had in a learning environment. I was really proud of her.

Please take all of your concerns or questions to your Elder. If you don't like your mentor's advice, don't search out someone else for a different response or for the answer that you want. It is best to stay within the tradition you are studying and complete the process with your Elder.

> I realize why books don't teach well. ...Spirits are invested in the transfer of knowledge. Spirits of [both] Elders and students are just as invested in the teachings as you are.
>
> - Shaina Golden

Fulfilling Obligations

Elders want committed and motivated students that will follow through on tasks given to them. Because learning is a process, they prefer students that are true to the teachings. Personal Elders give you tasks in relationship to spirituality, and sometimes it is not glamorous.

> You got to work for it.
>
> - Gene Rowand

Joy's story:

> When I first studied in indigenous traditions over 20 years ago, it was all hard, physical work and relying on oral teachings, i.e. seeing and then doing. It can be difficult at times to convey the importance of this direct form of teaching. Newer students believe if they can read it, they will know how to do it.

Seriously, be prepared to work. Sometimes Elders designate long assignments, for instance, a continuing task that requires work every day. When studying a tradition, there will be more than talking involved. Daily practices may include lengthy prayers, meditation, and puzzling through dreams and visions. Learning how to make offerings, memorize songs, and perform divination may go hand-in-hand with those. You may be required to do physical tasks like making 400 prayer ties, creating altars, building fires, or planning ritual and ceremony. All of this leads to understanding the cosmology within the tradition.

Perhaps the hardest requirements are the ones that necessitate our own commitment and monitoring. It is necessary to follow through on responsibilities and do your homework even when you don't want to do them. You will gain insight and knowledge from any consistent practice.

Joy's story:

> I went to a gathering and I met a Native American Elder while I was there. She would do the morning prayers and it was very moving to hear her pray. She was funny

— it was playful but very reverent. When it rained she sang for the rain and the thunder beings. I felt her connection to creation. At the end of the week, I told her I was interested in native spirituality and asked if there was something she could recommend that I could do. Before she would tell me what to do, I had to commit to doing it every day. I promised her that I would. She suggested that I take my sage bowl every morning and honor the directions. It was an honoring ceremony, not asking for things I thought I might need or would like to have. She also told me that in order to honor the four directions, I needed to study their attributes so that I could articulate something respectful. She wanted me to be able to say something like "I honor the place of the East, the place of the sun rising." After I learned something about the directions and became more comfortable, she told me to speak from my heart, allowing the prayers to be fluid and then later asking what kind of guidance I needed for that day.

She also told me to pray out loud because when I started to pray to creation, I needed to know what I was saying. I learned that to enable creation to understand, you have to be able to hear what you were really praying, not just what you thought you were saying from the thoughts in your head. Through speaking out loud, you would hear your own lack of clarity, where you are stuck, and learn to pray clearly through articulating your own truth. She told me that is the art of prayer.

I did that every day at the same time for a year. It took sustained effort and commitment. It's not just one event. As the year passed, I experienced a greater connection to creation and received more information.

She gave me a test that became my own test: am I getting more information, is it evolving? She didn't have to call me every week because we both knew how my lessons and learning were progressing.

Being mentored may show you not only your gifts and unique skills but where you are lacking in maturity. Although many Elders will be patient with your experience or stage of life, and your knowledge so far, they will still expect students to be responsible for their actions.

> One of my most recent experiences is in the first Fire Initiation in our tradition where one learns how to make Sacred Fire. ... After explaining the protocols surrounding fire, how to make it, and how to respect It when It came, she then demonstrated how to make it. After showing me, she left me to work at it, and only corrected me when I was clearly struggling or asked for help, leaving that power to ask within my boundaries, giving me respect and space to figure it out on my own. She encouraged me to keep it up, to take a break when I needed it, and keep with it when I was starting to get it. Sometimes the most profound thing an Elder can give you is the trust that you will own up to your limits, acknowledge them, respect them, and work past them as needed, each in their own time. She gave me that. Within a few hours of starting the work, I had my first fire lit in our Tradition.
>
> - Sarenth Odinsson

Sometimes students many feel they did not meet the Elder's expectations. Please don't blame the Elder when that happens — and don't assume that the failure is permanent. Although it can be a lesson, we have learned that failure doesn't mean a student is unworthy. It doesn't even really mean that the pupil was unsuccessful. Each person will develop along the path at an individual speed. There is no shame in moving slowly towards a goal. In addition, some steps require more maturity, a certain amount of healing integration or a different perspective. Often indigenous Elders say they are waiting for the right time — how does one explain that statement? They might be watching for signs that the student has progressed in healing or maturity to a certain level. It is based on a feeling, an energy arising from complex circumstances, and a knowing that both Spirit and the living people are ready.

In fact, if the student is not ready, pushing the individual could be dangerous. Certainly, Elders cannot prevent students from making mistakes or even from the decision to follow a precarious path. However, genuine Elders are concerned about risk and do all they can to guide the student away from situations that may be harmful.

Some tasks may feel nonrelated and difficult to focus on. The students may be unable to see the value in what they are doing. Examples can include: gathering twigs for a fire, carrying rocks, washing dishes and large pots, picking people up from the airport, last minute errand running, cooking and cleaning. These tasks also reflect your dedication and commitment.

Joy's story:

> I feel a responsibility to my students. I believe that I need to guide them, nurture their souls and keep them moving forward on their own unique spiritual paths. The promise of "a life well-lived" is sometimes not good enough anymore. Often, I spend too much time stroking egos and giving them jobs that they view as designating them as "special" somehow. I believe the core knowledge they need can become diluted because of these hindrances — and then I become disillusioned myself. When I was learning under an Elder I was happy to just not get corrected, or worse, yelled at or have my simple job taken over or given away to someone else.

Students are accountable for the outcomes of their assignments, and they decide whether or not they complete the tasks. There is a lot of truth in the fact that an Elder is likely to require the individual to finish an assignment before being given another task.

> I'd have to say that the Elders ... [want] to see if you were going to continue with your commitments, to see how much further you were willing to go. ... Were you going to use the information and wisdom? How did you use the wisdom that was passed onto you? ... They would ask, "Did you remember what we talked about? When was the last time you poured the sweat? What are you doing with this?" They were checking in with you before imparting more wisdom. If you don't use what you've been told, it kinda pisses the elder off.
>
> - Jase Peck

Plunge in, trust yourself, and be patient. It takes time to grow. You are responsible for your own progress. Believe in yourself.

Advice for Elders

Relationships are at the heart of learning, and they are also the foundation of the development resulting from that involvement. This is especially true with spiritual interactions. It is important to take the time to build a bonded and stable relationship. This can push both parties to give all they have to the process of teaching and learning. It is an obligation but also an adventure to have the responsibility of mentoring others. Have fun in the process and stretch yourself as well as your students.

Continue to be patient toward those that have come to study with you. Due to their inexperience, learners will ask questions that may seem foolish. Sometimes they really don't know what they actually want to ask. Try to answer as clearly as possible and do the best you can since other questions will follow.

In any situation take care that you don't jump to conclusions since cultural assumptions might cause communication issues. Listen to your students and be willing to hear their explanations. The people you teach will make mistakes and many of their errors will be very creative. It is good to develop a sense of humor with regards to situations that happen during instruction of others.

Joy's story:

> I remember giving a traditional spiritual bath remedy to one of my students. It was: a bowl of water, some milk, flower petals, and sugar. Later when I asked her how the bath was, she lamented that she really did not notice the difference. I was confused so I asked her to explain to me how she had prepared the bath. She told me that she was out of milk, so she used almond milk; she did not have any flowers, so she used essential oils, and she didn't have sugar so she put artificial sweetener into the bath. That was a really creative and relatively humorous solution, but of course it did not work, as those exact items for the bath offer specific blessings on a spiritual level. We both learned something. I learned to be really clear about the process, and precisely convey what was important about the whole recipe and execution of the bath. And my student learned to follow directions.

Be willing to give of your time and remain available as much as possible to your students. Make a clear commitment with your students on when and how you are accessible and keep those commitments. It is also helpful to have some flexibility built into the schedule. Often students will need to talk just to dispel confusion, to complain, to receive encouragement or to share an understanding or a revelation with you that is related to the teachings.

Present the truth of your knowledge even if the student struggles to understand what you are saying. When those you mentor are confused or frustrated, it is easy to judge yourself and think you are not doing a good enough job. Be persistent and consistent with your words. Elders need to trust in the process of growth for those that come after them. Just keep trying. Don't hold back, especially if it is a situation where repetition will bring insight and learning. Assume that the information the student needs will be conveyed and understood at the right time.

Many times, people that you are not responsible for will end up being part of a ritual or teaching. They might be unable to listen to you or grasp what is happening. Instead of focusing in public on the mistakes that any student or others make, fix them and keep moving forward. This is of primary importance when a ritual is involved.

If possible, make sure that the conveying of your spiritual practice is more than just explaining "how" to do your practice. Explain the "why" and teach students the means to incorporate the how and why into their learning. For example, when creating a ritual, define whether you pray and how, and to whom you pray. If you get advice from others, including other Elders, explain that. Give the full scope of what your practice entails so your students can grasp the heart of the teachings and how everything really fits together.

It is important that Elders that have committed to passing on knowledge and taking on students are capable of accepting the responsibility of caring for the individual and the community. This does not mean that it will be easy, and that you will not occasionally fail in achieving this goal. The key here is that you accept this responsibility and the unknown situations that may arise. There are many resources available to learn new skills, such as conflict resolution and mentoring guidelines. Remember that the Elders used to talk among themselves. If someone had a problem within the community, it was the job of the Elder group to settle it because it affected the whole community. It was also the responsibility of the group to support and guide each other. Connect with other Elders and get advice if you need it.

Encourage your students from a place of true sincerity as much as possible. Inspire them to achieve "more" and give them the tools so they can think and perceive differently. Celebrate their victories on their path of learning. Ultimately, give them themselves. Be kind and accepting of people. Remember to guide those that come to you in a way that allows them to discover their own path in life, their own dream.

> Do not interfere in someone else's future ... You can nudge them a little here or there or say things like, 'Perhaps you might want to consider this.' But that is the most you should do without changing future history.
> - Carlo HawkWalker,
> Native American Traditional Elder

As your students learn, acknowledge their progress and commitment. Allow them to share in more responsibility, for example, in the training of those that are less experienced. Speak kindly of your students to others and acknowledge the personal wisdom they have acquired through your teachings and their own knowing. If possible, find ways they can move up within the group. This could be through creating and doing ritual and perhaps even running parts of the group or organization in some capacity. Trust them to carry on your teachings.

> A couple of years after, the nine years of the first phase of Isaac [Bonewits]'s plan had passed. It is greatly to Isaac's credit that he did in fact open the Board of Directors to direct election, while retaining the Arch-Druid-for-life status that he had written into the original documents. I was the first elected Vice-Archdruid. I think I have never bragged on it much, but Isaac recruited me to run for that post, telling me that he trusted me with the vision of ADF. I served on the Board of Directors in some capacity for the next 7 or so years.
> - Ian Corrigan

Be grateful to have had the opportunity to be an Elder and share yourself. Have faith that your students will learn enough; after all, they are not Elders yet. The teaching will endure and grow as they mature, and eventually they will become Elders. When that happens, continue to speak highly of them and support them in words and actions. Give them the respect that they deserve even if they do things a little differently.

Joy's story:

> I have seen some of my Elders that were taught in a good way be ostracized or disrespected by those Elders that taught them and mentored them. Sometimes the up-and-coming Elder may have made a mistake, but more often their Elders could not allow the former student — and the student's teachings — to become as important to others as theirs were and therefore they withheld continued support. In turn, these new Elders don't know how to give respect and support to those that they mentored. A sickness forms when Elders are not respected, supported, and appreciated by their Elders, and this spreads to those they teach. To be truly supportive, infinitely related, and embracing to all in the circle of life, we need to walk with this knowing and behave toward others at all times with awareness of these connections. If we fail at this, the circles of knowledge, of people, of life will drift further apart and all of creation will suffer.
>
> The world and cultures shift and change, and as culture changes, different parts of the teachings will become more important. Watch with a great curiosity as the world changes and the teachings move forward without you. You can't own a culture; you can only own your own truth. Support those that come after you with love, respect, and honor.

Remember that cultures are fluid; they keep evolving. In addition, spiritual practices, in the best possible way, are meant to help and serve people. As long as the heart of the teachings — your teachings — survive, that is all that one can truly hope for.

How Elders Change the World

Perhaps one of the distinctive aspects of the Pagan worldview involves acceptance of altered states of reality. Participation in altered states ranges from utilizing meditative positions to trance states and from guided meditation through traveling on otherworldly journeys. Events incorporate chanting, drumming, trance dancing, lucid dreaming, and deep shamanic experiences. In the Pagan viewpoint, the expectation to learn about and control altered states holds true even in situations that the mainstream culture would not view as spiritual.

For instance, Ladyelle's Elder, Eugene Lion, included a number of unusual practices in his theatre classes. She explained that learning to navigate altered realities was part of how she was trained in "the metaphysics of theatre." In the Pagan perspective, reality includes both the seen and the unseen, and Elders assist others in learning about both.

> Yes, some of the trials we went through involved astral projection. On one such journey, I was in a place in dark space between two monoliths. Years later, another adept from a different tradition spoke of "the place between the veil, the place of the two pillars" which I found interesting. There was also a guide there, but this person was little more than a reassuring presence. Returning to the physical body was trickier than expected, but successful with slight adjustment.
>
> - Ladyelle

> Of the many aspects of magical events, traveling in time with the Frost and my coven was one of the most eye-opening experiences in my early education. And, yes, I can become invisible still to this day, thanks to Yvonne's encouragement!
>
> - Penny Goody

When the Elder summons power or accumulates energy, it helps others to see in new ways, to grasp a concept or to open up to unusual communications. The participants can feel an expansion of their own awareness. Because students are in the presence of an Elder, they develop heightened consciousness and perception.

Joy's story:

> I was able to approach my Elder with a question just as the daylight was dimming toward the night. It felt like a good moment to share a harsh and troubling dream with him. I have dreams on a regular basis and they are a tool I use in my spiritual work with others and myself, but this dream was not about me or a client. It seemed that it was a message for all the people of the planet. I wanted to know what his thoughts were.
>
> I told him about the dream. The road I was walking on was filled with all kinds of debris and stones, which made it a difficult place to find my footing. I saw people fighting on both sides of the street totally unaware of this central path, of me, and my destination. I was walking toward the Eye of God, a bright light that was above the whole scene. It was burning bright and steady.
>
> After I finished, my Elder looked at me very intently. Then he asked me if I would like to know about his dream. I nodded in agreement. Just as the sun dropped below the horizon, he placed his hand on my forearm. I was literally surrounded by images and pictures that were not my own; they were the vision of my Elder. I saw my dream as part of a larger circle of awareness, connected to many other layers of events. I also saw that these wars were happening not only on the planet, but also in the heavenly dimensions. I saw the Eye of God, that light too, surrounding everything and creating a web of roads that was capable of carrying everyone and everything home to that source, that light of knowing in the eye of God.
>
> He gently withdrew his hand from my arm. I had a lot to think about.

Many people reported that when the Elder created a sacred space or manifested energy, it allowed others to perceive in a new way and to participate in amazing events. Thus, people became more open to the teachings while in sacred space. Additionally, the

Elder activated more accessible connections to mystical experiences, magic, and Paganism.

> In my early experiences with my high priestess Teresa, the first circle I was ever in, I saw the circle as she cast it. It was visible and glowing blue. I was amazed and truly transported between the worlds. She cast it with her pointer finger. It was incredible.
>
> - Tina Frick (Freya Hlin Vrana)

> I feel that magick [sic] and Paganism has been demystified some by my communication and friendship with Daemon. Furthermore, I feel empowered by that which she has taught me so far.
>
> - Anna Calhoun

Numerous respondents considered the experience of working with an Elder transformative. Although the event may have occurred in a kitchen or other mundane place, possibilities were unlocked in the individual's life. A few mentioned that something was ignited, and through their interactions, the Elder connected individuals to their true selves.

> He and I entered into our teaching relationship, and our friendship, and that changed how I viewed the world. I could almost say that he introduced me to me.
>
> - Mary Hudson

> She taught me to believe in myself.
>
> - Lisa Owen

> He started me on a journey of believing in myself.
>
> - Rocio Darlene Arriaga

> She opened the door to Wicca for me; it was like a light had been switched on in my mind.
> - After the experience with the Elder, the person thinks differently and has a new perspective.
> More accurately, they can no longer be the same.
> The world was the same. I was different.
>
> - Eli Thorn

She made me self-aware. I see the world as not as linear continuum with cause and effect as a binary but as a vastly complex network of forces pulling and pushing each other through barely visible gossamer threads.

- Tehron Gillis

Daemon has a very down to earth approach to her teachings. She has shown me many more possibilities than I had known and enlightened me to information others may not be so quick to share. My world is more open, my eyes see more.

- Anna Calhoun

I think it had a lot to do with his/her life experiences. I learned how to think differently. How to look at things/experiences from a different perspective. These lessons are lifelong.

- Bernadette Montana

She taught me about the ancestors and how to connect to that side of me. ... She taught about the ways of her life and the spirits she connected to from her traditions.

- Lisa Owen

Meeting Joy and being introduced to spiritualism was a very life changing experience. My views on religion changed, I felt I did not have to go to church to pray. I also learned that I could be more closely connected to my ancestors by building an altar for them in my home.

- Alejandra Licea

As Alejandra Licea mentioned, change often results from the lessons. While teachings, regardless of topic, provide one way that Elders have an effect on people, they can influence an individual, a group, and a community — even strangers at a public event. Many people mentioned that the Elder's work brought about a change in their own energy levels. Participants were able to experience in a different way. They achieved a heightened clarity and became more aware of nuances in people, places, and events. For instance, learners experienced an unusual emotion, a feeling of empathy, or a sense of unity. Some reported increased sensitively while others noticed a change in the intensity of community rapport.

I remember the first time he [Craig Parsons-Kerins] asked me to participate in a healing. This was a group healing with practitioners up and down the East Coast. It was at a designated time with a focused intention. All I was told as that I was to concentrate (in a specific ritual setting for him and I) of directing energy to a particular location with the intention of healing. As I did so, eyes wide open and looking into the face my Elder, I began to see an overlay of another person, a young person. The image was complete and the left side of the shoulder, arm, chest and face where darker in color. It was amazing energy and off it was sent to its intended target. When it was done, Craig asked what I had experienced, and I told him what I saw. He smiled and explained that it was a boy we were sending the healing energy to and that his left side was afflicted. It confirmed that first I was on the right path and second that I wasn't crazy.

- Mary Hudson

How did the world seem different afterwards? Magic awoke all around the fire circles!! Actual rituals were instated, blessing the fire circle and the magical/spiritual work done there. Now drummers really took their Art seriously and learned rhythms and ancient heartbeats. Dancers, no longer shy about dancing their prayers, blossomed and helped to carry the drumming to new heights. Chanting and flutes and didgeridoos charged up the energy, and the fire tenders kept us all safe and took ... loving responsibility for their Tribe.

- Penny Goody

Eugene [Lion] taught me how to become sensitive to subtle energies. The prism with which I viewed the world changed because I began to understand how human energy behaves: consciously, unconsciously, subconsciously, cause and effect, a unique way of understanding how life energies interact. How smaller patterns intersect with grander ones. How to consciously create an "art experience" that people would value as being authentic, cathartic and genuinely moving. This is akin to ritual that succeeds in elevating its participants to higher spiritual awareness and insight.

- Ladyelle

The Elder's presence in people's lives continued after the interactions ended. They continued to be important role-models through their character and their teachings.

Each Elder in his or her own way has helped me to find insight into the deeper meanings of the way things are and also affected an experience which caused me to look into the deeper understandings of life.

- Jase Peck

Her [Sweet Medicine] view was that there was always a gentler way to do something. Her main teaching was to "go with the flow" and quit fighting the current. I had just come out of the military. I had a lot of hostility and anger. She put me back on the Native American path and brought a lot of things together for me. She set me on a course. That course now is why I am where I am at. I feel that the path I am on now is completing something that she started.

-Peaceful Rivers Rainbow Warrior White Wolf

Joy's story:

The Elders taught me that I was important and a part of everything. They also taught me that I was small in relation to the world and responsible for how I build connections to all creation. It was humbling and empowering at the same time. I became aware that my life was one of service to people and Spirit.

Because of their awareness of the microcosm and macrocosm, that is, the position of an individual in the vast cosmos, Elders demonstrate characteristics such as humility and faith. They live with a sense of truthfulness. Others may talk about faith, but do they really live their beliefs? Do they live with humility?

If you are meant to do it, Spirit will find a way.
- Beautiful Painted Arrow[32]

That kind of faith sets an Elder apart from others. Instead of egotistically brandishing their position, Elders seem to be humble because of the power at their disposal. They have self-confidence, but they also have certainty based on past experiences. They believe that the powers of the universe can transform situations.

Of those we interviewed, a few literally credited their Elders with salvation from bad situations, poor health, or destructive lifestyles. An extraordinary experience can change beliefs.

So, there I was, a high school junior, first chair in the Trumpet Section, nerd extraordinaire, and budding teenage witch, and into my life sweeps a larger than life Elder named Mrs. F. She was a Band Parent Booster and involved in a full-scale witch war with the assistant president of the same club. Of course, I knew none of this at the time; I only knew that she would look at me with a knowing expression. ...

She told me to bring my friend, Saxophone Section First Chair, with me to her house later so we could all chat and see where we were at in our studies. ...

Then came the revelation that the reason some of us were so sick and there was so much pain in the boys of the baritone section was that their mother was draining the life force out of them. She was also feeding on the ambient energy of all the kids in the band. That was why they were always staring each other down, they were at war... Then one day, the boys were extremely ill and began missing school. We were concerned. She sent us over there to visit, on a covert mission, to check on them and to get a taglock from the house. We did this, and she went to work. ...

―――――――――――――――――――

[32] Beautiful Painted Arrow personal communication to Lillith ThreeFeathers.

Mrs. F was ... missing for two days. We finally got her to answer the door, only to find that she was in her housecoat. Why? Because she had been astrally fighting with Mrs. A, the mother vamp, and was wiped out. She had finally brought in a root doctor to assist her and that made all the difference. He was also her fiancé, so he was more than ready to throw down. As is typical in Detroit, they were also both ministers. They explained to us that we should take extra precautions at practice, since the woman was out for blood at this point, and no limits were observed in her feeding.

Soon, the boys were back just fine, but the mother's stage 4 cancer had resumed its march throughout her body like it had been before.

- Kenya Coviak aka Mistress Belledonna

Just as Mistress Belladonna believes her Elder released several children from improper use of magic, other respondents believed their Elders had rescued them too. Some individuals witnessed Elders healing people, an experience that shifted their worldview. In both situations, Elders created a context that was conducive to growth and healing. This happened even when contributors shared events that were less supernatural but prevalent in today's world.

Witnessing several feather healings, seeing the Elder go right to the spot of illness, reach in and pull the illness from that person. The person had a marked difference in how they were carrying themselves afterwards. If they had a hurt knee, they walked better afterwards. If they had a breathing problem, they were breathing better. I witnessed a remarkable change in the person afterwards in every case of feather healing.

- Jase Peck

Lillith's story:

I can say that I would not be the person I am now if the Elders had not challenged me to change — no, that is not accurate. They did not simply challenge me to change;

they assumed that I would do so since I needed to change in order to heal.

Several individuals directly experienced healing through their interactions with Elders. The way the Elders acted and their understanding of how the individuals suffered created a space for recovery. They realized the Elders understood unspoken hardships from the past and accepted them. That acceptance, in itself, brought relief and healing.

> When I met Elisheva, I was a deeply troubled and wounded young man. I was in my early 20's and was planning on entering Art School. I already had a failed marriage and a couple careers under my belt and was battling fairly intense PTSD. My fallback plan, since getting out of High School, was that I could immigrate to Israel and join the army. When I met Elisheva, it was like being introduced to the prototypical Israeli. To my limited understanding, she was everything that I aspired to be. It was only natural that I would look to her as a mentor. Finally, I had a friend that didn't find me "too intense" or get freaked out if my PTSD got the best of me. She was even instrumental in getting me to acknowledge the diagnosis. There is no way that I can really convey the importance of her impact on my life. It was not just that she saved my life, however trite that sounds, but that she reminded me who I could be.
>
> - Kenn Day

> How do I explain? The second thing I learned at the Shaman event had something to do with seeing, and being seen. … It's consciousness and mindfulness on a larger scale, or maybe a smaller one.
> When the Elder said, "We see you. We see you doing the work, and we know you are alone," there was something so powerful in that. … There was something about being seen in that moment. … I can't explain it, like such a burden was sliding off my shoulders, I was so grateful. I did not know how much I was carrying. I did

not know how important it all was. There's a reason that message spread so far, so fast. Because it speaks to us.

It seemed like everything the Elder said made me cry. I felt so helpless, so hopeless in the face of everything. They told us stories of their travels through different states as they went to Standing Rock, or to Flint, how they were chased and isolated in a state where the laws have changed to make it legal to hang Indians (his word). How their lawyer had to travel with them. They were laughing and joking about how they got away, but I was so horrified at the events taking place so recently, at the fact that it was so commonplace for them, that this was their day to day lives as they did the work that was meant for ALL of us. Water really is Life, and water companies were prepping for this long before Flint became news. I remember reading articles in my news feed about it, claiming that drinking water isn't a human right, it's a commodity. The less it becomes available, the sooner we're all paying through the nose to survive.

Anyway, I tried to talk to the Elder about my tears. I felt selfish. There are members of various communities that feel that some people use tears as a way to avoid having to fix things, kind of a, "look, I sympathize, and I'm overwhelmed by your pain, I'm a good person, you can see that because you've moved me to tears, but I'm not going to change anything today.... it's all too much." That's not who I am. I wanted some direction, I felt like that poem where the girl is looking at the map saying, "show me where it hurts," and the answer is, "everywhere." Where do you start? How do you begin...?

He took my hands and looked into my eyes and said, "Don't heal the pain of others to avoid having to deal with your own. Heal the self and the way becomes clear." I was crying ... and I wanted to pull my hands back to wipe my nose. He didn't let my hands go. He kept talking. ...

"I will do the work," I said. "If you point me somewhere, tell me what to do, I will say the prayers, I will do the work, but there is so much! Where do I start?"

And the answer I got was to start inside. Not the answer I was hoping for. But an answer. And I will do the work. In that moment, I was really SEEN. I had never allowed that level of exposure. There was something healing in that moment, of having my hands held and just being seen and heard. ...

Being seen is more than something that just happens. It is something we crave; it brings meaning to things that are otherwise meaningless. The creation of art needs an observer. A dancer can dance for their own joy, but that same performance can multiply the joy with observers. A painting without an audience might as well be a rug.

And our pain, our weakness, our frailties...without an audience they are Shame or Doubt. But WITH an audience, they are Compassion, Sympathy, Humanity. There is a connection that happens when we are seen in our entirety, a circuit closes and some sort of electrical thing happens that is emotionally moving, and is literally:

Emotion
    moving
        from one place to another,
           transforming from Pain to Hope.

We can do that for each other if we will just be still. If we will hold each other's hands and look into each other's eyes and say, "I see you. I see what you're going through, and I see that it hurts you, and I am so sorry that you are having this experience."

- Mowglellan

As represented by the stories in this chapter, Elders can open up a person's abilities, organize an experience so that a vision can be fulfilled, or channel the divine to bring sacred knowledge and awareness into the physical world. Elders can train people about altered states of reality, and they can provide access to those mystical states. They can connect others to divine realms through ritual. Most importantly, Elders help individuals find their abilities, guide them towards a good personal destiny, and encourage people to be faithful to their authentic selves. Elders can help individuals to live better lives.

Amazing Events

Elders can help us achieve a way of being in the world, accomplish a shift in awareness, and travel though dimensional realities. As we have seen, they can reveal insights, create enthusiasm, teach an individual a new way of looking at life, or open a doorway to altered perception. Additionally, Elders can create extraordinary manifestations. A few people reported odd events and incredible experiences. Some of these materializations appear in physical form; some affirm aspects of ordinary reality that are not commonplace. Elders can create spiritual experiences that carry others along, leading to remarkable situations and astounding real life experiences.

> The greatest first experience with Auntie Dame was at a public ritual. I have had physical difficulties the last several years, which has made mobility difficult. I entered her circle in an electric wheelchair and transferred myself to a regular chair, moving the other one outside of the circle for proper energy flow. The purpose of the ritual was "what could you do if you had no fear?" As the energy built in the circle, people started dancing. Once I started feeling the energy in the circle, there was nothing to stop me. My physical pain was gone, and I found myself dancing with the others, completely and beautifully lost within this energetic circle. After about 3 trips around, I returned to my seat. That day will stay with me forever. Truly I had forgotten about any fear of pain and did what I love to do!
> - Anna Calhoun

> I was personal witness to an Inipi ceremony that was being poured by an Elder. During the rounds there were sounds of animals, what sounded like 30 gourds being shaken. The popping of lights like ball lightening. Also, the experience of a buffalo spirit in the lodge, we heard the snorting and smelled the smell of the buffalo. When

I reached out with my hand I felt the fur of the buffalo. This was during the healing ceremony for a young man.

- Jase Peck

I showed up to prepare the grounds for Sabbat ritual one Mabon afternoon with some other members, and one of my teachers under Lady Circe was especially demanding. I did what was asked and wondered if I was being tested again. Later I was told to prepare myself for a special ritual that would be preceding the Sabbat ritual.

I was then ushered outside to the sacred circle. It was dark except for the torchlights at the altar and at each quarter. I was told to kneel on one knee only. We had been taught that we were never to kneel with two knees in subservience to another. With her commanding voice, she called in the elements and invoked the Goddess. I raised my eyes to Lady Circe's face and she was glowing brightly. Though she was already of advanced age at this time, her face was youthful and resplendent. I gasped in awe at the Goddess before me! At the moment she spoke the words and performed the gestures elevating me to the title of lady, lightning flashed, the wind whipped at my robe, and the skies opened up in a deluge of rain. I was soon kneeling in mud. I didn't care about getting wet. I had just been blessed by all the elements and the Goddess Herself!

- Bona Dea Lyonesse

As Bona Dea Lyonesse mentioned, a divine being can overshadow or possess an individual. In a few traditions, especially those that evolved from the African diaspora, possession is a welcome and anticipated gift. Typically, the Elder has trained for hosting the deity during ritualized events and when it happens, the proceedings bestow special blessings.

In particular, I have experienced Trance-possession with Janet [Farrar] and Gavin [Bone]. It's a part of the Progressive Way. Connection with Deity. Very similar to Santeria and Voudun.

- Bernadette Montana

Speaking with my Father, Odin, through her, during
Etinmoot, was an incredible experience. ... The feel of His
Presence on her, and the 'smell' of Him was powerful. I
could see Him recognizably there, with His face looking
something between superimposed upon hers and
'twisting' her features, lacking a better term. When He
spoke through her, I recognized it as distinctly His
[voice]. I had not, until that point, seen Him seated in
another, and it brought me comfort as much as it brought
a sense of holy terror or awe.

- Sarenth Odinsson,
writing about the possession of his Elder,
Galina Krasskova

[During my time with Teacher] such amazing things
happened: visions, healing, and so much more. At one
point six months into this experience, she came to me
and said we needed to go for a walk about (vision quest
or mission of sorts) to the sacred land of the Native
American Indians: Devil's Tower and the medicine
wheel in the mountains around Cheyenne, Wyoming. I
was not clear why, but we knew that it would help the
healing of the greater good of humanity, that it was very
important we go during a cycle of the moon August
2002. We needed to have four people for the trip. ... She
had received most of the information for this trip and
confirmed it with me and through dreaming, but [she]
had no idea why four people. So I recruited two more
people and off we went on our journey. Teacher had a
way about her, [she could] take a trip and make it
something else. [We would talk] about what we needed
to know before we got to a place. [Searching for] intuitive
insights for what lies before us on this journey in as
much depth as we could get while driving. Before we
knew it miles passed. ... We drove through the night
talking about why we were on this journey as if we were
looking to the road to answer all our questions for
ourselves, our families, and the greater good of
humankind. This was the beginning of a practice [for
me] of receiving messages from the road/the journey.

We reached the foot of Devil's Tower at sunrise knowing we needed to do prayers to the ancestors and travel around the tower leaving sacred herbs and asking for blessings, permission for ceremony on the wheel, and insights to traveling to the medicine wheel.

On top of the Bighorn Range in Wyoming, a desolate [mountaintop] 9,642 feet high, and only reachable during the warm summer months, lies an ancient Native American construction: 80' diameter wheel-like pattern made of stones. It aligns with major celestial alignments throughout the year: Winter and Summer Solstice, Spring and Fall Equinoxes, and the Dog Star Sirius. ... It was used as a spiritual point of healing and for honoring ancestors of the ancient Native Americans. This was the destination. ... We moved forward in complete faith although we knew nothing of what was in store. We spent some time at the tower praying and giving offerings, but went on our way so we could make camp by nightfall. ... We had signs from the eagle, hawk, coyote, and crow, bringing messages for our safety, our swiftness, and the up-and-coming fullness of the moon.

With food, water and camping supplies ... we headed up Bighorn Mountain, twisting and turning within the switchbacks, climbing ... to 8,000 feet, an experience of its own. ... The climb was intense: the car overheating every 3 to 4 miles of climb, and [we] worried we would not make it to the top. Everything about the journey had signs in it, said Teacher, and I didn't disagree. Sleep deprivation, light on food, and heavy on the hydration, it was only our sheer will, faith and prayers helping us to the top of the mountain.

Facing [my] fear of heights, Teacher taught me to focus on the road even if the fear arose because it is only a temporary feeling that would be over soon. Sure enough it was and the journey continued. Asking the ancestors for assistance to find camping, we looked for direction to where we needed to be. Understand we had no Google, GPS, or cell phones, but we did have a good old paper map that gave us general info. Ancestors sent animals to show us [the way] ... maybe it was the old way's version of Google. We [planned to] camp for the night, prepare ourselves… and hike the wheel the day after on the full moon.

We found the medicine wheel site at the top of the mountain and scoped out potential camping spots. We had been guided by animals and insights of Teacher so far, and this was not different. She found a great campsite just below the medicine wheel … just in time to set up before dark came upon us.

The first night at camp was primarily to rest from the road, getting settled, and prepare for our trip to the top of the mountain. … Sleep that night was clear and deep, speckled with dreams of our endeavors to accomplish on the mountain. With the sunrise and coffee on the open fire, we discussed our dreams, what we all had to do for the first day, and what we wanted from the experiences. Teacher really wanted us to meditate into mindful clarity for this day and not to … come to any preconceived notions of realities…. When we are able to release the understanding of what is real and allow ourselves to be in the now of the experience we will not be disappointed with the journey.

This was the day the visions started for me. …I started hearing the [spirit] tribal drums, the singing voices of the old ones. It seemed to come on the waves of wind blowing through the mountain pines, speaking of how to honor the ancestors, honor humanity, and honor ourselves as we walk on the planet. I began to see the wise ones among the woods leading me to the path of my future. Something within that day was propelling me forward into a universal consciousness, understanding the greater good of the whole humanity, and was helping me purify my heart.

Teacher just let us be in the natural environment, connecting with the land, the elements; individually taking us aside if she saw we were fighting within ourselves. We each had our own fights within us on this mission. She helped us find our truth on one level or another within each of us. She brought us together to eat, do ceremony, and eat some more, building strength.

It was …strong energy compelling us forward. Now it was time for us to get real with our heads, hydrating, eating, and becoming sturdy and strong so we could manage the elements physically — as well as putting aside our egos for the sacred journey we had been placed upon. Teacher … would lead us through the challenges showing us strength.

[By] mid-morning we were packed and prepared for the medicine wheel. The National Park Service maintains and provides security over the medicine wheel …to preserve this sacred site. They greeted us as they opened the gate for the day. I knew that things were about to get very intense in a short amount of time; when we reached the main greeters of the National Park Service, Teacher was acknowledged by these strangers as an Elder … a wise one. I could tell this regal treatment even surprised her. She embraced this honoring very well, but for me as a student, I felt a subtle energy that I took as a sign for me to find my place rapidly, and keep … from interfering with the vibe Teacher was creating. By the time we were ready to make the 5-mile hike from 8,000 to 9,678 feet, she not only had permission to do ceremony on the medicine wheel, but to have the whole ceremony in total privacy. They made the offer, and we accepted all they were willing to give.

I got so excited with the manifestations that were affirming the messages we had. I knew we were called to do something very big. With water and packs on our backs, we headed to the top of the mountain with great enthusiasm. The altitude and my physical weight challenged me quicker than I anticipated. I tried to find a rhythm in my breath and walk, building a meditative state of being. I walked with Teacher most of the first section, with the others in front or behind. No one had conversation during our walk. Just trying to keep up with the rhythm of breath was challenge enough. I found myself in a zone of awareness where I could hear the [spirit] drums and singing again as if they called me towards the top.

...I began to see visions of Native Indian spirits guiding horses with the sick ones carried on gurneys. Medicine men dressed in worn buckskin clothing, beads, and feathers, the old ones, and mothers carrying their sick children, were all walking with me. They turned and looked at me as I gazed at them. We knew we had all traveled from very far away for this healing. We all walked the mountain together.

...We had discussed what directions we were to take when we got to the wheel, and the animals we would call upon to guide us and support us. I took the west, the bear cave, the place of introspection and healing. Another woman in the group took the east of new beginnings; the north, house of the ancestors, was taken by the only man on our trip. Teacher took the south, the place of community and family. We burned sage, honoring the directions and calling in all our relations, the grandmothers and grandfathers to be with us and help us with this healing for the greater good of all humankind, our communities, our families and ourselves.

It ...did not take long for the bear to take me over, and I found myself on all fours praying to all our relations, Creator, love, health, blessings. The drums began, the singing started ... at one point I looked up and saw the Ghost Dancers dancing around our circle. [I saw] warrior spirits protecting us from harm and giving us guidance.

Teacher made her way to the center of the wheel. As she moved her physical form began to change. The closer she got [to the center], the more she took a spirit form and turned from her physical being into White Buffalo Calf Woman.

Dressed in a white buckskin dress, long raven black hair, eagle feather in one hand and pipe in the other ... hands raised to the heavens praying to Creator for the healing of all our relations past, present and future. I could see a mist rise from her as if she allowed all the world's grief to be released. She stood with hands raised for moments and the mist returned ... golden in light and immense. It drew down upon her, into to the wheel, lighting all the wheel spokes. I closed my eyes and felt energy surge through my body and fill me up.

As Teacher resumed her original form, she nodded to me to open the circle. I gave thanks to the Creator and all those who worked with us. Asking for blessings on our journey home, we finished the circle. Calm came over us and a sense of peace ... whatever was done that day was accomplished.

One message Teacher and I both received ... was after we finished [the ceremony], thousands would come from all over the world to walk the wheel. When you get a message from spirit, you don't always know how it plays out to be true; you just know the message will be true. Well, this was truth, because when they let people through [the gate], there were thousands of people. Chinese, Japanese, Italians, Russians, Israelis, Africans, and people from all over the world ... came on that day. Other Native Americans, veterans, children, grandmothers, grandfathers, mothers, fathers, they all kept coming.

We stood off to the side in awe and amazement. What was it that we really did? And will we ever know? We all left that day knowing we had done something and received a gift for it, but did not know what it could be. ... We all said our thanks to the ranger, leaving gifts for our appreciation for their hospitality. ... We had talked and walked with the old ones, we were blessed to meet the Creator on the mountain in the center of the universe [the medicine wheel] ... and come back to the planet.

- Lisa Owen

The importance of Lisa Owen's encounter cannot be viewed as limited to the visions they received. The entire experience was an amazing gift. Not only did Teacher recognize her student's message, she also organized a trip to a sacred place and (perhaps most importantly) asked for divine guidance to help Lisa experience the fullness of the vision. Based on that information, Teacher focused the group to create a safe and protected space for their spiritual work. During their work at the Medicine Wheel, nobody bothered them; no one interrupted. The Elder created a space which allowed all of the participants to establish their own connection to the vision and to the Medicine Wheel. Through the ceremony, all who were present were able to connect to the divine healing energy that emerged.

When people desire a change in their spiritual paths, individuals might participate in a spiritual quest, such as the healing trip up the mountain Lisa Owen's Teacher instigated. Perhaps a more common occurrence in the Pagan community is when people wanting to boost their spiritual awareness request a dedication or initiation.

> We began what was supposed to be a simple student/mentor dedication ritual — one that so many others have gone through in formal and informal traditions — and what transpired was the beginning of the most amazing journey of my life. During the ritual a force came in, a different energy, and it used Craig as a conduit. It was the Fey. By the end of my "student dedication" ritual, I was being introduced to the four directions, the four winds, the four mystical cities or whatever you would like to call them by my formal name given by the Fey. As we finished, he looked at me, told me he didn't know what had happened, and he needed to make a few phone calls. When he had finished speaking with those he considered his Elders, it was clear I had been initiated directly from the Fey; no student/mentor dedication occurred, and he explained he would be with me to teach what he knew until it was time for me to move forward on my own.
>
> - Mary Hudson

A number of people reported unusual experiences in ceremonial situations. However, a few mentioned events that happened in daily life. Such situations may be unexplainable.

Joy's story:

> My teacher, Mr. William Molnar (Bill), called me one day and told me he was having a problem in his apartment. He had a large carpet that wouldn't stay still on the floor.

Bill said he would leave for work and when he returned, the carpet would be in a different place; it would move towards the couch. Each day, it was getting worse. The day he called me the carpet had actually started moving up the front of the couch. At that point, I said, "I think you're kidding me."

He said, "All right, we'll put the carpet back and you can see for yourself."

Bill picked me up at my house and drove me to his apartment. The carpet was slightly wavy looking, and one side did appear to be moving up the front of his couch. We placed the carpet back in the center of the room and left for about two hours. When we returned, the carpet was no longer flat on the floor and it had moved about a foot closer to the couch. So we sat down to watch. Soon the carpet began to move towards us: it would rise up in one area and then slide forward.

At this point, two friends came to visit with a child. The child began running around the room, but stopped dead at the edge of the carpet, staring at it like he was on a cliff. The family, slightly bemused, left and we went back to our vigil.

I said, "It looks like something is under there, moving the carpet." It really looked like there was something crawling underneath the carpet; as it moved, the carpet moved.

I asked Bill, "Do you see that shape moving under the carpet?" This quickly changed to "There is someone under there!" It looked like a person was struggling to stand up. We freaked out! Bill frantically suggested we throw it out the window, but it was too big, and we didn't know where the non-corporeal person was going to go. Finally, it occurred to me to just roll up the carpet and Bill happily agreed. After we rolled it up, the carpet stopped moving.

However, Bill no longer wanted the carpet. So he called a friend who had always admired it and asked if he wanted it. "Could you come get it now?"

The friend and his buddy arrived to get the carpet. Bill and the two men carried the carpet down the stairs, out of the building, and across the complex to the new apartment. It was a long walk and I was curious about what would happen, so I tagged along.

As they carried it, the new owner of the carpet said, "This carpet is really heavy. What you got in here, a dead body?"

With a perfectly innocent face, Bill replied, "Why would you ask me something like that?"

The carpet was installed in the new apartment, and it never moved again. Ever.

In addition to introducing learners to the wonders of the world, Elders have the ability to recognize a person's skills and gifts. Based on the individual's facilities, Elders can see if a particular practice is helpful or not. Because they have more experience, they can understand the steps involved and they can keep people from moving ahead of their safety zone — a situation which could cause problems in the future. Actually, Elders might decide that a specific type of training would not be safe for the individual. They can stop apprentices from calling in spiritual forces they do not understand, cannot contain, and do not know how to remove. When the mentored person could be harmed, an Elder would need to be capable of taking a stand.

As the year crept on, she [Mrs. F] found more and more ways to find time to mentor me unofficially, until one day, she just flat out asked me, "Are you a Witch?"

"Yes," I said, fully expecting the typical censure that the African American Detroit Community had been giving me for years.

To my surprise, she said, "Good, because I thought something was wrong with you if you weren't. At least now I can talk freely to you."

She told me to bring my friend, Saxophone Section First Chair, with me to her house later so we could all chat and see where we were at in our studies. Of course, this was unexpected, but I jumped at the chance. At last someone was not threatening to pray on me or sanction me, but actually interested in what I believed was my path.

So off we went, band practice first of course, riding our bikes like chariots of fire, straight to the east-side neighborhood where this enchanted house was waiting. Once we were inside, I knew that something was just right. For the first time in my life, I actually attained a level of Angelic vision, and could see their energy signatures flitting all throughout the house. It was awesome.

After sitting us down and giving us Kool Aid, since we refused tea, she went on to check our auras. Shaking her head, she then went about the business of repairing some holes and instructing us how careless it is to run around without shielding. Lesson one was just that. We did it so much that it became instinctual. Which is why to this day, I can honestly say I do not shield. It is just there. … She gave us some chants and laid hands on us and sent us on our way. Every day that summer, without fail, rain or shine, we spent at least one hour at her house after school or in on the weekends. Every day.

Meanwhile, I had decided to venture out into the magickal [sic] world on my own a bit and decided that it was a great idea to start studying Enochian Magick [sic] and hanging out at a certain shop on 7-Mile Road that sold seals and talismans. Well, as could be expected, I wound up conjuring up something I could not get rid of on my own.

Frustrated with me for being a pain in the butt, she went to the shop with me and looked through the door. And I MEAN looked through the door, with her hand. She never opened it, just held up her hand, and described the inside perfectly. Then she nodded and said something to the woman who ran the shop as if she were on the sidewalk with her. She then reached into my shirt and found the sigil I had bought from the woman and shook her head. Did I mention I was a pain?

Well, after helping me get rid of it, and its attendants, she decided that she needed to see all the High Magick [sic] books I was studying. She bid me bring all of them to her house that weekend. So I did. After looking over the stack, she put it on the table and said that she would keep them for a while, and that as soon as I came back over, I could have them back.

I never remembered my way back to her house after that moment. To this day I cannot remember it. I saw her later, and the words were the same. As soon as I came back to her home, I could have them back. But I never could. I guess her words still ring true even now, "Sometimes, I have to save you from yourself."

- Kenya Coviak aka Mistress Belledonna

As that story depicts, occasionally Elders keep people from being stupid. They can stop learners from calling in spiritual forces they do not understand, cannot contain, and do not know how to remove. Just as Elders lead people towards helpful experiences that will bring them closer to their chosen destinies, they can guide individuals away from dangerous practices and areas of study that would be negative. In addition, they provide connections to remarkable events, synchronicities, and mysterious phenomenon. Through divine communications, astounding real-life experiences, and other amazing incidents, Elders open up perception and improve understanding of the world around us.

Rites of Passage, Honoring and Initiation

Initiation is a mysterious process of coming home to self.

Throughout history, most tribal cultures have enacted ceremonies to designate a person as an Elder. Now a number of Pagan organizations follow that practice too, and they are looking for ways to distinguish the Elders of their community. Many groups will choose either an honoring ceremony or a rite of passage, which is also called an eldering initiation. Both types of ceremonies delineate a time of transition. An honoring ceremony gives respect to and recognizes an Elder's accomplishments while an actual initiation or rite of passage delineates a time when obligations and bonds between communities and the Elder become more distinct. A rite of passage may be better suited to meet the true needs of both Elder and community.

> If we cannot give an Elder respect while they are living and make them aware of our gratitude, what is the use of gathering at a person's grave, offering them our heart and tears? Tell the Elder now, today, and do not focus on their passing!
>
> - Penny Goody

Well-planned initiations will add meaning to life and provide a sense of direction. All initiations have a defined or divine purpose. They create a territorial passage and navigation of both community and cosmic roles. Initiations create a change in social position, not only for the Elder, but for all those involved. They sustain and support the Elder and community members as they strengthen connections to ancestors, deity, and each other. Because initiations help us to understand where we are in time and space, both during the ritual and afterwards, they can help to preserve the stability of the collective culture of the community and ensure that it will continue to serve its members even after the Elder is gone.

Initiation is (should be) a moment in time that changes everything after it. It is not the end, it is the beginning. Well-organized rites inspire communities, and successful eldering rituals allow enough time and space for all involved to adjust to the changes that will come. Everybody participating in the process will move forward because when one person gets initiated, the whole community also gets initiated. As a consequence, the Elder's role changes, and the positions in the entire group shift as well.

Historically, there have been basic differences between men's and women's initiations. Although current gender roles are more fluid, these concepts can be helpful in creating an Eldering rite that will fit the needs of the community. Men desire rank and the acknowledgement of accomplishment; they mark their progress through life in this manner. It is a change of their previous authority and responsibility as a new title is conferred, showing an upwardly mobile societal placement. Men expect an outward symbol, such as a sash, belt or pin to give a visual reminder of the new status.

In contrast, women's initiation helps them understand their importance to their culture and therefore, seeks to develop the qualities that will benefit them in fulfilling their future obligations. They are usually nurtured during the initiation in order to be beautiful, generous, compassionate, courageous, and embody similar qualities. Since women are literally the manifestation of the life force becoming tangible, the birth of the future, they are given the wisdom and confidence to sustain life, not only their own but the life of the people and the cosmos. Women bring order to the universe by birthing it in a tangible way.

In African tribal cultures, it is believed that men and women switch roles and viewpoints after their initiations as Elders. Men become caretakers of children and look out for people, especially younger men, to train and teach. Women become the spiritual warriors, fighting for the spiritual wellbeing of their people and society. They become the caretakers of the female mysteries of life. In this way the traditions of the community are kept alive. These simple differences help to make the process meaningful for men and women and the communities they serve. Still, an Elder in either role becomes responsible for the welfare of the community[33].

---

[33] For further information on initiation styles, see Chapter 7, "On the Nature of Women's Initiation" in Bruce Lincoln, *Emerging from the Chrysalis: Rituals of Women's Initiation* (Harvard University Press, 1981).

There are some basic ways to format a ritual that will help everyone understand the process. A structured ritual allows all participants to gain a clearer insight and understand how these new roles will affect each of them personally.

Groundwork

The following tips are for planning an Elder Initiation.

Take some time at the beginning of the planning process to create a strong foundation for all aspects of the ritual, and identify the primary goals of the initiation. How will the person's life change? Consider the new social and spiritual roles. Make sure the Elder participates in identifying the primary intention of the rite. Both initiators and initiate need to have input. In addition, allow the community to have input into the Elder's roles. How can the ritual influence and meet the requirements of all involved?

When planning the actual ritual, consider how the ceremony will enhance the initiate's life journey. Also remember to honor and pay respect to the Elder's ancestors for they are supporting this person on the long journey of life. In fact, an Elder often thinks of those that have come before. Remember to include the initiate's tradition; the ritual should have spiritual meaning and be in keeping with the individual's practices. It may also be important to find a way to include other traditions that may be part of the community as a whole.

There may be some work to prepare the initiate to be ready for the new position. Have all previous phases of life and experience been integrated? Can anything be done ahead of time by the initiate to help with this transition? An Elder may need to let go of a fear of death, concerns about having made a difference, grief over losses, and sometimes bitterness and anger about old events and relationships. Look for resources to help the initiate, such as other Elders, books, and environments that will allow for a steady integration of the new self before the actual initiation. A therapeutic ritual or simple ceremony can be especially helpful and can become an important addition to the Transformation phase. For more information about that, read the section called Transformation included in this chapter.

It is best to have one person coordinate the ritual. Of course positions and tasks can and should be delegated to others. Rely on the community and prepare them for the work that the initiation will require. What are the available talents and resources? Who are the participants and what can they do? Get others involved. Include set up and tear down, decorating, cooking, music, drumming, praying, or being guardians and watchers for the ritual. The creation of the initiate's clothing can include skilled people in the community to sew, embroider symbols, make other regalia, and through their work, infuse the garb with blessings. Clothing chosen for the redressing should encompass the symbolisms of the tradition, the Elder's spiritual progression, relationship to divine beings, and community placement. Many groups have capable ritualists as well. Invite their input for the planning of the ritual.

During the rite of passage, it is ideal if each of the participants fulfills only one role. This allows for better focus from all involved and gives a stronger personal sense of how their own lives will change if each is only worrying about one role to play. If the group is small, try to do as many things ahead of the ritual date as possible.

The people involved in the ritual should be able to keep their focus on the proceedings and on the new Elder. It is best if the initiators are already initiated Elders and comfortable in that role since they will know the power they are passing on. These wise Elders will enhance the experience and guide the way.

There are four main parts to an initiation ritual: seclusion, transformation, a public rite, and integration. The elevation of the initiate takes place during the transformation phase, which is supported by the other stages. Typically, the first steps, seclusion and transformation, take place in private with those performing the initiation while the last two steps are usually public.

Seclusion

The initiate is separated, contained, and secluded from other members of the community. This time alone is for contemplation of the life passage. In addition, it distances the person from the current group identity and status in order to begin to leave those behind. The initiate enters a state of being that is neither of the world nor removed totally from it.

In this beginning phase, surprise creates a mysterious process that works to benefit the initiate. Historic examples would include children being carried off from the village or stolen in the night. In our society, everyone knows when the ceremony is scheduled, and the initiate assumes s/he knows what will happen and when. Therefore, a better option for a rite of passage is to plan the proceedings so that the Elder will not know exactly when the ritual will start. For example, if someone is to pick up the initiate at 7:00, show up at 6:00 instead. This marks the period of restriction as not being totally under the Elder's control. Lack of control supports the individual's ability to surrender to the proceedings.

Transformation

At this time, the initiator is responsible for the private process of changing the individual into someone transformed or different than they were before they entered into seclusion. The change that happens, hopefully, will be internally on a spiritual level, and also externally visible through clothing, hairstyle, adornment, etc. This is the in-between time for the initiate. They are not who they were before they arrived, and yet they have not become who they will be at the end of the eldering rite. The person is either symbolically or literally stripped of previous physical forms of the self.

One way this can be accomplished is through ritual bathing. The initiator can prepare a bath with herbs and other ingredients, and other members of the community can assist with the intention and charging. This bath will help facilitate the final release of the previous phase of life that will no longer serve the Elder. It can be taken by the initiate just prior to the ceremony in private or with the initiator and other ritual members present. Either way, it is a good time for the new Elder to state out loud what is being released.

After the bath, and if the initiator or others are present, the new clothing created for the ceremony can be given to the initiate to dress themselves or the new Elder can be dressed in a ceremonial fashion. The ritualized redressing of the new Elder can also be part of the public ceremony. If so, after the bath, the initiate would be clothed in simple new attire.

Whether the ritualized redressing is completed in private or included in the public rite, it is an important part of the transformation. During the dressing, each piece of clothing or regalia is given a specific designation. For example, when passing or placing a robe on the initiate, state, "This is the robe of an Elder; let it be a reminder of your life and your importance to this community." If the colors have symbolic meaning, mention that; for instance, they represent a connection to Mother Earth or a specific deity. The new clothing endows blessings, designates status, and symbolizes the transformation. In this way, the old identity is removed, and the new stage is marked.

Another option for symbolically and physically stripping away the old identity is to have the initiate relinquish any previous signs of the old status. This can be accomplished by a statement that the person gives up a prior name or title from a previous initiation. For instance, the initiate could say, "I release my responsibilities as a third degree initiate to others and take on the duties of an Elder." As the initiate releases a name or an object, stating the change in words provides meaning for the new Elder, encapsulates the past identity, and allows for its release.

Community Ritual

Each community can decide whether all or part of the ritual will be public. Some groups will choose to perform the entire rite of passage in private. Afterwards the initiators would present the new Elder to the entire community at a party. If you choose the private method, move to the section titled Integration. Other communities want to actively participate in the Eldering, and they will want to plan and perform a public ritual.

Consider the location of the rite. Will it happen outside or inside a dwelling? Perhaps a corner or more private area is desired. Make sure the ritual can be observed by all those involved.

The appearance of the ritual space is important. Create a scene that allows those watching to understand what is happening. Think about clothing style so others can quickly be aware of the difference between the new Elder and those doing the initiating. Make the area as beautiful or mysterious as those involved would like. It should be special in some way and distinctive from a typical ritual. Create settings that enrich the new Elder's concept of self in a manner that makes sense and gives a feeling of order to the ritual.

We have included examples of rituals in the following chapters.

Integration

This stage is necessary to allow both the new Elder and the community to settle into the changes that have just taken place, get a feel for shifting roles, and interact with each other. Since this is the transition from ceremonial to secular space, it is important that everyone involved in any part of the initiation ritual and preparations are present. It publicly affirms their places together at the current time and for the future. Integration reinforces new roles, connections and bonds in addition to those that were in place before the ritual.

During this final stage, the Elder and the initiators reenter the community; there is an announcement of the new status and a celebration. The initiate emerges and is greeted by the village as a new person. The individual's presentation makes the transformation immediately visible to the community. The initiate and the community will not only begin to assume their new roles but also feel the depth of the change that has taken place. This happens through the happiest of events: an important celebration of togetherness.

Having a party is an excellent way to commemorate the milestones of the day. If possible, tailor the party to the initiate's interests. For example, if the new Elder enjoys drumming, that could be included in the event. Also, try to serve cuisine from the Elder's tradition, feature favorite items, and foods that their ancestors would have eaten. Special music that honors the traditions of all members of the community might be a pleasant addition.

Many groups choose to invite relatives of the initiate, giving the family an opportunity to experience a celebration concerning their loved one and to interact with the community members. Becoming an Elder will change the way the affiliated group interacts with the family too. People who were not involved in the Eldering and those with children can also participate.

If emeritus Elders are not able to participate as initiators, they would be esteemed guests during this stage. Their participation is important since they are welcoming a new member into their ranks. In the future, the initiate will need their support and advice. Having previous Elders in attendance gives a connection to a lineage, offers a sense of placement, and helps raise the novice.

The following chapters provide examples of initiatory rituals for Elders. The first one, Eldering Ceremony and Rite of Passage, is easy to adapt to any belief system or gender and gives a basic idea of the steps that are involved in the actual ceremony. The second one, a Croning Ritual, includes many tips on creating and performing public ritual while the third is a man's Saging Rite.

Eldering Ceremony and Rite of Passage

Lillith ThreeFeathers

Guidelines

This ceremony was developed for a community that bases its rituals on the seven directions: north, east, south, west, above, below, and spirit. Notice that grandparents were called in each direction to help the person who is becoming an Elder. In this tradition, it is very important to have interactions with the spirits of those who came before, and they are recognized as guides who support the new Elders and help them to perform duties properly.

Adaptations

The rite can be adapted to remove binary gender references by changing *Grandmothers and Grandfathers* to *the Grandparents* of each direction. In other words, the leader would call to Grandparents of the East, Grandparents of the South, and so forth. Alternatively, your Officiant could substitute the title *Elders* or use the designation *Ancestors*. Remember to change the pronouns from s/he in the ritual to match the individual's preferences. This would be particularly important during the Closing of the Circle when the new Elder is blessed.

The ceremony can easily be modified to fit other traditions. For instance, instead of petitioning Grandmothers and Grandfathers, the Officiants can replace them with particular deities or divine beings. Since elements are not associated with directions, the ritual should fit with any traditional format. If you typically follow a specific order of ceremony, you can merge the two by incorporating the aspects of the eldering rite into your customary procedures. Whatever adaptations you make, the body of the ritual should distinctly focused on the reason for the event, that is, a rite of passage to acknowledge and create a change in status for an Elder for the community.

The best location for this event is outside since this rite uses smudge to prepare sacred space, cleanse, and focus participants on the ritual. Appropriate changes can be made for a particular spiritual tradition, due to limitations caused by the location of the event, or because of allergies. If burning plants would be a problem, a suitable substitution should be made. There are a variety of methods to help people settle into the ritual. Some groups utilize blessed water, sprinkling everyone to refresh them. Others prefer to ring bells, chant, or dip their fingers into salt water. Regardless of the method used, it is important to prepare for the service and delineate the beginning of the ceremony.

Officiant(s)

Since the Officiant holds the ritual together and performs as the initiator, the individual should be an experienced person previously recognized as an Elder. If the community is lucky enough to have more than one Elder, they can divide up the Officiant responsibilities. For instance, they could divide the calling, questioning, and blessings by alternating between two people. Alternatively, four individuals could stand in the cardinal directions and handle the corresponding parts.

If possible, all of the ceremonial roles should be filled by Elders. In groups where there are not enough Elders to act as ritual leaders, the Officiant can pick assistants from younger people who have chosen to walk a path of service to community and who are in training for leadership roles.

Duties should be shared between Officiants as needed. During the eldering, the initiators will work together to ensure that everything moves smoothly and to keep vitality high throughout the rite.

Companion

The initiate is continually accompanied by a companion who performs an important function; other than the companion, the initiate remains alone. Prior to the ritual, the initiate should be in seclusion, should speak very little (if at all), and should spend the time before the ceremony in mediation and prayer.

As intermediary between the initiate and the community, the companion will protect the initiate's privacy. For instance, if the initiate would like water, the companion can request that someone bring it for the initiate. The person bringing the water would give it to the companion who would in turn give the glass to the initiate. If the initiate needs to use the restroom, the companion would accompany the initiate and remain outside the bathroom door unless the initiate calls for assistance. When the initiate leaves the bathroom, the companion will again escort the initiate to the place of seclusion. At all times, the companion should respect the initiate's privacy and need for silence without leaving the initiate alone.

Before ritual, the companion will smudge the initiate. Throughout the ritual, the companion will assist the initiate to move to the correct place and face the right person. This is especially important if there are four initiating Elders.

Ceremony

Prior to the event, prepare area, and set up the altar in the North.

Smudge participants and gather in a circle. Chairs should be used for those who need them. Please see the section called Adaptations *for other options.*

The initiate has been smudged and prepared for the ritual, stands outside the circle with the Companion, but remains separate. The initiate should be able to hear the rite, but it is not necessary for the initiate to see everything that is happening.

Beginning the Circle

Officiant lights the candle in the center of the altar and begins the ritual.

Officiant: "Greetings, friends and families, it is good to see you all. It is wonderful to be together in the circle again. We gather here at this time to acknowledge the seasons of life and to recognize and honor _____, who is taking a step into a new role as an Elder. Come forward, _____."

The companion brings the initiate from seclusion into the circle. They stand in the north in front of the altar. Throughout the ritual, the companion will offer direction to the initiate.

Officiant: "Ancestors, those who walked the Earth before us, we ask your help that we may see the Seven Generations and understand the role we each play within them."

Officiant: "Grandmothers, Grandfathers of the East, we call to you and ask for your help. We ask for your vision that we may see how to live our lives in a better way, that we may become more balanced individually, and that we may become whole."

Officiant: "Grandmothers, Grandfathers of the South, we call to you. We ask for your help. We ask that you be with us when we have hard lessons to learn, lessons of trust and faith. Be with us and guide us through difficult times so that we may be strong, brave and loving."

Officiant: "Grandmothers, Grandfathers of the West, we call to you and ask for your help. Help us to manifest our best dreams so that together we may create good lives for ourselves and the other creatures of the Earth."

Officiant: "Grandmothers, Grandfathers of the North, wise ones, we call to you. We ask your help that we may learn from the errors of the past. Help us to respect ourselves and to respect those who teach us. Help us to build a new future."

Officiant: "Grandfather Sun, Grandmother Moon, Father Sky and Star Ones, we call to you for help. We ask you to be with us, to share your energy with us so that we can stand tall on the Earth and under the heavens. We ask you to share your cosmic awareness with us that we may see more clearly."

Officiant: "Mother Earth, grandmother of all life on this planet, we call to you. We ask your help that we may be thankful for the gifts we have received. We ask that you teach us some of your nurturing ways so that we can learn to live within the hoop of life and learn to walk softly on the Earth."

Officiant: "Father Sky, grandfather of all life here, we call to you. We ask that the sacred light of sun, moon, and stars revive us when we feel weak and sad. We ask your help that we may have the energy to move forward in this life."

Officiant: "Great Spirit, Great Mystery, Creator, Divine Beings, who have blessed us with free will, we ask your help that what we create is an improvement over what came before us. Help us to live well, and to create well while we are on the Earth, so that when we leave this plane of existence, we will have no regrets."

Officiant: "[Initiate's name], you have walked many roads to this place and this time. Just as the seasons change and shift from Spring to Summer to Fall and on to Winter, you have moved through many stages of life."

Officiant says something specific to the individual such as: you have raised children, you have created a successful business, you have worked as [vocations], etc.

Officiant: "Over the years, you have served family, friends, and community as a teacher, warrior, healer, counselor, spiritual leader, and priest."

The statement should match the person's service and work within the community.

Officiant: "Both life and community have tested you. You have persevered. You have learned from mistakes; you have fallen and gotten back up to continue the journey. Your community finds you worthy of this rite of passage into a new stage of life as Elder."

Officiant: "[Name], you have been called here today to be recognized as an Elder. Do you accept this role of your free will?"

Initiate answers "I do" or "I accept."

Officiant asks: "To the best of your abilities, will you serve as an Elder in the service of the Divine, in the performance of your higher purpose, and in the service of your community?"

Initiate answers: "Yes, I will serve the divine, my higher purpose, and my community, to the best of my abilities."

Officiant asks: "To the best of your abilities, will you share your knowledge, abilities and skills as an Elder, with the help of the good Spirits and the Divine Beings?"

Initiate answers: "Yes, I state my purpose to serve as an Elder, to share my knowledge, abilities and skills as an Elder to the best of my abilities, with the help of the good Spirits and the Divine Beings."

Officiant asks: "Will you work as an Elder for the good of yourself, your family, your friends, your community, and the Earth?"

Initiate answers: "I state my purpose to work as an Elder for the good of myself, my family, my friends, community, and the Earth."

Officiant: "[Name], do you swear to perform this role to the best of your abilities, working with good character, clean hands, and heart?"

Initiate answers (something like): "I will work as best I can with good character, clean hands and clean heart."

Officiant says, "May the good Spirits and Divine Beings support you."

Officiant gently touches the initiate's forehead to anoint it with blessed water or oil.

Officiant takes one of initiate's hands, turns it palm up, touches the center with blessed water or oil.

Officiant says, "May the good Spirits and Divine Beings guide you and help you with your work."

Officiant does the same with the other hand.

Officiant touches initiate's throat and anoints with blessed water or oil.
Officiant says, "May the good Spirits and Divine Beings guide you
and help you with your work."

Officiant touches initiate's heart and anoints with blessed water or oil.

Officiant says, "May the good Spirits and Divine Beings guide you
and help you with your work."

*At this time, the initiate is invested with any special robe, belt, jewelry,
or device symbolizing Elder status.*

Closing the Circle

The closing includes blessings for the new Elder.

Officiant: "Ancestors, thank you for participating in this ritual and
for the many ways you help us in our lives. Please walk with
[initiate] as s/he moves forward into new responsibilities as an
Elder. We ask you to help and guide him/her so that the path will
be smooth, and the new duties will be leavened with the joy and
kinship that comes from community."

Officiant: "Grandmothers, Grandfathers of the North, thank you
for your presence at this ceremony and in our lives. Thank you for
your help. Please continue to guide [initiate] so that s/he may
grow in wisdom. We ask that you continue to support him/her as
s/he moves forward in service as an Elder."

Officiant: "Grandmothers, Grandfathers of the West, thank you
for your help during this ceremony and in our lives. Thank you
for bringing dreams into our lives. Please continue to guide
[initiate] so that s/he will create only the best dreams in this
world. We ask that you continue to support him/her as s/he
moves forward in service as an Elder."

Officiant: "Grandmothers, Grandfathers of the South, thank you
for your presence and your strength at this time and as we leave
this place and go back to our daily tasks. Please continue to guide
[initiate] so that s/he will remain calm in times of turmoil and be

able to mediate when others have need. We ask that you continue to support him/her as s/he moves forward in service as an Elder."

Officiant: "Grandmothers, Grandfathers of the East, thank you for sharing your vision with us. Thank you for being here at this time. Thank you for showing [initiate] the pathway to this moment. This is a new beginning, but it is a new beginning based on the foundation of a lifetime of experiences. Please continue to guide [initiate] so that s/he will walk as a good Elder. We ask that you continue to support him/her as s/he moves forward in service."

Officiant: "Grandfather Sun, Grandmother Moon, Father Sky and Star Ones, thank you for sharing your energy with us during this ceremony. Thank you for the place you have in our daily lives. Please continue to guide [initiate] so that s/he will serve as a beacon of light when others are in darkness. As s/he takes his/her place as an Elder in this circle and in the larger community, we ask that you continue to support him/her as s/he moves forward in service."

Officiant: "Mother Earth, grandmother of all life on this planet, thank you for the abundance and diversity of your gifts. Thank you for the support you have given us during this ritual. Thank you for the sustenance and foundation you give us every day. Please continue to guide [initiate] so that s/he will have all that s/he needs: strength of purpose, flexibility like the seasons, and the ability to nurture others. As s/he takes his/her place as an Elder in this circle and in the larger community, we ask that you continue to support him/her as s/he moves forward in service."

Officiant: "Great Spirit, Great Mystery, Creator, Divine Beings, thank you for the abundance and wonder that surrounds us. Please continue to guide [initiate] so that s/he will have the connection to the divine that is necessary for an Elder. Please grant her/him the ability to come to you for answers when s/he has doubt or needs direction. As s/he takes his/her place as an Elder in this circle and in the larger community, we ask that you continue to support her/him as s/he moves forward in service."

Officiant: "It has been spoken."
Officiant: "Rise [initiate's name]."

This can be a special Elder's naming or a title of recognition such as Grandmother, Grandfather, Elder or other appropriate title. New Elder rises.

Announcement

Officiant: "Please welcome [new Elder's name and/or title] as Elder of our community."

People can respond with "welcome" or applause and cheers, whichever is considered acceptable by the group.

Companion and Officiant walk with the new Elder slowly around the circle. People in the circle receive blessings from the new Elder. Participants can offer a few words of congratulations and well-wishes. Although humor is permitted, comments should be respectful.

If gifts are permitted in the circle, the new Elder acknowledges the gifts and thanks the giver (hugging is also fine), and then hands the gifts to the companion (or someone else who has been designated for that role). This leaves the new Elder's hands free so that s/he may continue around the circle offering blessings. Otherwise, people may give gifts to the new Elder during the community meal and celebration.

Community meal follows.

Croning Ritual:
Eldering Ceremony for a Woman

Lady Vala Runesinger
(Elizabeth Hazel)

Introduction

This ritual was written for a coven-sister who decided she wanted her croning ritual in early December, on her 60th birthday. She initially discussed it with me in early summer, so we had plenty of time to plan the event. I did a great deal of research on croning rituals. Although I found plenty of suggestions, I was unable to find a fully written ritual anywhere. Suggestions from the Circle Sanctuary website and an adapted crone-piece from *Circle Magazine* kick off the beginning of the ritual (noted in the text). The vows are original and personalized for the coven-sister who was ready to become a crone.

By the time we arrived at the event date, everything was customized. We used original art for the mailed invitations and the ritual included an original soundtrack. Everything that could be made or created for the event (and this coven is blessed with immense talent) was contributed by individual members. Once it gained momentum, it was truly a group effort.

The coven did a few walk-through rehearsals before the actual event. Everyone knew what they were supposed to do, and where they were supposed to be in the space during the ritual. Advance choreography is a huge bonus! Participants know what they're doing and the ritual flows smoothly and without big, noticeable gaps that cause watchers to get restless. A background in the theater is a real asset in creating and staging rituals.

Our group includes a high priest and high priestess (me). The other members wanted to actively participate in the ritual, so there are several parts that can be assigned to coven members. The ritual also includes responses written for attendees. Everyone at the event was involved in the process.

The original performance of this ritual included the crone-to-be's family members and friends. These non-Pagan people were nervous about attending. The invitation made it clear that it would be an interesting event, followed by a feast. Curiosity won! The ritual was designed to be fully Pagan and ceremonial, yet non-threatening to Muggles. Everyone who was invited attended, and the ritual got rave reviews, especially from the crone's older friends who all wanted croning rituals of their own.

The unity and cooperation of the coven members made a big impression on the guests and left them with a fabulous impression of their first Pagan event.

Ritual Space

We were lucky to have a very large, long living room to stage the ritual. Chairs were placed on either side of the room, facing inward and creating an aisle through the middle of the room. A large, throne-like chair was at the focal area. A table with our tools was nearby. The celebrants were provided with scripts with the full ritual text, while the attendees were given a program that included responses and an "order of ritual" description so they could follow along.

The beginning of the ritual takes place just inside of the entrance to the room. The celebrants lead the crone-to-be into the room, near the aisle formed by the attendees. Once the vows have been spoken, the crone processes down the aisle to the crone throne. The rest of the ritual takes place in this area. Modify the choreography to suit your space and needs.

Before the Event

A designated Greeter welcomes attendees at the door, directs them to their seats and gives them a ritual program. When everyone has arrived, the greeter or hostess assigns individual attendees or multiple people to respond to the directional calls (north, east, etc.) The Crone-to-be is sequestered in another room.

Before the ceremony begins, the greeter and other coven members can smudge the space with sage or substitute a spray with a few drops of clary sage, rosemary, and white thyme oil in water. Someone should turn on the stereo to start the music soundtrack at low volume. The music should be instrumental and unobtrusive. Once all of this is completed, coven members should take their places and prepare for the procession. The high priest and priestess enter the ritual area to give the greeting to the attendees.

Abbreviations

HPS – high priestess
HP – high priest.

The celebrants can be modified to suit the coven's leaders and members. Passages can be assigned in ways that are suitable to the coven members.

Welcoming

HPS: Welcome to this Croning Ritual! We gather here, at the dark of the moon, to honor (name) and support her passage into elder womanhood. Each of you has walked a part of (name)'s path with her, each in a different phase and place of her life. By coming here this evening, we are creating an intersection of (name)'s many paths and many friendships. We form the gateway to this pivotal crossroad, the crossroad where she will assume the mantle of Cronehood. Let us join our good wishes and intentions as she makes this momentous transition.

HP: Take a few deep breaths and close your eyes. Breathe deeply. Connect to the energy of the divine as you know it. Feel the energy in your space and join it to the person standing next to you.

HPS and helper spray herbal potion and sage-smudge the people in the circle.

HP: Feel the cleansing spray as it removes all sorrow and worry. Feel the sage smoke as it heals and reinforces your aura. Let the music penetrate into your being. Silently meditate and ask your blessings for (name) as she proceeds through the ritual.
Remain silent until the cleansing ritual is complete.

HP: Now we will cast the circle of protection by calling on the Elements and the Four Winds. Answer as you are called!

Casting the Circle

HPS: I call the powers of the North!

North (assigned attendees): Crone of Earth, Crone of Soil

HPS: I call the powers of the East!

East: Crone of Air, Crone of Winds

HPS: I call the powers of the South!

South: Crone of Fire, Crone of Flames

HPS: I call the powers of the West!

West: Crone of Water, Crone of Sea

HP: We are protected in the North!

North: Crone of Land, Crone of Planet

HP: We are protected in the East!

East: Crone of Heavens, Crone of Cosmos

HP: We are protected in the South!

South: Crone of Spirit, Crone of Soul

HP: We are protected in the West!

West: Crone of Dreams, Crone of Mystery

HPS: This is a gate of time and space where the veil is thin;
The meeting of the four winds, where the ancients listen and are heard.
This is the Crossroads of the Crone!
The Seeker must pass through this portal
To find her way to the Throne of the Crone!

HP: May the Seeker enter this space, to be tested and tried, to be found worthy of the title and take her place as an Elder of this community.

Procession: Led by coven members, the Crone-to-be enters the room and

greets the guests. She stands, flanked by the HP and HPS, and speaks about her life and her passage into old womanhood.

The Rite of Croning

Adapted by Lady Vala Runesinger (Elizabeth Hazel) from "I Am a Crone" by Holly Heart Free, published in *Circle Magazine*, Winter 2003 issue.

Coven-member 1:
I am a Crone.
I have been called many things;
Hag, Wise Woman, Grandmother, Spinster.
I have lived many times, have grown old many times.
I have a hundred lifetimes of stored rememberings and wisdom inside my mind and heart.
Through all of these times I have known pain and love.
I have felt the rain on my face as I walked softly on the earth.
We welcome the Crone.

All: We welcome the Crone!

Coven-member 2:
Somehow deep inside myself,
I forgot that I am also Goddess.
I forgot to stand for myself and was shunted aside.
Once my wisdom was sought, my voice heard.
But then I remembered. I had power.
I was a Goddess. I was a Crone.
We welcome the Crone.

All: We welcome the Crone!

Coven-member 1:
Then the times changed me, and I became a burden.
This happened because I stopped listening to my inner voice.
The lessons of the ancestors, the voices of the women of my people, were lost in my mind.
There was no one to pass these learnings on to, because the children no longer came to me.
I was the Crone.
We welcome the Crone.

All: We welcome the Crone!

Coven-member 2:
Healing comes in many forms and wisdom is often part of healing.
I am trying to heal. In many cultures I am still a useless old woman.
But this time, this time I go to death with a light heart, for this time
I remember.
I know again I am Goddess. When next I come, I come with Power.
I will not forget the magic of the plants, the wonder of the dreams, the
splendor of the stones.
I am a Crone. I am an old woman.
We welcome the Crone.

All: We welcome the Crone!

Coven-member 1:
I take back my power. I acknowledge my Goddess.
I walk my path with lust and fire.
I balance this with the tears of many.
I weave the fabric of my life by myself and for myself.
No other will weave my life for me again.
I will not forget the life lessons of all the ancestors.
Their hearts lay heavy on my spirit. I will not forget again.
I am Crone.
We welcome the Crone.

All: We welcome the Crone!

The Crone's Vows

HPS: And now I ask you, she who stands at the gateway to
Elderhood: Will you walk your path with honor and dignity?

Crone: I will walk my path with honor and dignity.

HPS: Your dignity shall never be taken from you, except if you
give it of your free will. Are you a strong link, preserving the
chain linking ancestors and generations to come?

Crone: I am a strong link in the chain of life.

HPS: And will you keep the circle?

Crone: The circle will never be unbroken by my hands or deeds.

HPS: Will you ever surrender your Self, your Spirit, or your Power?

Crone: I will never again surrender my Self, my Spirit, or my Power.

HPS: You have many gifts. Will you use them to unify and heal?

Crone: I have many gifts, and I will use them to unify and heal.

HPS: Will you teach and listen?

Crone: I will teach and listen.

HPS: Will you use your power to balance?

Crone: I will use my power to balance.

HPS: Who are you? Declare yourself!

Crone: I am not an old woman; I am a Crone.

HP: You have made your vows, and the Ancient Ones have heard your words. Proceed through the gateway of the Crone and approach the Throne. You will now be garbed in the robes of the Elder, with the tools of your new station in life.

The new Crone slowly moves through the passageway formed by the people, followed by the HP and HPS. As she approaches the throne, each person lines up to present her with the new garb of her role. This will include a new robe, necklace, scarf, pouch, belt with tools, etc. Each person approaches her with one item and puts it on her. Once she is garbed, the crone remains standing, with the priest and priestess on either side. The final item is the crown of the crone, which is held apart until after she is named and anointed.

HP: By the power of the God, with this wand, I name thee Crone (magical name).

HPS: By the power of the Goddess: with this chalice, I anoint you Crone, and join you to your purpose. May your thoughts and words be a source of good sense and peace bringing; and may the works of your hands bring wholeness and healing.

HPS anoints her forehead and the palms of her hands.

HPS: By the turning of the earth, the moon and stars, you are now one with the Ancient Goddess, she who has seen all and remembers all. Serve her with all of your powers, honor her with all your heart.

Crone: I, (name), serve the Goddess with all of my powers and all of my heart.

Crowning

HP: Receive now this crown.

HP holds it aloft and says: "This crown is a symbol of the privileges, rights, and duties of the Crone."

HP places the crown on her head, backs away from her, and says: I now present to you all: (name), **Crone at Large.** You may be seated upon your throne to receive the admiration and well wishes of your friends and loved ones."

Everyone applauds when she sits in the throne.

HPS: The Crone will receive her people and their gifts; and give her blessings to us all. Before we so honor her, I will give one final blessing.

Final Blessing

HPS: (name), may you be at one with the Goddess, and may she guide you in your path always. May the blessings of wisdom and respect be yours, now and for the rest of your life. I thank the Crone Goddess, our most Ancient Mother, the Holder of Eternal Wisdom, and release the guardians of the four quarters who have given their protection during this ritual.

ALL: Merry meet, merry part, and merry meet again. The Circle is Open, but Never Unbroken! Blessed Be!

Ring bells.

Afterwards

Once the ritual is complete, guests and coven members form a line to greet the new Crone. In our crone's ritual, coven-members contributed her ritual garb as gifts, and some of the attendees brought small gifts. The new Crone made gifts for everyone. To keep it simple, she made ceramic leaves with ribbon hangers and wrapped them in tissue paper. Coven members went through the line first, and when they were finished, they rushed to the kitchen to bring the food and drink to the table. After people had moved through the greeting line, they were directed to the buffet. Coven members helped serve the food and drink as needed. Another coven member went to the stereo and put on livelier music appropriate to a celebration.

The ritual took about twenty-five minutes, perhaps a bit longer. This is a good length for a group that includes attendees that are unfamiliar with Pagan rituals. Although the circle-casting is truncated, it serves the purpose by opening the ceremony and including the attendees in the quarter-calling.

Considerations

The Crone-to-be thought about her little speech ahead of time and knew what she wanted to say. Her remarks included the mention of events or things that had led her to the path of Paganism or had molded her life in significant ways. As I recall, her speech was about five minutes long. Since we had an opportunity to rehearse parts, the ritual text wasn't rushed or garbled by the readers. Parts were assigned in advance, so people had a chance to practice reading their parts at home. Clear, strong speech helped the attendees follow the ritual.

Coven members contributed to making the crone's new garb items and her crone's crown. This was a really simple circlet with silk leaves and some trailing ribbons glue-gunned onto a twelve-inch, pre-made vine wreath. We went to the crafts store and bought a lot of silk flowers, but when we put it together, it was clear that a simple crown was easier to work with and it looked better on her. She acquired her own new velvet cloak, but the other items were made or provided by coven members as gifts.

This was one of the most special rituals I've ever put together and conducted. We were able to integrate non-Pagans into the ceremony, make them feel welcome, and create an enjoyable and memorable experience for them. One reason we felt it was appropriate to invite her family and friends is because it was important for them to witness her transition into Cronehood.

Whether they are involved in her Pagan experience or not, it was important for the people closest to her to realize her status within the Pagan community and acknowledge it.

The Crone's Vows are an idea I came up with as we were developing the ritual. It wasn't enough just to plop a crown on her head and shoot her out of a croning cannon! Her crone's role, responsibilities, and duties needed to be clearly stated. An initiation can be a fairly private affair. But ordinations, cronings, or elderings (like marriages) need to be witnessed because these rituals confer public titles, status, and purpose onto individuals. Vows are made in front of witnesses for a reason. People who take on the responsibilities of priestess, crone, or elder promise to serve a community, so the community they are serving should be a part of those rituals.

By including family and friends as witnesses, this public ritual also serves a secondary but no less important function of enhancing the value of elders in society. Covens generally acknowledge the status of elders and give them due respect. Society in general does not. Each person who is given a public croning or eldering ritual creates more status for all elderly people. This is a hidden but critical consideration that makes the role of the crone – and preparation for that role – all the more valuable and important for the Pagan community. In contemporary society Pagans are the one of the few groups that honor, celebrate, and reward aging.

It is difficult to fully describe the impact that this ritual had on the non-Pagan guests. Our crone's age-peers expressed a lot of good-natured envy during the feast. Her family members didn't really know how to react, but over time, the croning ritual served to elevate her in the eyes of her children and grandchildren. They give her more respect and take better care of her. The co-workers she chose to invite were those she knew would be discreet and sympathetic. Since the ritual, her career has blossomed in amazing ways, too. She's become an acknowledged innovator in her field and is traveling constantly to give lectures, although retirement is just around the corner.

The coven members were geeked, as usual, to focus their abundant talents on an elaborate and unusual ritual that's not a typical part of the Pagan year. Our crone is fifteen years older than the next oldest group member, so she's way ahead of us on the croning curve. In a subtle way, the attitudes about aging have shifted. It isn't such a horrible, scary thing to approach old age. It's just another step in life. Since she was able to reach the crone's crossroads with such grace and courage, we're all inspired to live up to her example.

Whether readers choose to use this ritual text or create their own ritual, performing a croning ritual that's witnessed by guests is a more amazing experience that can be imagined.

Saging Ritual: Eldering Ceremony for a Man

Lillith ThreeFeathers

Preparation

Both the ritual and party areas would have been cleaned, tidied, and decorated prior to start. Before people gather, set up the altar with elements representative of directions according to the group's tradition. One candle in the center of the altar will represent both the sacred connection to the divine and the initiate's transition. At the beginning of the rite, prepare the initiators with smudge, incense, water or other preferred method of cleansing.

Please remember to incorporate decorations, music, and food for the party area that will have special meaning to both the new Elder and the community. It is convenient to have the social celebration separated from the ritual space so that any guests who will not participate in the rite can gather there. Let them know to arrive at the festivities at a specified time. In particular, the comfort of families with children should be considered. If needed, a few toys could be provided, or the helpers could show parents a nearby play area. Several community members will welcome people, provide snacks or beverages, and handle any questions. They will also set up the tables with covered food that will be served after the new Sage is announced to the community. In addition, they would offer food and beverages to Elders who have physical limitations. After the new Sage and initiating Elders are seated, community members can bring food and beverages at regular intervals since they might not be able to eat otherwise!

Since the community is acknowledging his experience, knowledge, and worthiness for the position, the Initiators can discuss the Pledging with the Sage-to-be. In addition, the new Elder will have time to determine his personal remarks.

Before the final blessing, the new Sage would be given one or more symbols of initiation. Pick clothing or a special object such as a belt, stole, cloak, staff, garland or crown. Although these items will have been magically blessed or charged prior to the initiation, they will also be consecrated again during the Blessing of the Elements. This is an important part of the initiation and should not be stinted. If possible, active participants would include the initiators and other experienced Elders, especially any who were Elders or teachers of the Sage-to-be.

Dressing the newly initiated Elder in ritualized garb is very important; make this part of the rite specific to the new Sage. Incorporate the initiate's beliefs and the concepts significant to the group. It would be nice to include the gift of a staff to represent the new status. If so, consider what the staff will mean to the new Elder and add that to the ritual: it will connect him to the Saging, the community, Elderhood, and to the divine; it will support him in times of need, and so on. The person bestowing the staff can expound on each of those connections as well as other meanings. In addition, share the origins of the staff and talk about the members who worked on it. Of course, the explanation ought to include what the staff represents within the spiritual tradition, how it is viewed as symbol of a position, and so forth.

Officiants and Initiators

Priest and Priestess will act as the initiators during the ritual; they will be supported by the other officiants. The positions would be handled by people who are recognized as experienced Elders. Both can hold staffs.

Staff-bearer and Swordsman

Since this is an eldering for a male, the person who acts as Staff-bearer must be male. Swordsman can be of any gender, but it is appropriate (but not required) that the position is filled by a veteran or martial artist. Both people ought to be those who have previously been recognized as Elders; if this is not possible, they must be experienced members of the group.

The Staff-bearer is required to use a staff, and the Swordsman carries either a ritual sword or athame. Just as the blade represents that the holder has been initiated to a certain level within the group, the staff would signify Elder status.

The initiate will be kept out of the circle until the priest calls for him to enter. Before the entrance, the Staff-bearer will act as guide and escort, accompanying him to the ritual space. After Swordsman passes the initiate into the circle, Staff-bearer will enter and stand in a position beside the initiate. Swordsman will remain in the circle standing behind the initiate as watchman and witness.

Advocates

During the planning stages, two people will be picked to fulfill these functions. Advocates may be any members of the community who know the initiate. It is fine if they are friends, students or family members.

Officiants for Blessing of the Elements

As you plan the Saging, determine who will perform the blessing of the elements. If possible, it is best if experienced Elders fulfill these functions. If the group is small, Staff-bearer and Swordsman can handle the blessing.

Adaptations

Feel free to modify words to fit your customs. If the group prefers, another title can be substituted for the title of Sage, for example, if the community uses a specific designation for an Elder from a different language. If the community is one that uses modified elements in the directions, such as, air in the north instead of earth, you can easily rearrange the casting and closing of the circle to accommodate that.

When God and Goddess are mentioned in the ritual — when the priest and priestess say "May God and Goddess support you" — the statement can be replaced with "May the gods support you" or with the names of the specific deities worshipped by the group.

Saging Initiation - Casting the Circle

Priest and Priestess can alternate the parts of calling the circle. Initiate should be standing outside of circle with Staff-bearer.

"Kind and helpful Ancestors, Ancient Ones, we call to you. We greet those who have gone before. Bless us with your presence. We call to the good ancestors of [initiate's name] and ask them to be present. We ask you, divine ancestors, to give us your guidance and to support this ritual. Blessed be."

Everyone says: "Welcome and blessed be."

"As we turn to the East, and call to the winds, we think of the gifts that Air brings. We give thanks for the breath of life. We give thanks for the inspiration of our thoughts.We give thanks for wisdom from the winds of change. Welcome are the gifts that you bring. Please join us in this ritual of transformation. Blessed be."

Everyone says: "Welcome and blessed be."

"As we turn to the South, and call to the flames, we think of the gifts that Fire brings. We give thanks for the power of will and desire. We give thanks for the warmth from the sacred fire, which lights our lives. We give thanks for the fire of inspiration. Welcome are the gifts that you bring. Please join us in this ritual of transformation. Blessed be."

Everyone says: "Welcome and blessed be."

"As we turn to the West, and call to the rains, we think of the gifts that Water brings. We give thanks for the richness of cleansing and healing. We give thanks for the water of life, which flows through our blood. We give thanks for our dreams and emotions. Welcome are the gifts that you bring. Please join us in this ritual of transformation. Blessed be."

Everyone says: "Welcome and blessed be."

"As we turn to the North, and call to the stones, we think of the gifts that Earth brings. We give thanks for the seeds and the harvest, the fruits of the Earth. We give thanks for the deep rocks that provide stability in our lives We give thanks for the many ways you shelter us. We give thanks for the cycle of life and the wisdom of the years. Welcome are the gifts that you bring. Please join us in this ritual of transformation. Blessed be."

Everyone says: "Welcome and blessed be."

Priestess: "Mother Goddess, sweet mystery and beautiful mother of the green earth, Great One of the Stars and Moon, Great air mother: vast and unbounded, giving the breath of life. Great fire mother: bringing warm passion of life. Great water mother: flowing through the blood of life. Great earth mother: supporting the bones of life. Mother of us all, bless us with your loving presence. Blessed be."

Everyone says: "Welcome and blessed be."

Priest: "Father God, divine protector, spark of life, Great Sun God who watches over us below, God of the calm breeze and God of the powerful wind, God of the rushing waters and God of the abundant land, Father of the green wild places, master of the mountains, God of change and God of strength, join us in this place. Father of us all, bless us with your loving presence. Blessed be."

Everyone says: "Welcome and blessed be."

Challenge

Priestess: "We are gathered here in community on a landmark day for [Name], known to us as [Title, if he has one] [Magical Name]."

Priest: "[Name], come forth."

Staff-bearer and initiate begin walking to the circle.
Swordsman blocks initiate from entering with his blade and stands in front of the initiate.

Swordsman says, "Stop."
Swordsman asks: "Who are you?"

Initiate responds with his name.

Swordsman asks: "Why do you come here?"

Initiate replies: "I come to be initiated into service."

Swordsman says: "You may enter the circle and be examined."

Swordsman lets initiate and Staff-bearer enter, and escorts them to Priest and Priestess.

Staff-bearer states, "This person, [Name], who is known to me, comes to be initiated into service."

Priest: "Thank you, for bringing [Name] to this circle. Why do you recommend him to Elderhood?

Staff-bearer makes a statement in his own words.

Priest thanks him. Staff-bearer steps back and stands behind and to the side of the initiate.

Priestess: "Will anyone else stand to speak on behalf of [Name] and recommend him for Elderhood?"

Advocate 1 comes forward and announces, "I do."

Advocate 1 states name [magical name is fine] and explains relationship to initiate.

Priestess: "As advocate of this person's initiation into service as Elder, what do you say in support of his request?"

Advocate 1 speaks here in his/her own words about the initiate and why he is ready to take this step.

Priestess: "Thank you for your words."

Priest: "Who else will stand as advocate on behalf of [Name] and recommend him for Saging?"

Advocate 2 comes forward and announces, "I do."

Advocate 2 states name and explains relationship to initiate.

Priest: "As advocate of this person's initiation into service as a Sage, what do you say in support of his request?"

Advocate 2 speaks here in his/her own words about the initiate.

Priest: "Thank you for your words."

If others wish to speak on behalf of the initiate and have requested to do so, either Priest or Priestess would ask for another advocate to step forward. If the community is present, it is necessary to give them the chance to speak positively about the initiate, but the initiators must be careful to limit the number of advocates and the length of their statements so that the energy of the ritual is not dissipated by random talking.

Questioning and Pledging

Staff-bearer and Swordsman continue to stand behind and to the side of the initiate. If a group includes the observances of Drawing Down the Moon and Drawing Down the Sun, those rites can be performed here.

Priest: "[name] today, you have arrived here to become initiated to the service path of Elderhood. Advocates have spoken on your behalf and have testified to your preparedness. The position of Sage is important to all of those present and for continuity of our community. An Elder is challenged to serve in ways. As a Sage, you may be called upon as a mentor, a guide, an adept, and a mediator.

Priestess: "The responsibilities will be two-fold: your obligations to this community [group's name can be inserted] will be transformed and our duties to you will also change."

Priest: "Is it your intention to accept the challenge of Elderhood today?"

Initiate answers, "Yes."

Staff-bearer asks: "Have you chosen a new spiritual name?"

Initiate answers as appropriate. In some traditions, the person continues with the same magical name; those systems tend to add a title to the name. Therefore, if he will continue using a previously given name, he states that. If there is a new name, he responds with it.

Initiate says: "I have chosen [name]" or "I have been given the new name of [name]."

Priest asks: "[Name], will you do your best to serve your community as Sage?"

Initiate answers: "I will do my best to serve my community."

Both priest and priestess say, "We acknowledgement your pledge of service."

Priestess asks: "Will you do your best to uphold your personal ethics and those of this organization?"

Initiate answers: "I will do my best to uphold my ethics and those of this organization."

Both priest and priestess say, "We acknowledge your declaration."

Priest asks: "Will you do your best to maintain the highest standards of spiritual work?"

Initiate answers: "I will do my best to maintain the highest standards of spiritual work."

Both priest and priestess say, "We acknowledge your declaration. May the ancestors guide you."

Priestess asks: "Do you state your purpose to serve God and Goddess and to serve your higher purpose for the good of yourself, your family and friends, your community and the Earth?"

Initiate answers: "I state my purpose to serve God and Goddess and my higher purpose for the good of myself, my family, my friends, my community, and the Earth."

Both priest and priestess say: "We acknowledge your declaration. May God and Goddess support you."

Priest: "[Name], to the best of your abilities, will you share your knowledge, abilities and skills in the service of God and Goddess, in the performance of your higher purpose, and in the service of your community?"

Initiate answers: "To the best of my abilities, I will share my knowledge, abilities and skills in the services of God and Goddess, in the service of my higher purpose, and in the service of my community."

Both priest and priestess say: "We acknowledge your declaration. May God and Goddess assist you."

If the new Sage wants to speak to those doing the initiating, he would do so now.

If initiate will receive one or more special symbols of initiation, Staff-bearer and Swordsman will assist Priest, Priestess, and other Elders in placing them on the new Sage. If a staff will be given, do so at this time. Please refer to Preparation section for more details.

Blessings of the Elements

Priestess: "It is time to receive the blessings of the elements."

Priest: "[Name] and [Name], will you perform the blessing?"

Officiant 1 brings smoke [from incense or smudge stick]; passes smudge around [Name].

Officiant 1 says, "May the element of air protect and guide you. You are not alone, for the breath of the Earth is with you."

Officiant 2 brings a candle, passes it around the Initiate.

Officiant 2 says, "May the element of fire protect and guide you. You are not alone, for the passion of Spirit is with you."

Officiant 1 brings a chalice of water, sprinkles the water onto the Initiate.

Officiant 1 says, "May the element of water protect and guide you. You are not alone, for the waters of the Earth mingle with yours."

Officiant 2 takes a bit of ash from the smudge or a tiny bit of dirt, touches the Initiate's forehead and his/her hands.

Officiant 2 says, "May the element of earth protect and guide you. You are not alone, for the bounty of the Earth is with you."

Priestess: "[Name], you stand between earth and sky. You stand here sheltered by the four directions. Remember this, so that they may continue to nourish and sustain you."

Priest: "[Name], we have come to the end of this initiation of Saging, but it is just the beginning of this stage in your life. It is important for us to see that you represent a new time in the cycle of life. As you have journeyed through this life, you have moved from youth to father, and now you enter the time of Elder. As your community, we will do more than ask of you and your talents; we will work side-by-side with you and strive to support you in the days to come."

Finish the circle, thanking every element and being that was called.

Announcement and Celebration

Initiators, new Sage, other Elders, and those who participated in the Saging will process to the celebration area. It is good to send someone ahead to let those waiting know that they are close by. Upon arrival, they would arrange themselves around the new Sage, Priest and Priestess. Since this is the first view the larger community has, don't rush.

Staff-bearer raps on the floor and states "Hear ye, hear ye," (or something similar).

Priestess: "Friends and members of [Community name] I am thrilled to present, our newest Sage [Name]."

Everyone can applaud or cheer.

If the new Sage would like to offer thanks, a blessing or address the community, he can do so now.

Priest: "Please come forward and greet our new Sage [Name]."

A receiving line might work well. Of course, the family must be part of the initial group of special guests to offer acknowledge and congratulation. They would take their places with the Sage so that both he and his partner/family can be introduced to everyone. In addition, the first group to greet the new Sage would include any experienced Elders who were not able to participate in the initiation and any visiting Sages or Crones.

Community celebration with shared food follows.

Parting Ways

As with any other relationship, interactions with Elders can evolve through all phases of life. The strong ones forge connections that last a lifetime and may stop only with the Elder's passing. Other relationships end in separations due to difficulties that arise from distance or health issues. Some fall apart because of misunderstandings and disagreements, and a few terminate due to purposeful decisions. What happens after the relationship ends?

Separated by Distance

In our mobile society, individuals can travel to far-away places to study with an Elder. Although this provides excellent opportunities for individuals to pursue their dreams and to establish a connection with an Elder in a specific tradition, it puts additional stress on those relationships. Although some people manage to maintain contact through diligent use of email, telephone, and Skype, such mediated contact might not provide the type of mentorship you need. Even in the best of circumstances, it is unlikely to withstand long periods without personal contact.

If you set up a mentorship with an Elder who lives far away, realize that you will need to commit to regular contact through various methods. Definitely, it will require diligence and clarity in communications. Most people in such associations travel at regular intervals to meet with their Elders; a few of our respondents moved to live in nearby locations.

Even with the best of intentions, long distance study doesn't work well for everyone. Not only can individuals face difficulties due to financial issues, but also misunderstandings can arise due to the distances separating people. It might take hours of honest dialogue to mend misconceptions, but that commitment is necessary in order to maintain a good relationship. Communication is always important. For example, if economic or family changes prevent you from traveling, please tell the Elder. Don't just disappear and assume it won't matter.

Growing Apart or Moving Beyond

Many people choose to work with an Elder due to proximity. After a while, the fact that the Elder is nearby is not enough and the person may feel a need to focus on other studies or have different experiences. Over time, personality differences might emerge. The question becomes: is this still the right Elder? Perhaps the interaction was correct for a time, but it no longer fits.

> When starting on a new path, it is human to want to learn everything quickly and move along, to fit in with a new community. The fact that an Elder has shown interest is often enough. It's only later, in looking back, that I can question why I wanted to work with this person — and I know that availability played the largest role of all.
>
> - Kurt Hohmann

Eclecticism is common in the Pagan community. When the quest calls again, the individual may move on to different studies with a new person. Sometimes the student recognizes the need to move on. However, at other times, the Elder believes the relationship must change, and might even instigate the separation.

> She taught me what I knew and saw where I needed to go and kicked me to the door. We started to get visions of the seven African powers and she did not want anything to do with me.
>
> - Lisa Owen

Even when the Elder withdraws from interactions, out of respect for the mentoring, training, and friendship given, the individual ought to continue to honor the Elder. Whether or not the lessons were basic, or they were mystical and life-changing experiences, recognition can still be given. Although the learner can choose to separate from the relationship, what the Elder offered should be acknowledged and respected.

> I worked with Craig [Parsons-Kerins] for two or three years learning all I could, but a time came when he told me that there was nothing left for him to teach me; we

were equals. I can't thank him enough ... and to this day I'm still shifting and learning and amazed by everything that comes my way ... I love him with all my heart for who he is and what he passed on to me, but more importantly for being a friend.

- Mary Hudson

Retirement and Sickness

In mundane employment, no one is surprised when employees retire to take care of children or parents. The same is true of people who retire from a job due to age, although the retiree may return as a part-time consultant to help during a busy time of year. It is of primary importance that we realize the same things can happen with spiritual and community Elders.

Whether due to age, illness or other circumstances, the majority of Elders who function as spiritual leaders will eventually step down from active duties and move into an advisory role. They may turn over much of the work to their students or the spiritual group may be asked to pick a new leader. Eventually, most will turn over teaching and ritual facilitation to those they have trained.

Teacher was my elder and I honor her, her family and all her relations, but a time came that her responsibility as my Elder came to an end. It was time for her to focus on her family and the raising of her grandchildren. She chose to step out of the spiritual teachings and practices ... she sent me on my way. I was very perplexed at the time... I do know now that I am an Elder in training, and I understand the responsibilities of caring, teaching, and doing my own work can be overwhelming. I embrace it every day but I have the choice to lay it down like my teacher. I am so grateful for her guidance. She knew the teachings would continue on with me. Mei guitch, thank you.

- Lisa Owen

It is not realistic to expect that older people would continue to be as active as they were when they were 30 or 40 or 50. Certainly,

Pagan beliefs would sustain expectations to keep in touch, to be willing to stop by to pick up groceries, mow the lawn, or clean up the kitchen. Such kindness seems a small repayment for the Elder's years of service. However, it seems that Elders who no longer actively serve the community are sometimes ignored or undervalued. Why should retirement lead to changed acceptance of the person's Eldership? After people retire, the community has an obligation to maintain contact, be a support network, and not forget about them.

Consider Isaac Bonewits, who founded and led Ár nDraíocht Féin (A Druid Fellowship); his role in the Pagan community extended beyond that organization. He was considered an Elder and teacher by others outside that organization. Eventually his health prevented him from continuing in a direct leadership role. At the time he stepped down, he was still recognized by the ADF group as an Elder and awarded the title of Archdruid Emeritus.

> Under Isaac's direct leadership ADF survived its first decade in a pattern of modest growth, building organization and spiritual depth. When the time came, Isaac stepped aside, and allowed the organization to find its feet without him, until returning as an honored emeritus member of ADF's clergy and spiritual work. Since his departure as our formal first officer, his vision, plans and specific teachings have remained a central guide of ADF's growth.
>
> - Ian Corrigan

Although the roles change when someone retires, the connection between the emeritus Elder and the younger ones brings continuity to the community and its traditions. They continue to provide advice, experience, and act as a vast resource for newer Elders and everyone in the community. Their continued involvement, at whatever level, is a blessing.

Honoring

Some individuals are lucky to have a long-term relationship with an Elder. However, due to the typical Pagan's individualized quest for a spiritual path, many people interact with a specific person for a couple of years or only a few months. Regardless of the length of time, there is a vast difference between separation from a teacher and parting from an Elder. Although the names and faces of teachers may be forgotten, people recall abundant details of their time with Elders. Even after they part, those mentored feel a sense of gratitude.

Lillith's story:

> After passage of time, I was not able to maintain interactions with certain Elders. Although they were my Elders then, and they continue to be Elders to other people, I might not consider them my Elders now. However, if I were to meet them at a public event, I would treat them respectfully in honor of their status and in acknowledgement of our past relationships. Even though I no longer train with them, they continue to be Elders and I offer them the respect of acknowledging their roles in my evolution. Elders do not stop being Elders simply because I am no longer studying with them.

When people separate from good Elders, whether the parting is due to choice, distance, retirement, sickness or death, those Elders should continue to be in our thoughts and prayers. If we do have a chance for a reunion, they deserve our respect and appreciation. Regardless of the time (or distance) that separates us, common sense dictates that we remember them for their teachings. Truly, we should communicate our appreciation to them while they are living.

Leaving a Bad Elder

The Pagan community is very accepting of non-mainstream views and lifestyles. Sadly, a few unethical people have used that tolerance to establish themselves in the position of acting as an Elder within a Pagan tradition or subculture. While individuals may hide their true nature for a time, eventually the group will discover immoral acts, inappropriate behavior, or incompetence. Sooner or later, people will recognize duplicitous character. Each individual must consider the pros and cons of a particular relationship to weigh their experiences and interactions against beliefs about appropriate interactions.

In our experience, sexual relations between students and Elders are not productive and should be avoided. Adding a sexual component to a student/Elder relationship may create unclear boundaries and undermine trust between both parties. If sexual activity is part of your path, know that this relationship will be extremely complicated. Many conversations will be required to create a relationship that is successful for both parties. This assumes consensual sex. When a person in a position of authority uses that position to manipulate others into sexual actions, it is a reprehensible misuse of power.

> In the early days of training, I held this person in highest esteem and believed that what he was telling me was factual or, given the metaphysical nature of our training, at least valid in practice. Toward the end of our working relationship, I recognized him as a man who was willing to say or do anything in order to feed his own physical desires, and I no longer believed much of anything he said or wrote.
>
> Today, if I see someone who is being influenced by an Elder (or anyone else), I caution that person to step back and look at the relationship objectively. Even the most respected of individuals can have an agenda which may or may not be in line with the student's best interests.
>
> - Kurt Hohmann

Sometimes individual Elders develop alcoholism or drug addiction, situations that exacerbate the issues in any interactions. Although certain Pagan traditions reject them, alcohol and drugs can be important elements or sacred components in other belief systems. Regardless of whether or not you use them, unacceptable or uncontrolled consumption will hinder events. Try to view the situation impartially. If you are new to a tradition, you may find it helpful to talk to others who have more experience in participation. Even so, you must decide your own comfort level. Ask yourself some questions. If alcohol is a part of the tradition, how do you feel about that? Is it used in an appropriate way? Does the Elder drink a few beers after the work has been completed or does alcohol interfere with the event? Does substance use stop the Elder from completing commitments?

A few Elders may constantly ask for money while some individuals charge exorbitant fees for services. Although different Pagan traditions handle payment in differing and contradictory ways, there is nothing immoral about providing money, food or physical assistance to your Elders. Certainly, contemporary culture includes the concept of payment for workshops, lessons, and travel expenses. Additionally, many indigenous-based systems expect the student to bring gifts of food, provide supplies, and handle chores. Still you shouldn't feel like you are playing the role of a bank. Although there may be a valid reason for the request, do some research and ask about expenditures. Is the Elder traveling a long way to perform a ceremony for you? If so, it is not unreasonable to be expected to cover expenses, provide lodging, and pay an equitable fee. However, if typical fees are $500 and you are asked for $2,500, you have the right to question the increased amount and ask (politely) for an itemized accounting or explanation.

We all know that there are people in the world whose energy is just plain negative. If you act naive, people might do things that you might not like. In addition, there are plenty of well-meaning individuals out there who will do something harmful to an individual because they think it is the right thing to do. Perhaps they believe what they say, but maybe they are trying to manipulate others.

Lillith's story:

> There were two women who were fairly well known in the local area and considered knowledgeable. The two decided that energetic barriers surrounding people were preventing spirit messages from "getting in," and so they decided that they should break such barriers wherever they found them. Professing it was the right thing to do, they went about breaking this barrier whenever they could. Since it was supposed to help build their personal skills, quite a few people agreed to let them do it, sometimes without asking what the two were going to do. The effects were not always pleasant. Eventually, individuals realized what the two had done and got angry — but who should have been angry and at whom?

Excessive ego can lead to the same place: don't be too proud to say you don't understand. Ask questions. If someone claiming to be an Elder wants you to do something that is truly dangerous, please remember that you always have the right to refuse.

Lillith's story:

> I was talking on the phone to an individual I'll call Donald. He was telling me about his experiences with a man who claimed to be a South American Elder sent to heal everybody in North America. Enthusiastically, Donald said that everyone was so excited (although I was not sure who everyone was).
>
> Happily, Donald told me, "He's so astonishing. I think he's a real shaman. He's going to cure my migraines!"
>
> Of course, I was very interested in his method to cure headaches. Before I could say anything, Donald rapidly launched into a recitation about his costumes, songs, and rituals — and how amazing he was.
>
> Finally, when Donald stopped talking, I was able to ask: "How will he cure your migraines?"
>
> Donald announced: "He just has to bury me in the ground for three days and I won't have migraines ever

again!"

I said, "If he buries you in the ground for three days, you might not have to worry about anything ever again."

Donald: "What do you mean?"

Me: "Headaches might be the least of your problems: you might die."

You should be able to discuss your concerns with the Elder. If "the Elder" responds by ignoring you, talking about you in demeaning terms or bullying you, evaluate your situation. You can decide not to continue to interact with that individual. You don't have to stay if it isn't safe. You may feel that your progress will be stunted, but there are always other teachers.

Don't worry about giving your Elders power; worry about giving the wrong people power. Worry about giving power to those who manipulate others, who abuse others, who purposefully hurt others. Don't continue to give authority to those who call themselves by fancy titles in order to use their positions to betray their stated beliefs and deceive their followers.

Perhaps the most difficult issue to pinpoint in the Pagan community is when an Elder does negative magic on students. Although it happens rarely, this is one of the most demoralizing occurrences, a betrayal of the very foundations of Eldership. If you truly think the leaders of the group are working malicious magic, it's time to think objectively about them. If your practice includes spirit guides, ancestral helpers, and divine beings, check in with your known allies. Do a cleansing bath. Talk to people who have left and ask them why they departed. When you listen carefully to their answers, you may be able to discover if your misgivings are supported. Take a break to participate in different gatherings and compare the experiences. Search out another Elder and ask if what you suspect is possible.

Another reason to leave would be if the head of the group supported cult-like or totalizing behavior. The leaders of a totalizing system establish a belief that there is one (and only one) valid way of being; they claim entitlement as the only determiners of the proper conduct and methods. Setting themselves up as prime arbiters of the tradition, they manipulate others to foster confusion and increase dependency. Those same individuals use religion as the justification for exerting control over subordinates, and they evict those they cannot control. When power-hungry people take over leadership of a group, they may move it towards totalization.

Both Isaac Bonewits[34] and Robert Jay Lifton[35] have offered evaluation systems for determining if a group has cult-like or totalizing behavior. Bonewits' tool is readily available online and includes rating categories such as external control, isolation, and sexual manipulation[36]. Lifton described eight themes that constitute totalistic behavior. He detailed how leaders seek to control information, hinder their followers' ability to solve their own problems, and change people's behavior through guilt, shame and fear. Ultimately, the totalistic group supplies the only justification of behavior and faith standards in order to pressure individuals to remake themselves according to the group's doctrine[37].

In the case of someone who posed as an Elder but committed nefarious or harmful acts, separation makes sense. After establishing and accepting the fact that there were improper actions, each person or assembly should have little problem leaving. However, there will always be some who choose to see what they want to see instead of recognizing the truth. Whether or not all those involved agree, move forward with your decision.

Lillith's story:

> Since I have had so many teachers, my experiences have varied widely. Sometimes I placed my trust in the wrong person — for instance, a teacher who acted improperly or immorally — and so I had to walk away. Many others were wonderful Elders, and I was sad when they retired from teaching or ritual work. The best of them offered their time, their knowledge, their wisdom with a bit of patience and stability.

---

[34] Isaac Bonewits, "The Advanced Bonewits' Cult Danger Evaluation Frame (Version 2.7)" *NeoPagan Net* (2008) http://www.neopagan.net/ABCDEF.html (accessed 04/10/2016).

[35] Robert Jay Lifton, *The Broken Connection: On Death and the Continuity of Life* (America Psychiatric Press, 1979) 298.

[36] Bonewits, http://www.neopagan.net/ABCDEF.html (accessed 04/10/2016).

[37] Lifton, 298.

When Elders Pass

An Elder's passing has a profound effect on those who have studied with them. It is difficult for communities to say goodbye to a person who was as important as a family member and has influenced beliefs, studies, life choices, and interactions with others. When an Elder dies, people feel sorrowful, but more importantly, they have a sense of loss of not only the person but their wisdom. They wonder who they can call with their problems and who will offer advice. Often Elders are the anchor; they are the foundation, and the glue that holds communities together. Several contributors mentioned the effects of the deaths of their Elders.

> I have had an Elder pass, but not Craig [Parsons-Kerins]. He is still alive and kicking! No, these were other Elders. One, I only attended the rituals put on by others, but the other, I helped to officiate at the ritual of their crossing. Both of these individuals still impact my life and probably always will.
>
> - Mary Hudson

> In regard to Isaac's [Bonewits] passing, it really hit the community hard.
>
> - Bernadette Montana

> I did experience a pillar of the community passing. ...Denessa Smith (Tempest Smith Foundation) who was not only a pillar of the community but a friend to me. ...It has been five years, but her passing has not been forgotten, nor has her contribution.
>
> - Anna Calhoun

Intuition

Perhaps because of an energetic connection to the Elder, a few people sense the Elder's passing without prior notification. On rare occasions, unusual events act as harbingers.

In 2004, I was walking through my house and a painting he had created that I brought from his collection fell off my wall. I thought something had happened and it reminded me of my lessons at the river. A week later I went to a powwow and found out he had died the same day. The day the painting fell off the wall.

- Rocio Darlene Arriaga,
speaking of the passing of her elder Grandfather Bear

Since members of Pagan groups often live scattered across widespread areas, it is common for people to participate in solitary rituals or prayers that are scheduled for a specific purpose. The goal is for all participants to do the work at a particular time so that they can be energetically united. Often calls will go out to help with an Elder's surgery and subsequent healing or with a particular rite such as support for Sun Dance or an initiation. In a similar way, some Pagans are asked to offer aid through prayers at the time of Elder's transition out of this life. The following story explains an intuition followed by a request for assistance.

It is Friday morning and I still have that nagging feeling. It is almost time to smoke pipe. But why, and when? For three days it has been on my mind. The call is in and the spirits are waiting. I just can't seem to connect to the true moment to respond.

It is early morning when the phone rings. Sun Bear is going to be taken off life support and prayers have been requested. Now is time to honor and pray.

I get my bundle. I am so grateful to be asked to connect with others and pray for this man as he crosses over. I ready my space. The sage feels good and healing.

When I start the prayers I hear not only my voice praying, but the voices of many other people praying and honoring their friend, their teacher, their Elder. There is so much love. As the ceremony moves through the directions, the prayers of the people keep circling and connecting with and to all things. Through time and space, all of Creation honors this man of vision.

I am standing on a spectacular mountain range all along the rim of the Earth Mother. She is a bowl moving through space, spinning and turning and rolling. The bowl is a beautiful and lush valley. On every mountain rim and peak, down the sides of the mountains, across the sloping hills and all throughout the valley, everywhere, there are people.

Across the valley I see the beginnings of light, the first rays of the new dawn. The sunrise speaks of a new day. I become aware that my vision is a shared one with my sisters and brothers with me on the mountain.

As we watch, the sun slowly rises. When the sun rises high enough in the sky to clear the highest mountain peak the light floods into the valley of the Earth Mother. It races across the land and moves like wildfire throughout the hearts of the people. With this one light comes a shared and common vision of Peace.

I hear the Ancestors praying. Now I hear the Ancestors calling. They are calling their brother home. They smile at him and invite him into their arms and toward his new way and place of being. Let him go, I hear spoken so kindly. Let him go now. The wheel is turning and still moving. Let him go now...

What a beautiful feeling! Free, peaceful, loving and safe. I feel the future that is possible because of the life of Sun Bear. The unfolding that is possible because of his death.

- Earth Wind Woman

Contact from the Spirit Realm

Countless Pagans believe in reincarnation, and so they feel they may meet their Elders again in future lives. Others believe in communication from the spirit realm. To numerous Pagans, the Elder's death is not the end of their interactions, and many people mentioned that the connection remained after their Elders crossed.

The great Lady Circe crossed through the Veil ... Many rituals were held in her honor. Witches from different parts of the world mourned her passing; her influence had stretched far and wide. She has visited me many times since then. I relish those moments, and she is still a vital part of my spiritual life.

- Bona Dea Lyonesse

Lillith's story:

One evening, Joy and I were leading a Misa, a spirit circle. Throughout the circle, spirits stepped forward with messages for the living participants. I received a series of messages from a spirit man who delivered his words in a serious tone. When I asked who he was, he replied in a solemn voice, "William." I thanked him and delivered his messages. At first, I thought he was an ancestor of one of the people in the circle, but no one knew of a relative named William. After a while, I turned to Joy and said, "I wish I knew who this was!"

Just then the spirit said, "Don't you know me?" He called me by his nickname for me, and he began to chuckle. As I repeated this to Joy, she exclaimed, "It's Bill!" Then we both had a hearty laugh.

When he was living, his business card read Mr. William Molnar, but I had always called him the Great Wizard Bill (as did many others). He had a delightful mischievous attitude, which he loved to display when he thought I was taking life too seriously. It was good to experience Bill's wit again.

In certain Pagan traditions, individuals who have passed are revered through shrines or rituals such as Blots or Samhain rites. Those who practice this method of honoring believe that Elders can continue to provide teaching or counseling after death. In addition, many Pagans believe that the deceased may appear in dreams, visions or mediations to offer assistance and advice. Some Elders actually continue teaching after death, and a few seem to focus on finishing tasks they could not complete before their demise.

Lillith's story:

> One night, Sun Bear appeared to me. In my vision, his face framed by his hair and topped by his hat. He was standing behind a number of glass display cases. With a beaming smile, he greeted me, "ThreeFeathers, how are you?" Then he reached into one of the display cases, pulled out a pipe, and handed it to me. He said, "Go and do the work you are supposed to do."
>
> When the morning came, the vision did not fade; it remained clear in my mind. Throughout the day, I wondered at the experience. Later, a friend called: "Did you hear? Sun Bear died."
>
> When I heard those words, I saw Sun Bear's face again and his arm reaching out to me with the pipe. Once more I heard his voice calling me. He had given me a task. What an amazing experience!

As the responses reveal, numerous Pagans do not consider death the end of interactions. At the least, training by the Elders lives on in those who follow them. The wisdom will continue to be shared with the next group of people who search for answers.

Remembering

Both the dominant culture and the Pagan subculture honor memories of Elders who have passed. As we have seen, Pagans believe that influence continues after death, and they anticipate that the value of the heritage will endure through the lessons and by remembering past experiences. This is particularly true when the Elder has founded a community or researched and expanded the tradition's knowledge.

> Our Elders — good and bad — become part of the legacy of our ancestors. I don't claim blood ties to all of my ancestors, but I consider them to be the ones who have influenced my life in some way.
>
> - Kurt Hohmann

Those that are passed are Elders. Everything is built on the bones of the ancestors. All those teachings came from Elders. It got passed on and they still are in the present. That is another degree of eldership.

    - Peaceful Rivers Rainbow Warrior White Wolf

I write today to celebrate the life and mourn the death of Isaac Bonewits, 20th century occultist of note, Pagan and environmental activist, author, bard, humorist and family man. Isaac has gone too young, but will be remembered fondly and with honor by more people than he, himself, could know. ...

Isaac considered himself a Druid, but that didn't prevent him from writing, teaching and practicing a variety of other Pagan ways. *Real Magic* is broadly theoretical and relevant to everything from Wicca to heathenry, in many ways it is Chaos magic ahead of its time. Isaac's personal spiritual adventure included Druidry, Neopagan Witchcraft, and a variety of other cultural experiments. Isaac's later writing ranged from energy work to Pagan anthropology to historical and descriptive surveys of modern Pagan traditions. ...

Isaac's name and ideas will be remembered in ADF. We'll remember with affection his humor and wisdom, his compassion and his effort. We'll remember with honor his work to establish our ways, his strength in the face of criticism and the wisdom of his initial designs. We'll remember with reverence the core spiritual and Pagan ideas that still light the heart of Our Druidry.

    - Ian Corrigan

People gather at memorials or funerals to celebrate the life and teachings of an Elder and to share the sorrow and loss. Of course, death is an emotional experience, but Pagans often view the cycle of life differently from the majority culture. We acknowledge their value and continue to honor them through our words and actions. The next chapter offers a ritual of remembering and bereavement called Death Rite for an Elder.

Death Rite for an Elder

Lillith ThreeFeathers[38]

When Elders die, their passing affects both individuals and communities. Consequently, we felt it was appropriate to provide a ritual for honoring their lives and mourning their passing.

Preparation

Everyone present should sit in a circle. It is fine to have several circles. If several are required, those closest to the deceased, the immediate family, and the officiant should be in the inner circle. Using a circle will permit everyone to share their experiences and talk about the Elder. If a casket is present, it would be placed in the north and the circles would radiate out from there.

Duties of the officiant can be divided up between several group leaders.

In the Blessing and Sharing, wine will be used. If preferred, the wine can be replaced with cider, blessed water or other beverage. In addition, bread can be added to the rite. It would be blessed and shared after the wine. If the tradition typically includes a similar ceremony, the officiant(s) can substitute their usual practice.

Throughout the ritual, there are several places where options are suggested. This allows for adaptation to fit the Elder's spiritual practices and beliefs. In addition, the officiants should consult with the deceased person's loved ones so that they can help pick the best choices.

---

[38] Death Rite for an Elder" is part of the official liturgy of the Circle of Living Spirit, founded by Lillith ThreeFeathers, and recognized as a church under 501(c)(3). This memorial service was revised by Lillith ThreeFeathers from "Rite of Passing into the Otherworld," part of the liturgy that was submitted to US federal government in partial requirement for 501(c)(3) non-profit status. In addition to changes that make the ritual easier to perform, the revised version focuses on the impact of an Elder's passing.

Altars

It may be fitting to build the altars in collaboration with those who mourn.

If the casket or urn is present, position it in the north of the circle with Altars 1 and 2 on either side.

If a specific altar is typically created for the group's rituals, that altar would be in addition to the ones mentioned here. When a fourth altar is used, the group altar would be situated in the east with altar 3 in the west.

Altar 1 for the Elder

Set up an altar for the Elder. Include candle, incense, and chalice or objects specified by the Elder's tradition. You can include photographs of the loved one, small personal belongings, a magical item, a piece of jewelry, special flowers or plants, and favorite foods. This becomes a creative way to honor and celebrate the life of the deceased Elder. Include a portion of any food to be eaten in the ritual. This altar should be placed in the North. If a casket is present, Altar 1 should be to the head of the casket.

Altar 2 for the Ancestors

This is a separate altar to strengthen the Elder's ancestors. Altar 1 and 2 can be set up on opposite sides of the coffin or urn. If neither one are present, Altar 2 can be situated at a convenient distance from Altar 1. Include a glass of the same beverage to be used in the ritual and offering for the Elder's ancestors. If the beverage used is not water, include a glass of water in the offerings. Any food or beverage placed on Altar 1 should also be given on Altar 2.

Altar 3 for the Community

Place a small table set apart from the other altars to hold the beverage and/or food to be shared by the community during the ritual. The beverage can be something distinctive to the deceased, specific to the Elder's tradition, blessed wine, apple juice or water.

Water is recognized as a sacred liquid in many cultures and it comes with the benefits of being family friendly. Additionally, it won't upset those with dependence issues or allergies. If food will be shared in the ceremony, it should be placed on this table too. Appropriate food for the ritual should be picked from seasonally available staples, dishes from the spiritual tradition, and cuisine from the deceased's family customs. In addition, the talking stick, wand or object to be used during the Celebration of Life should be placed on this altar.

The Circle

Officiant says: "We honor the ancestors of [deceased person's name] and the ancestors of his/her spiritual lineage. We ask them to greet and guide our friend, Elder, and beloved [deceased person's name]."

Officiant continues to cast the circle starting in the south using a system that would be acceptable to the deceased.

Evoking the Divine

Option 1: *Request the presence of the deceased's personal God and Goddess, if known. If the deceased did not have personal deities [or they are unknown], chose one of the following options.*

Option 2: *Ask Great Spirit and the Spirits of the directions to be present.*

Option 3: *Call to God and Goddess and ask them to be present.*

Option 4: *Angels may be called instead of deities.*

Explanation of Ritual

The Officiant should stand before the casket or urn, if there is one present; if not, the ritual leader stands by altar displaying photographs of the deceased Elder.

Officiant says: "We enter this sacred circle for the purpose of remembering and honoring our Elder [name]. We are gathered in this sacred space to acknowledge our love and respect for her/him, and to honor his/her lifetime. We are here to share our mourning and to say farewell to [name] until we meet again."

If the deceased was known by a magical name or nickname, that can also be stated. If necessary, the Officiant can explain the significance of the circle and share a brief teaching about the deceased's views of life and his/her spiritual path. A few words can be added about the deceased person's beliefs or the tradition's attitudes about the after-life.

Rite of Remembrance

Officiant or a designated family member stands by the altar or the urn.

Officiant or designated person will pick one of the following divine beings that will be in agreement with the casting of the circle:

Great Spirit, Great Mystery
Specific names of god and goddess or simply God and Goddess as titles
Angels

Officiant or designated person says: "[Divine being], in this sacred space, we recognize and remember [deceased's name], who came to this life _____ years ago [birthday can be mentioned too]. We ask for your presence and blessing, as s/he joins you in spirit and moves from the physical world to the space beyond the veil."

Officiant continues with either option 1 or option 2.

Option 1: Candle
Officiant lights a small candle and says: "This flame represents [name]'s journey."

Option 2: Incense
If the ceremony is outside, a large stick of incense (or incense in a beautiful burner) can be used in place of the candle.

Officiant says: "This smoke represents [name]'s journey."

Record of Accomplishments

The Officiant or designee should say a few words about the family members and acknowledge the deceased person's accomplishments in this life. This is a review of the deceased's life and accomplishments. It is a listing of the typical accomplishments, such as marriage, children, and achievements on the job and for the community. Before the ceremony, the family should decide who will be asked to talk. The officiant or the designee can say a few words to the gathering about the life of the deceased and then introduce the first family member to talk. Various designees can mention specific events.

For example, officiant says: "Several people have asked to speak, and we will now hear from [name of person who will be speaking; can also mention the relationship with the deceased]."

Celebration of Life

During this section, the officiant or designee will share a few words about the deceased's spirit, who he/she was, and how his/her personality and/or teachings affected those around them. After this, the officiant states that others may offer stories and memorial statements.

Officiant announces: "Our Elder [name] influenced many of us. We will now remember and celebrate his/her life. Please talk about lessons learned from [name] or special events shared with her/him. This would also be a good time to offer words of encouragement and love for his/her family."

A talking stick or object to pass is appropriate; the officiant should give a brief explanation of talking stick etiquette.

Transition

The purpose of this section is to provide the living with an opportunity to say good-bye to an important member of the community. It is especially important if this is a memorial service without the physical presence of the deceased's remains.

Officiant says: "Although [the deceased] has moved onto another level, our Elder is only gone from this physical world. We may be lucky enough to receive spirit communication from our beloved. We are grieving, yet we know that we expect to meet [name] in the future. Someday we will leave this life and travel to the spirit realm; we will once again join [the deceased] in spirit. Throughout the cycle of life, the continuity of life, death, and rebirth exists, and we expect to share experiences with our Elder again, perhaps over many lifetimes."

Depending on the number of people present, one of the following options can be included.

Option 1: Candles
Everyone present or a few individuals can light candles to place on an area provided on or next to the altar. If many people are present, only a few individuals should light the candles; as they light the candle, they should make a ritualized statement.

Suggested Declarations
We are grateful for your life and teachings.
We offer light to the spirit of (deceased).
We bid you farewell and safe travels.
Goodbye, dear teacher.
Similar declaration specific to Elder's tradition.

If everyone present will be lighting a candle, people can chant or sing during the lighting.

Option 2: Incense
Participants may replace the candles with incense. They would pick a declaration from those listed in Option 1. If everyone will light incense, the others should chant or sing during the lighting.

Option 3: Flowers
Participants can toss flowers or flower petals into a large container of water. Outside rites can include throwing the flowers into a river or other body of water. If the rite takes place in nature, make sure to remove any plastic or non-biodegradable attachments from the flowers. Each person can ask for guidance for the deceased and request blessings for the deceased's family and loved ones.

Option 4: Fire

If the ritual is outside in an area that will safely permit a fire, the participants can place herbs or flowers into the fire while offering a blessing or declaration.

Blessing and Sharing

Officiant holds a chalice filled with wine aloft. See the section called Preparation at the beginning of the rite for more details on substitutions.

Officiant says: "Great Spirit [can be replaced with Divine Ones or God and Goddess], bless this beverage that we may be nourished in our time of sorrow. Bless this wine that we may find joy in our celebration of the life of [name]. Bless this wine so that we may understand that we will be together again."

If the ritual is outside, the officiant offers a small amount of wine to the earth.

Officiant says: "Accept this offering as a token of our gratitude for your presence and help in this time."

Officiant pours a small amount of the blessed wine in a separate glass for the deceased and sets it on Altar 1, which was dedicated to the Elder. A shot glass works well.

Officiant turns to those present and says: "Let us share this wine in recognition of the blessings we have received by having [name] in our lives. Let us share this wine in community."

Officiant carries the chalice to the immediate family and offers it beginning with either the oldest person in the family or the deceased's spouse or partner.

If the group is not too large, the wine can be offered to everyone present. Assistants will help with passing the chalice.

If the group prefers, bread can also be blessed and shared. Any extra beverage or food is given as an offering.

Farewell

Option 1: Candle
Officiant, or a family member, holds the altar candle (lighting it again if it has gone out).

Officiant says: "This flame is a symbol of divine light. As this candle casts light on the surroundings, we ask Mother Goddess [or a specific deity, or Spirit] to come near, to be with our loved one. We ask you to guide [name] during his/her transition and to light her/his way to the Otherworld."

Option 2: Chalice
Officiant takes the chalice containing liquid, holds it aloft.

Officiant says: "Just as this chalice — beautiful as it is — is a container for this beverage, a body was the container for the one we called [name]. He/she has now taken a different form."

Officiant slowly pours liquid onto the earth as an offering.

Officiant says, "Now, he/she is on a different journey. He/she has now returned to the Mother of us all. His/her spirit has returned to that unknowable Infinite from which all comes. We were blessed by _____'s time with us, and we look forward to the time when we will be together again."

Option 3: Mother Earth
Either cornmeal or tobacco can be sprinkled onto the ground or scattered into the wind.

While sprinkling, officiant says: "During life [name] was nurtured by Mother Earth. Now he/she has returned to the love of Mother Earth. Our beloved [name] has traveled beyond the veil and now prepares for the next adventure."

Option 4: "Beloved One" by Joy Marie Wedmedyk

Officiant or designated person recites:

Beloved one,
Our hearts are filled with love and memories of you.
May our love carry you to the arms of your ancestors.
May their love comfort you on your new journey.
From love to love and from life to life,
May you be blessed.

Closing

If this ritual is being conducted at a cemetery and the casket will be lowered, this is the appropriate time to do that.

If this ritual is being conducted at a place where ashes will be scattered, now is the time to do that.

Prayer

Option 1: *Do Not Stand at My Grave and Weep,* by Mary Elizabeth Frye[39]

Officiant or designated person recites:

Do not stand at my grave and weep,
I am not there. I do not sleep.
I am a thousand winds that blow,
I am the diamond glints on snow,
I am sunlight on ripened grain,
I am the gentle Autumn rain.
When you wake in the morning's hush,
I am the swift uplifting rush
Of quiet birds in circled flight.
I am the soft stars that shine at night.
Do not stand at my grave and cry,
I am not there, I did not die.

---

[39] Mary Elizabeth Frye. "Do Not Stand at My Grave and Weep" (1932) (she did not copyright the work).

Option 2: *Hold on to What is Good* by Nancy Wood[40]

Officiant or designated person reads:

Hold on to what is good
even if it is
a handful of earth.
Hold on to what you believe
even if it is
a tree which stands by itself.
Hold on to what you must do
even if it is
a long way from here.
Hold on to life even when
it is easier letting go.
Hold on to my hand even when
I have gone away from you.

Option 3: *We All Come from the Goddess* by Z Budapest[41]

Officiant or other person leads everyone in singing. It should be sung at least four times.

We all come from the Goddess
And to Her we shall return
Like a drop of rain
Flowing to the ocean.

Officiant closes circle, remembering to thank any entity whose presence was requested. Officiant continues by picking one of the following divine beings that matches the casting of the circle:

Great Spirit, Great Mystery
Specific names of god and goddess or simply God and Goddess as titles
Angels

---

[40] Nancy C. Wood. "Hold on To What is Good" *Many Winters*, ©1974 (Nancy Wood Literary Trust, 2017). (www.NancyWood.com)
[41] Zsuzsanna Budapest. "We All Come from the Goddess" (1972).

Officiant says: "Our thanks and gratitude to the forces that have been present, to the Lord and Lady, to spirit, and to the guides and guardians. We ask for blessings of health and good life to all present. Thank you for guiding [name] in life and in this transition. We leave him/her in your care. We close this sacred circle and bid farewell to our loved one."

Community meal follows.

Luck

Joy Wedmedyk

It is said that when the student is ready the teacher will appear. The same can be said for the entrance of an Elder. What allows us to recognize that a student or Elder has arrived?

Students that are ready to move forward spiritually possess qualities that bring the Elder toward them. Knowing that the answers they seek are "somewhere out there," students have faith that something of the Divine guides them toward the answers they are seeking and the people they need to meet. They become open to receiving guidance. These students are willing to let go of what they already believe in order to learn more or uncover the truth of what is. Other qualities they possess are the willingness to engage in their own growth, curiosity, playfulness, and the ability to find humor within themselves and our collective human struggles, seeking with persistence and endurance for the process.

Elders seeking students have qualities that include recognizing and knowing the truth that guided their own lives, the desire to share what they have learned, love and compassion for people and the process of living, contentment with where they are in their own lives, a commitment to guide and listen, and knowledge that the students they mentor will bring change to their own lives as well.

When these qualities of both students and Elders meet, the magic happens and the most growth is achieved. Students and Elders that have connected with each other in profound ways, even if they worked hard to find each other, have tended to say that it was synchronicity or serendipity, divine will, or their ancestors or spirit helpers that made it so. Feelings of gratitude and thankfulness filled their hearts. As time moved forward and they had a larger context with which to view their own relationships as student or teacher, they were still surprised at the uniqueness of it all.

As I look back on my role as both student and Elder I am left with this observation. It was the force of the universe changing and creating an existence of possibilities: the right time, the right place, the right people all coming together in their own unique way. But even more than that, it is the unperceived and mysterious blessing of luck.

May we be so lucky.

Conclusions

As mainstream society has moved away from lifestyles based on small communities and extended families, adult roles have significantly changed. Functions and purposes no longer relate to stages of life, but rather to broad conditions such as wealth, parenthood or employment — limitations that severely restrict social acknowledgement of the range of humanity's experiences and contributions. For example, judging individuals solely by their employment means that civilization values only a narrow part of their lives. Although some people's existence does revolve around their work, few believe that employment ought to be the sole compass of determining their worth. Such a restriction ignores an individual's character, valuable interpersonal interactions, and any number of significant philosophical, ethical, and humanitarian classifications.

While conventional contemporary societies value experience in the area of employment, as inadequate as that valuation might be, they often discount similar experience when considering the life knowledge of "senior citizens." Perhaps because our society moves so quickly, younger individuals feel that older people are out of touch and might not understand their problems. Yet momentous events and difficulties happen in everyone's life; consequently, certain experiences remain worthwhile from generation to generation.

Inter-generational detachment weakens the community and the family — in short, everyone is diminished. When modern mainstream culture cuts off its oldest citizens, discounting their experience, it eliminates possibilities and opportunities. Traditional indigenous villages, regardless of their prevailing belief structures, have something that our contemporary mainstream society has lost: the belief that our Elders have knowledge they should share.

Although Pagans interact with mainstream culture, Pagan culture and attitudes are vastly different from the majority civilization. Despite its statistically small size, Paganism has a growing influence on the dominate society — and the Pagan community is increasing too. According to the US Census Bureau, the number of Wiccans in the US population has grown from

134,000 in 2001 to 342,000 in 2008[42]. In the same period, those self-reporting as Pagans grew from 140,000 to 340,000[43]. It will be interesting to see the numbers in the next census. These statistics do not include those who refused to respond to religious questions — a category that includes many individuals who are still in the broom closet.

Pagan culture is comprised of various subgroups in a robust fusion of individualism, acceptance of diverse lifestyles, and belief in the unseen. It is a unique blend of old and new customs based on political, social, and magical concepts. Pagans believe that positive changes come from interactions with nature and through respecting the circle of life.

Within this vibrant expanding community, all ages of people have roles to fill. The concept that Elders should teach younger people remains important in many organizations. Because every generation (and each individual) has a valid purpose, they believe that intergenerational interactions strengthen everyone. Therefore, Elders are not just older persons, but individuals tempered by a lifetime of experience. In fact, most Pagans respect experience and longevity even in people they do not personally know. Additionally, they are often considered to be knowledgeable in specific areas.

However, Pagans do not live in a vacuum: they, too, have to contend with the problems and ills of mainstream society. They strive to maintain their own ethics instead of adapting the attitudes of the dominant culture. When they are intimidated or puzzled by interactions with mainstream society, they consult their Elders. When gender, familial and other social roles become confusing, they do the same. Therefore, when picking a personal Elder, individual interaction is considered an important requirement.

---

[42] The most recent data available from the US Census Bureau was for 2008. Currently, those statistics are available at "Population" through US Census Bureau online at https://www.census.gov/library/publications/2011/compendia /statab /131ed/population.html (accessed 5/2/2017).

[43] The most recent data available from the US Census Bureau was for 2008. Currently, those statistics are available at "Population" through US Census Bureau online at https://www.census.gov/library/publications/2011/compendia/statab /131ed/population.html (accessed 5/2/2017).

In almost all instances, these people were presented to me and I chose to study with them. I wasn't looking for anyone in general. I studied many of the books that they had written (Janet [Farrar], Gavin [Bone] and Isaac [Bonewits]) so I knew who they were initially, but it wasn't until I met with them, that anything "clicked" for me. I had already considered them to be Elders in a community sense but, with me — I needed the one-on-one experience.

- Bernadette Montana

Pagans that continue to hold onto long-standing traditions and hereditary customs view family Elders, such as grandparents, as important guides for the youngest children. Senior relatives are expected to share their expertise and mentor younger individuals. As family Elders share chronicles and traditions, they provide continuity between the past and the youngest generation. Due to historical persecution, many Pagans acknowledge the value of oral customs. Even in contemporary times, when people tend to spread out over great distances, a family Elder continues to fulfill important roles.

As relationships have shifted and the concept of chosen kinship has spread, community and elected Elders have stepped into areas that were historically designated to family. Additionally, when people have physically moved away from their families (often due to employment), nearby spiritual or community Elders may step in to perform similar functions.

This is especially true when Pagans don't have positive contacts with their families. Particularly when individuals have walked away due to abuse, imprisonment or other difficulties, they look for someone else to act as an Elder. In challenging situations, spiritual or community Elders may provide counseling or encourage proper behavior, and suggest ways to improve conduct.

While many Elders focus on sharing their art or spirituality — vitally important roles — others accept the role of community Elder. Although community Elders can concentrate on interactions within a specific group, such as members of a coven or organization, they might decide to work on improvements to social, economic and political systems. For instance, Maggie

Kuhn, founder of the Gray Panthers, called on Elders to step into the five M's: the roles of mentor, mediator, monitor (of politicians and government bodies), motivator, and mobilizer[44]. Because of their long-term views, community Elders aspire to improve life and create a better future. Some are recognized through their commitment to a specific contemporary social problem, for instance, working to stop child abuse or to safeguard the environment. Such people can be famous, such as Starhawk, or largely overlooked and little known outside their community.

Lillith's story:

> I briefly worked with an immigrant woman named Vijaya Emani. She was amazingly positive, friendly, and enthusiastic. Since she was a new employee, I didn't think much about her exuberance. After all, everyone tries to present themselves at their best when they start a new job. I liked her and looked forward to getting to know her.
>
> One day we had a division meeting and the director asked her to stand so she could be introduced, but she wasn't there. No one knew where she was. Later that day, we heard the news. For some reason her car stopped on the way to work. She left the car and was walking along the shoulder when a semi killed her. It was a huge shock.
>
> Afterwards it was a great surprise when President Obama posthumously awarded her the Presidential Citizens Medal for her work fighting domestic violence in immigrant communities. That was an amazing lesson: anyone could be a champion. Vijaya was a community Elder not only in Cleveland, Ohio but also in Washington DC. Yet, she worked a job just like anyone else, raised her children, and paid her bills — and she helped many people.

---

[44] Ken Dychtwald Ph.D. "Remembering Maggie Kuhn: Gray Panthers Founder On The 5 Myths Of Aging" *Huffington Post* (2012). Retrieved May 5, 2017, from http://www.huffingtonpost.com/ken-dychtwald/the-myths-of-aging_b_1556481.html.

Pagans also recognize that Elders fulfill other roles too. They can be founders and elected heads of groups. They include individuals who create and maintain public sacred spaces, and scholars who research ancient traditions and historical customs. Some create meeting places and performance venues. Through these locations, they teach others the appropriate ways to participate, share life skills, and explain how to honor the traditions.

Spiritual leaders who grow into Elderhood are recognized for inspiring and guiding the community. Through their teachings, they provide not only education, but also continuity of tradition. In fact, they can be the glue that holds together an entire organization.

> [What are the spiritual Elder's roles?] Leader of ceremony and temple, guide to those seeking spiritual growth, teacher (an educator of the tradition and life in general) and mistress/master of their craft (able to produce consistent results with their magick).
>
> - Tehron Gillis

As ardent patrons of handmade items, Pagans recognize expert craftsmen and artisans as Elders and feel honored by studying with them. Although Pagans appreciate all art forms, they particularly respect jewelry making, leather working, ceramics and blacksmithing. Many are fans of Elder musicians, poets, dancers, and storytellers; they continue to be favorites at bardic and talent events.

Elders can also be teachers and leaders, but most do not function in all three roles. Some reject leadership, and numerous teachers do not develop into Eldership. As we realized during the writing of this book, individuals may lead rituals, and they may temporarily or permanently head an organization, but others do not view them as Elders. Elders have a quality that is difficult to define — although we have written this book to do just that. Superior characteristics make them more than just a teacher or a leader.

However, many Elders consider teaching to be their greatest tasks, whether the lessons happen formally or in casual situations, and whether teaching occurs at a podium, over coffee in a kitchen or while weeding the garden. Regardless, they can explain the doctrines and principles within the craft or tradition. They teach in many different styles: through words and silence, through active work and through patient waiting. They see the world with a different viewpoint, a wider, more expansive outlook.

Elders don't expect others to do a task by rote; they know why it should be done that specific way. Similarly, Elders might tell someone, "Don't do that," and they would know the reasons why it shouldn't happen — although they may or may not be willing to explain at that moment. Trust, respect, and dedication are necessary for both Elders and those they mentor. When those attributes are present, the learner can accept there is a reason and wait until later for the explanation.

Since Pagans value the concept of doing no harm, respect is both a common courtesy and an important character trait. Even if you will interact with a certain Elder for a limited time, you should acknowledge the individual. This is true whether or not you choose that person as an Elder or plan to interact again.

> I treat people the way I want to be treated: with honesty, compassion, graciously, and with a positive manner.
> - Rocio Darlene Arriaga

Those we interviewed encountered their Elders in many different ways, but a number of them knew immediately that the person would be instrumental in their lives. Others established a relationship slowly over time. Regardless of how the association began, our contributors said the interactions changed their lives by transforming their viewpoints and providing intriguing experiences. Quite a few also felt their Elders healed or protected them.

Whether Elders work as leaders, teachers, advisors, or guides, they want to explain things, share stories, communicate concepts, and offer a lifetime of lessons. They might teach through practical tasks, esoteric ritual or philosophical discussions. They may pray for others, offer comfort or strive to help in other ways. Elders are not perfect, but they strive to continually better themselves, to be good examples, and to be caring citizens of this wonderful planet. They seek excellence through a connection to the source, whether they call it Goddess, God, Spirit, Nirvana, Tao or Art. They connect to the greater knowing through theater, music, ritual, devotion, meditation, political action or advocacy.

The Pagan community is comprised of numerous small groups, and each may have specific expectations for participants, such as ritualized greetings, studying different languages or acquiring specialized vocabulary. When an Elder accepts a pupil or apprentice, both of them have responsibilities. These obligations include commitment, honesty, and a level of trust. The Elder might require the learner to follow rules; in fact, the rules might be established by the tradition. Above all, people are expected to listen and do their best to learn. Although levels of commitment can change over time, respectful behavior and communication will remain an important part of appropriate contact between Elders and learners.

Because Pagan culture is an amalgamation of diverse traditions, practices, and skills, the ways that people become an Elder are not consistent. Certain traditions include a path of training for Eldership. Within those groups, an individual may chose a path of service and preparation that will, over time, lead to that role. In other situations, people may be thrust into Elderhood when a group picks them. Occasionally they are called to step into the position by spirits, divine beings or those who walked before us.

Pagans recognize that knowledge and training merges with life experience to create an Elder. In addition, they may determine specific individuals are worthy of respect and appreciation because of their work, wisdom, and service to the greater community.

Many groups acknowledge the transition through initiation or ceremony. Afterwards, both the Elder and the community realize that positions have changed, bringing new responsibilities, experiences, and connections.

As with any important relationship, the one with an Elder may evolve or shift. Either party might decide that another course of study would be better for that learner. Distance might prove too much of a challenge for continuation or the Elder might turn over duties to others. Regardless of the reason, separation will require an adjustment, and most likely, encompass a sense of loss.

Due to their lasting influence, Elders were respected and acknowledged within the Pagan community, even when time or distance intervened. In fact, many of our contributors continued to honor theirs despite a long separation. This was especially true if an Elder had passed on.

Certainly, Elders can be controversial. They want others to learn, aspire, grow and change. That makes them provocative and sometimes challenging people. Although they possess disparate personalities and fill various roles, this book offers a number of ways to recognize them. When in doubt, evaluate their actions. In particular, look at how other leaders view them.

> Elder is a title bestowed upon an individual not only by the people that they lead spiritually but also by the people that trained and guided them.
>
> - Tehron Gillis

> Old age is not a disease — it is strength and survivorship, triumph over all sorts of vicissitudes and disappointments, trials and illnesses.
>
> - Maggie Kuhn,
> founder of the Gray Panthers Movement[45]

Due to all they have encountered, living through good times and bad, Elders gain a broader and extended viewpoint. Their goal is not just to make people feel better, but to guide younger people to see the larger picture and greater perspective.

Anyone who has tended a garden knows that roots are important to the health of plants. Elders provide those roots. In fact, the overall health of society depends upon interactions between the generations, which include the sharing of experience, significant history, and stories. No civilization exists for long without Elders.

> Progressive Witchcraft is more of a philosophy then a tradition. It's going back to the roots.
>
> - Bernadette Montana

---

[45] Maggie Kuhn's well-known quote has been used in multiple books, websites, and columns; original citation unknown.

Despite mainstream society's propensity to separate generations and isolate the elderly, Pagans believe that interconnectedness is necessary. In fact, even practitioners from widely different paths acknowledge the importance of Elders in maintaining traditions, teaching, and telling the stories.

Paganism's inclusive beliefs and attitudes combine the need to heal and transform the individual with the desire for the evolution of community and society. Because of that attitude, Pagans believe we can discover ways to heal the ills of our civilization through embracing a diversity of viewpoints. Therefore, Pagan culture continues to be the testing ground for new, unconventional, and unorthodox associations.

Although some Elders may act as ministers, many don't use that title; however, they assist with ethical demarcations and help to resolve issues. Based upon a lifetime of experience, they have made the journey from book knowledge to wisdom, and so they can inspire, lead, question, and offer a lifetime of understanding and abilities to their family, their circle, and the community.

In addition, Pagans recognize that Elders have the ability to open up awareness of the world in new ways and they can help others discover how to improve their lives. Perhaps Elders can do that for the majority culture too, functioning as beacons leading us out of the dark ills of our society. Although they may not physically build the change, they can suggest alternatives, provide a link to the beneficial elements of the past, and teach about transitions. Perhaps, Pagan intergenerational acceptance can now move into the dominate culture so that Elders will once again be recognized as an important part of our society. Their wisdom is sorely needed. As a forerunner for mainstream society, Paganism has already shown it is up to the challenge.

Appendix 1: Method

As authors, we wanted to see how Pagans differed from mainstream society regarding viewpoints about Elders. Were their attitudes and interactions similar to or different from mainstream culture? Rather than attempting a statistical analysis of the Pagan community, we wanted to provide a philosophical and sociological review of the community. To us, such a comparison would be more useful to the Pagan community, and to those outside the Pagan community, because it could provide identification of authentic beliefs and understanding of related actions.

We examined the ways that Elders were defined and how their places were viewed within the culture. Were they vital in Pagan groups? If so, how were they significant? What could we learn about Elders' roles? More importantly, how were they chosen?

We constructed a questionnaire and asked many individuals to answer it. We spent a great deal of effort to obtain answers from a variety of Pagans. We contacted some respondents directly and connected with others through social media. In addition, we asked people to forward the questionnaire to their friends and teachers.

Those who replied came from different subgroups within the community. They embraced various spiritual traditions (or no religion at all) and followed different lifestyles. Several people did not answer the specific questions, but used them as a starting point for expansive writings. Sometimes we requested more details or asked for clarifications. In addition to sending out questionnaires, we interviewed a number of people by telephone or in person. All interviews followed the same format.

Most importantly, we had long dialogues about the topic. We initiated conversations with small groups of Pagans and with individuals, especially those who were viewed as leaders or Elders in the Pagan community. Typically, those exchanges took place at social occasions in private homes or at public Pagan events. Due to the unrestricted access with a book, some of the people we talked to were not comfortable with us quoting them or mentioning their names. Yet, even those discussions were important because they gave us information that was instrumental in identifying or confirming perceptions within the Pagan community. As we gathered the answers, we noticed similarities, and investigated the differences. Throughout the research, we were mindful of our own experiences.

Please see the List of Contributors (in the Appendix) to learn more about those we quoted. The descriptors used to define them are their own words. You'll find some of their Elders listed there too. We are grateful to all of those individuals who helped us by talking to us, answering our questions, and sharing their personal stories.

Appendix 2: Sample Questions

How do you define an Elder?

When does a person become an Elder?

Do you consider your teachers to be your Elders?

How do you define the Elder's cultural role?

What Elder influenced your spirituality?

Were you officially designated as a student?

What responsibilities or duties were associated with student status?

How did you meet the Elder?

Why did you end up with that Elder?

How did you know that Elder was the one for you?

How did the Elder interact with you?

If your Elder is still living, do you keep in contact and still rely on them for guidance?

Did the Elder test you?

Did you experience amazing events with the Elder?

Did the Elder give you a name?

What did the Elder call you?

What was the significance of that name or title?

How do you treat your Elder?

Did you experience an Elder's passing?

Did you participate in a ritual for their crossing?

Does your elder still impact you?

Are you an Elder?

Why do you call yourself an Elder?

How did you become an Elder?

Do you like being an Elder?

Appendix 3: Elders of the Authors

The authors are grateful to many Elders who mentored, taught, and guided us over the years. In this section you will find information about the Elders mentioned in the book.

Joy's Elders Referenced in the Book

Joy Marie Wedmedyk has studied shamanism, mediumship, divination, and mysticism for over forty years. Initiated in Regla de Ocha (a Diaspora tradition), Native American and African shamanic traditions, Joy is an accomplished teacher, Medium and dreaming Shaman. Her life's work is to disseminate the teachings of the ancestors and offer support, guidance, and healing to others.

Joy was a quoted source for the book *Drawing Down the Spirits* by Kenaz Filan and Raven Kaldera (2009) and is a contributing author for *Walking the Path of the Ancient Ways* edited by Corvis Nocturnum (2012) and *Calling to the Ancestors: An Ancestor Devotional* edited by Sarenth Odinsson (2015).

As an Elder of the Western Cherokee Nation, **Carlo HawkWalker** lives the ceremonial and traditional ways of Turtle Island. He is a decorated veteran with distinguished service in both Army and Navy. Carlo has traveled the world to forge Peace between people, cultures, and religions, carrying the teachings of the Medicines of the Heart. He sat on the CSAP Native American Steering Committee for Substance Abuse in Washington DC and was co-facilitator of the Indigenous Round Table of Russia in St. Petersburg. Carlo is an officer of the Order of the United States Grand Priory of the Hospitaller Order of Saint Lazarus and acted as their representative to the United Nations in a Peace Keeping and Medical Capacity at Standing Rock. He is also Chancellor of the Indigenous Grand Priory. In addition, he founded Willow-Hawk Valley Sanctuary Branch of the Oklevueha Native American Church. In 2016, Carlo received the President's Lifetime Achievement Award.

Marge McCabe preserved and practiced the spiritual traditions of the Indigenous peoples of the Americas. In addition, she was a devoted Bahá'í. She was an intelligent, curious and avid student and expected commitment and dedication from those she mentored. By sharing her love of god, four-legged furry ones, nature, and the sea, Marge was, and continues to be, an inspiration and example to others striving for spiritual connection within themselves and their community.

William Molnar, also known as the Great Wizard Bill, was an incredible spiritualist with skill in physical mediumship, that is, he could manipulate ectoplasm and provide physical manifestations, sounds and other materializations. He was also an old-school ceremonial magician. His favorite divination tool was a faceted crystal ball that he affectionately called Junior.

An elder of the Seneca nation and a 1999 recipient of the Living Treasures Heritage Award, **Grandmother Twylah** was the founder and leader of the Wolf Clan Teaching Lodge. In the early days, she opened her home to the seekers of ingenious wisdom. Since her passing, her teachings have been kept alive by her children and the Wolf Clan has evolved into an international organization.

Her Seneca name, Ya-weh-node, means "She Whose Voice Rides the Four Winds.

Lillith's Elders Referenced in the Book

Lillith ThreeFeathers has studied dreamwork, shamanic practices, alternative and ceremonial healing, the Toltec Way, and Goddess spirituality for more than forty years. Her training with indigenous Elders spans North and South America, Europe, and Africa. In addition to shamanic initiations, she is an initiated priestess in Regla de Ocha. Lillith is founder of the Circle of Living Spirit, a multi-faith Earth-based church, and she functions as Director and Elder for that church and other groups. She works as a shamanic healer, medium, writer, and visionary.

In addition to being a quoted source in *Drawing Down the Spirits* by Kenaz Filan and Raven Kaldera (2009), her publishing credits include hundreds of articles. Her writings were included in the anthologies *Calling to the Ancestors: An Ancestor Devotional*, Sarenth Odinsson, editor (2015), *With Arms Wide Open Anthology* (2009), and *Lilith Queen of the Desert*, Anya Kless, Editor (2010).

Joseph Rael, Beautiful Painted Arrow, (Tslew-teh-koyeh), is recognized by the Ute and Tewa (Pueblo) people as an Elder and healer. He is also an author, artist, and vision-holder of the Sound Peace Chambers. Creator of fasting dances for non-natives (the Sun-Moon Dance, the Long Dance, and the Drum Dance), he has bridged the distance between earth-based teachings and mainstream culture. From his original vision, the Sound Peace Chambers have grown into a world-wide movement of sacred spaces focused on using sound vibration and chanting to heal the planet.

Sun Bear definitely influenced the course of my life. As Medicine Chief and founder of the Bear Tribe Medicine Society, he offered a connection to contemporary Native North American traditions during a time when there were limited opportunities to interact with or learn about indigenous practices. He always asked, "Does your philosophy grow corn?" That question continues to be a great indicator of whether or not something is beneficial.

As an Elder of the Western Cherokee Nation, **Carlo HawkWalker** lives the ceremonial and traditional ways of Turtle Island. He is a decorated veteran with distinguished service in both Army and Navy. Carlo has traveled the world to forge Peace between people, cultures, and religions, carrying the teachings of the Medicines of the Heart. He sat on the CSAP Native American Steering Committee for Substance Abuse in Washington DC and was co-facilitator of the Indigenous Round Table of Russia in St. Petersburg. Carlo is an officer of the Order of the United States Grand Priory of the Hospitaller Order of Saint Lazarus and acted as their representative to the United Nations in a Peace Keeping and Medical Capacity at Standing Rock. He is also Chancellor of the Indigenous Grand Priory. In addition, he founded Willow-Hawk Valley Sanctuary Branch of the Oklevueha Native American Church. In 2016, Carlo received the President's Lifetime Achievement Award.

William Molnar (affectionately known as the Great Wizard Bill) was an incredible spiritualist with skill in physical mediumship, that is, he could manipulate ectoplasm and provide physical manifestations, sounds and other materializations. He was also an old-school ceremonial magician. His favorite divination tool was a faceted crystal ball that he affectionately called Junior.

Nagual Dreaming Woman and author of four books, **Merilyn Tunneshende** continues to be a provocative teacher despite the lack of public appearances for more than a decade.

Appendix 4: List of Contributors

What follows is a list of quoted contributors with the information they were willing to share. When available, the list includes their traditions, the names of their Elders, and the traditions of those Elders. The information is given in the contributors' own words. Due to personal concerns, some respondents requested anonymity in this book, and their wishes were followed. Others used a magickal name or nickname. For the same reasons, many have chosen not to share their spiritual traditions, life paths or the names of their Elders. We, the authors, are grateful to all who shared their experiences with us, whether they are listed here or not.

Arriaga, Rocio Darlene - Tradition: ancient, indigenous, traditional. Elder: Grandfather Bear. Elder's tradition: Ute medicine man and artist. Elder: Mother Meerra. Elder's tradition: Darshan, a blessing of light and love.

Calhoun, Anna - Tradition: Celtic/Native American Witch. I personally am an eclectic Witch. Elder: Daemon Wilburn a.k.a. Auntie Dame. Elder's tradition: She holds a 3rd degree from the Elder Faith Tradition Craft. She also holds a 1st degree in the Raven Myst tradition.

Cameron - Tradition: Agnostic.

Corrigan, Ian - Tradition: Ár nDraíocht Féin: A Druid Fellowship (ADF). I'm a Neopagan of the Druidic sort, interested in Celtic polytheism as it might manifest for modern people in North America. I'm also an occultist, broadly interested in arcane and magical systems and ideas, from medieval grimoires through Hindu Tantra and Asian shamanism to Thelema and Chaos Magic. Elder: Isaac Bonewits. Elder's Tradition: Druidism, Witchcraft, magic (with a degree from University of California, Berkley), and the occult. He founded Ár nDraíocht Féin and wrote significant books on Druidism, magic, ritual, and Paganism.

Coviak, Kenya aka Mistress Belledonna - Tradition: Eclectic Magick/Sacred Fool. Elder's Tradition: African American HooDoo/Ceremonial Magick.

Day, Kenn - Tradition: I am Sheya, Post-Tribal Shaman and AMHA. Sheya and PTS are both founded on received teachings that focus on awakening and integrating the whole self. AMHA is a reconstruction of pre-diaspora Hebrew Earth Spirituality. Elder: The most influential would be Elisheva Nesher, Shofet of AMHA. Elder's Tradition: AMHA (Primitive Hebrew Assembly).

Earth Wind Woman - Tradition: Indigenous North American traditions. Elder: Sun Bear. Elder's Tradition: Cherokee (Objiwe) Elder, founder and Medicine Chief of the Bear Tribe Medicine Society, an organization for people of any skin color to join together to live in harmony with the Earth. Author of eight books, he passed in 1992.

Euphrates. Euphrates came to Paganism in the age of BBS communication in the '90s, after spending 12 years as a Born Again Evangelical in her teens and early 20s. Her first teachers were various friends on PODnet (Pagan Oriented Discussion net), including several folks who've gone on to be fairly well-known authors, among them Dorothy Morrison, Trish Telesco and Isaac Bonewits. She has dabbled in many paths over the years, currently content as a "solitary eclectic" who celebrates holidays with her mate, children, and grandson, and that's more than good enough for her.

Frick, Tina (Freya Hlin Vrana) - Tradition: I jokingly tell people that I'm a Tinanian because my tradition is a tapestry of many different beliefs. Elders: I have been very lucky in learning from the most amazing people. I was able to spend time with Isaac Bonewits. He was a great man; a spiritual hero of mine. Also Lillith ThreeFeathers, an amazingly grounded and whole person. Ian Corrigan, my favorite Druid. And Teresa, who was my high priestess in the first coven I was in. Elder's tradition: Teresa was Dianic.

Gillis, Tehron - Tradition: New Orleans Voodoo. Elder: Lilith Dorsey. Elder's Tradition: New Orleans Voodoo, Haitian Vodou, and Santeria.

Golden, Shaina is a millennial who has been a practicing medium, psychic, and healer for the past 12 years. Raised in the

Pagan community, she has studied shamanism, Buddhism, Espiritismo, and Africana traditions, and has practiced many forms of divination and spiritual healing. She completed a degree in anthropology at Oberlin College, where she focused on the spiritual traditions of indigeneity. A perpetual nomad, she has lived in over 10 places in the past 10 years, from New Orleans, to Paris, to West Africa.

Goody, Penny - Tradition: American Wicca (Celtic tradition). Elder: Yvonne Frost, Wiccan practitioner, author, and teacher. She and her husband Gavin Frost founded Church and School of Wicca in 1968. Together they wrote many influential books on Wicca. Elder's tradition: The Old Religion (Celtic tradition).

Hazel, Elizabeth. See: Lady Vala Runesinger.

Hohmann, Kurt. Although his tradition is primarily Norse/Heathen, Kurt does not hesitate to knock upon the doors of other pantheons as needs present themselves. The Elders in his life come from a wide variety of backgrounds and have helped shape his rather diverse worldview.

Hudson, Mary - Tradition: I'm a Celt and I've always been a Celt. So, I work with the Celtic Pantheon, specifically the Tuatha de Dannan, and am currently studying Druidism. Elder: There were several to be sure, but the one that I will forever be grateful to is a gentleman named Craig Parsons-Kerins. Elder's tradition: I know that our culture is big on labels, but honestly I couldn't tell you what Craig's tradition is. He is Pagan, as well as Jewish, Gardnerian, Alexandrian, Druidic, Hermetic, Fey, BTW, Agnostic, Celtic, Hebrew and physicist. I have never really asked for a definition of his tradition and he never tried to define mine. He was/is more interested in the connection to spirit or deity and how the universe connects to everything and how all choices are not singular.

"J" - Tradition: Energetic Earth Energies. Elders: Joy Wedmedyk, Gene Rowand, Lillith ThreeFeathers, [Don] Waterhawk.

Johnson, Sheree is the founder and Director of Gestalt Counseling and Training Institute of Ann Arbor. She is a licensed psychotherapist and a certified alcohol and drug prevention specialist. Sheree has received the Jukai rite of passage empowerment in Buddhism.

Johnston, Fred. There are so many who inspired me and helped me along the way. I have been deeply influenced by ADF Druidism, taught to me by Earrach Canali and Diana Paar, and I also credit Isaac Bonewits and Ian Corrigan for inspiring the way I approach Paganism and magic. I learned Ceremonial Magick and Thelema from Frater Baraka, who initiated me into the OTO. Dawna Hulslander taught me Reiki and energy work. I learned coven-based Wicca from Taliesin and Willowe. For a few years I studied Kenn Day's Post-Tribal Shamanism, but went in my own direction. Many conversations with Lillith [ThreeFeathers], Joy [Wedmedyk], and Gene Rowand also helped me to deepen my understanding of more shamanic based work, ancestors, and spirit guides. My practice now is my own system of spirit based shamanic witchcraft, Energy healing, and divination.

Ladyelle - Elder's tradition: Live theatre. Tradition: The metaphysics of theatre – moving energy in live engagement/performance and the process of sharing the human experience. Elder: Eugene Lion, published playwright & writer, theatre director, acting teacher for stage & film, metaphysician and explorer of the human experience. Briefly employed by The Guthrie in Minnesota until a controversy over his staging of "Waiting for Godot" caused his departure. [He] also worked professionally in New York, Hawaii and British Columbia.

Licea, Alejandra - Tradition: Traditional Mexican. Elder: Joy Wedmedyk. Elder's tradition: Lucumi Orisha Worship, Espiritismo, and Shamanism.

Lyonesse, Bona Dea - Title: Elder High Priestess, founder of Circle of the Sacred Grove. Tradition: My personal tradition is a combination of several influences but is best described as mostly following the Circean Line of the Romano-Celtic Tradition of the Old Religion. Elders: There are four women who were influential spiritual Elders for me. The one I was privileged to spend the most time with was the Lady Circe. Elder's tradition: Lady Circe was a

5th generation hereditary witch who blended the teachings of her great grandmother with contemporary Wiccan ritual practices and founded the Sisterhood and Brotherhood of Wicca in 1971 as the first legal church of Wicca registered in the state of Ohio. Several covens descended from her initiatory lineage, affording her, by tradition, the title of Queen. She was born Jeffrey B. Cather in 1921, was a dancer, a WWII veteran, and a registered nurse. She died in 2004.

Meyer, Collin - Tradition: Atheist.

Montana, Bernadette - Tradition: Progressive Witchcraft is more of a philosophy than a tradition. It's going back to the roots. Wicca (as a tradition) is fairly new starting with Gerald Gardner. Those that practice a 'progressive' form of witchcraft, strive to [go] back further and study and incorporate the practices of the ancient ones. Connection with deity and the ancestors is one of the main focuses of this form of witchcraft. Elders: Janet Farrar and Gavin Bone. Elders' tradition: Progressive Witchcraft (though Janet was originally an Alexandrian before evolving into the progressive movement). Elder: Isaac Bonewits. Elder's tradition: Druid/Neopagan. Elder: Tara Wolf. Elder's tradition: Alexandrian Wicca. Elder: Wind Daughter. Elder's tradition: Native American, Sun Bear Tribe.

Mowglellan - Tradition: Eclectic.

Odinsson, Sarenth - Tradition: Northern Tradition Pagan and Heathen. Elders: Galina Krasskova and Raven Kaldera are the influences on my religion and spirituality. Galina Krasskova is my primary Elder as she is also my teacher. Elders' traditions: Northern Tradition Pagan and Heathen.

Owen, Lisa - Tradition: In the Native American tradition they teach of the Medicine wheel, where the main concept of the teachings is 'we are all connected, Red, Yellow, Black and White; we all come round the circle in this connection.' My path is following the wisdom and teachings of the ancestors who have walked this circle. Elders: On the White Road, my grandmother was the first person in my life that told me I had magic hands that helped heal pain. She was one to believe in the stars and how they affect our lives, and she believed in me with love. She taught me to believe in myself. When I discovered the Red Road, Black Elk writings, and Winona LeDuke speeches, two Spiritual Leaders from the Anishinaabe people taught me the ways of the traditions, our connection in the circle of life, and the responsibilities we have to keep it sacred. On the Yellow Road, the writing and speaking of His Holiness the Dalai Lama taught me about compassion. On the Black Road, the traditions of Ifa and Lukumi Regla de Ocha have taught me of the languages of the secrets of life and the ways of the mysteries.

Peck, Jase - Tradition: Mixture of North American and Central American and South American Shamanism. Elders: What Elder influenced your spirituality? All of them. My grandmother on my mother's side, Grandfather Wallace Black Elk, Don Jose Matsuwa, Moon Thunder, and a youth elder. Elders' traditions: Lakota, Ute, Quechal, Seneca, Objiway... a conglomeration between many traditions, finding the similarities, the truths, between traditions of North and South America – it has coalesced into some core truths.

Quarrie-Bendis, Deanne - Tradition: Feminist Dianic Witchcraft practiced through The Apple Branch – A Dianic Tradition. Elders and their traditions: Z Budapest: Feminist Dianic Wicca. Morgan McFarland: McFarland Dianic. Mark Roberts: Dallas Dianic, Faerie Faith. Searles O'Dubhain: Druidism.

Rowand, Gene - Tradition: Dakota. Elders: Iron Moccasin and Ervin Cook. Elders' traditions: Dakota.

Runesinger, Lady Vala (Elizabeth Hazel) is an astrologer, tarotist, author, and speaker. She has created many rituals for her coven and has conducted original rituals as a guest celebrant for other groups. Her work includes the book *Tarot Decoded* and the *Whispering Tarot* deck and book. She writes the Third Rock Almanac weekly horoscopes for newspaper publication. Liz lectures on astrology, tarot, and mystical topics in the Ohio-Michigan region and at regional conferences.

Shadow Walker - Tradition: Toltec Sorcery. Elder and Tradition: Merilyn Tunneshende, Nagual Dreaming Woman and Toltec sorceress. Elder and Tradition: Robert L. Spencer, Warrior Path teacher and author of *The Craft of the Warrior*.

Stormcrow. I am a Pagan. A female human being.

Thoms, Karen - Tradition: The tradition I practice is a fusion of several practices. My grandmothers and great-grandmothers were Pennsylvania Dutch, Mennonite, Native American, and Appalachian Baptist. I practiced Ceremonial Magick and was drafted into working with Spirits of the Land and several other Spirits. My tradition reflects the cultural blending and experiences of my Ancestors.

Thorn, Eli - Tradition: American Witchcraft. Elders: Rev. Jica, Grandfather BearHeart, Grandmother Lucy, Chasky Denny, Toni Grey, Richard Rice. Elders' traditions: Christian, Cree, Dakota, British Traditional Witchcraft, solitary.

White Wolf, Peaceful Rivers Rainbow Warrior - Tradition: Since 1993, my practice is Native traditions of tribes from the Clans in Canada — and Lucumi Orisha worship. Elders: Sweet Medicine, Joy Wedmedyk. Elders' traditions: Canadian native traditions and Lucumi Orisha worship.

Appendix 5: Glossary

ADF: see Ár nDraíocht Féin.

Afro-Caribbean Paganism: this is a general term used to describe the African diaspora religions of the Caribbean.

Ancestor reverence: devotion and respect given to people who are blood relatives, adopted relatives, and people from spiritual lineages.

Animism: the belief that everything in the world has a soul; this includes animals, plants and so forth.

Animist: one who believes in animism.

Archdruid: a person who is a leader in a druidic tradition.

Archdruid Emeritus: an honorary title for a person who has retired from active leadership.

Ár nDraíocht Féin: name of an organization of druids; it means "A Druid Fellowship" and is also called ADF.

Aromatherapy: the use of scents and oils derived from plants in healing work.

Astral projection: the experience or feeling when a person has left the body to travel to other places.

Athame: a sacred knife used in rituals to direct energy.

Atheist: a person who does not believe in a god or gods.

Aura: the energy field surrounding a person, place or thing.

Awen: a common sacred symbol in Druidism, it represents the connection between individuals, divine spirit, and nature. Most simply, it symbolizes all of the important triads within Druidism such as the three realms (land, sea, and air).

Bahá'í: a monotheistic religion that believes in the spiritual unity of all humanity.

Bard: a story-teller or poet associated with oral traditions.

Beltane: a Spring festival usually celebrated on May 1 in the Northern Hemisphere.

Blot: a ritual for followers of Norse, Northern European, Heathen or similar traditions. It may include toasting, boasting, praying, and an offering of beverage to the gods.

Boline: a small knife used for cutting herbs, which can have a white handle or a blade shaped like a sickle.

Broom closet: a term meaning that an individual is not public about religious affiliation, spiritual practices or beliefs.

Bundles: see **Sacred bundle**.

Ceremony: a procedure performed alone or in a group for religious or sacred reasons.

Chakra: a Sanskrit term that signifies energy points in the body.

Chaos magic: a magical system that rejects confinement, orthodoxy, or habitual practices.

Clairsentience: a psychic or supernatural method of sensing or feeling.

Clairvoyance: extrasensory perception.

Coven: a group of people who work together, learning and celebrating typically within traditions of Wicca or witchcraft.

Crone: a term referring to an Elder woman.

Croning: a ritual recognizing a woman as a Crone; a rite of passage for a woman becoming an Elder.

Dark of the Moon: the new moon.

Divine beings: a term that can refer to elevated spirits, guides and gods.

Dreamer: a person who works with dreaming to receive information and effect change.

Druid: a follower of certain Celtic traditions.

Druidry: a system of nature-based religious practices that have evolved from Celtic traditions.

Earth traditions: a tradition that honors nature.

Elder: a person recognized as carrying on the traditions of the culture, family or community including spiritual practices.

Esbat: a meeting of the coven for the full or new moon.

Espiritismo: see **Spiritism**.

Fey: supernatural beings commonly referred to as fairies.

Fivefold kiss: a Wiccan ritual in which kisses are given to five parts of the body with associated blessings.

Folk curing traditions: traditions of curing passed down in families who lived in isolated areas such as kitchen magic or Appalachian remedies.

Folk magic: see **Folk curing traditions**.

Goddess worship: various practices worshipping the divine female or divine feminine.

Gods: see **Polytheism**.

Gray Panthers Movement: in 1970, when Maggie Kuhn and five others were forced to retire, she founded the Gray Panthers Movement, a multigenerational advocacy group, to work on fighting ageism. It lobbies on social issues including corporate reform, workers' rights, and universal health care.

Groves: a sacred space in nature or a dedicated place created in a wooded area.

Heathen: a person who practices a reconstructed religion based on ancient Northern European beliefs.

Hecate: Goddess associated with crossroads, witchcraft, magic, and the land of the dead.

Herbalism: the use of plants in healing treatments.

High Priest: a title given to a male spiritual leader after years of work within an initiatory process.

High Priestess: a title given to a female spiritual leader after years of work within an initiatory process.

Hindu: originating in India, Hinduism is a religion that accepts multiple deities. It incorporates the beliefs of reincarnation, karma, and liberation with dharma (loosely defined as ethics and duty), compassion and responsibility. Worldwide it is the third largest religion.

Hoodoo: a tradition of folk magic that evolved out of a merger of African, American Indian and European beliefs and practices. Also called root-working or conjuring.

Ifa: an indigenous religion of the Yoruba peoples of West Africa based on Spirits commonly referred to as Orishas.

Imbolc: in Wiccan and European traditions, Imbolc is a festival celebrated on February 1 or 2. It is one of the major Sabbats.

Immanent: the belief that the divine pervades the entire universe.

Indigenous culture: indigenous people are aboriginal or first peoples of a land, and their cultures were formed prior to colonialism or invasion of a territory.

Inipi: a Lakota term for a sweat lodge, which is rite of purification.

Initiation: a ritual admitting an individual into a group or organization; a rite of passage marking a change of status or a new role.

Karma: a term borrowed from Hinduism and Buddhism. In Paganism, it refers to the belief that good actions will be rewarded and that bad actions will bring negative consequences; some individuals believe that good deeds will counteract the karma from negative ones.

Kemetism/Kemeticism: Kemetic traditions are reconstructed religions based on ancient Egyptian beliefs and deities.

Kith and kin: this term is widely used to respectfully designate chosen long-term relations as well as family.

Lucumi (Lucumi Orisha Worship): an African diasporic religion codified in Cuba worshipping the Orishas; also known as Regla de Ocha.

Mabon: a harvest festival celebrated on the Autumn Equinox by Wiccans and followers of other European Pagan traditions.

Magick: an alternative spelling of magic used to differentiate the spiritual and ceremonial practices of magic from staged illusions and performances.

Medicine man: see **Medicine person**.

Medicine person: an indigenous traditional spiritual or ceremonial leader, often a healer.

Medicine wheel: in North American indigenous traditions, a medicine wheel is a sacred circle of stones that symbolize parts of the universe, such as the directions, Earth, and Sky.

Metaphysics: deals with the topics of existence, cause and effort, space and time, and perceptions of reality.

Misa: a ceremony that evolved as a way for people to pray for and receive messages from their ancestors or from those that have crossed over. It takes many different forms in the Afro-Caribbean diaspora.

Muggles: contemporary slang term to define an individual without magical powers, practices or beliefs.

Mysticism: esoteric traditions that the experience of oneness with nature, the divine or the cosmos.

Neopagan: a person who follows Neopagan spiritual beliefs.

Neopaganism: the umbrella term for various traditions that incorporate reconstructed or historical practices that include reverence for nature and multiple deities.

Neoshamanism: a contemporary practice of shamanism that does not follow the methods of a traditional or indigenous group.

Occultist: someone who studies hidden spiritual mysteries; a person with knowledge of or ability to control magical, mystical or supernatural powers.

Odin: the father god in the heathen traditions.

Oklevueha Native American Church: located in Utah, it provides protection for those practicing indigenous Native American spirituality.

Old ways: ancient traditions.

Olorisha: an individual who has been initiated as a priest of the Orisha.

Orisha: manifestations of the source energy revealed on Earth and differentiated as divine beings, qualities of the world, and aspects of nature.

Otherworld: a world other than ordinary reality; the place of spirits.

Ovate: a Druidic term for a person who studies divination or herbalism; a seer.

Pagan: please refer to the chapter "Pagan: Disclaimer and Definition" for the definition used in this book.

Pantheistic: the belief that everything is part of god or part of the divine.

Pentacle: a five-pointed star signifying earth, air, fire, water, and spirit. A common symbol in Wicca. A talisman.

Pipe ceremony: a sacred ritual utilizing tobacco and similar herbs. The ceremony connects the physical and spiritual worlds together through prayer.

Polytheism: the belief that more than one god exists; the worship of more than one god and/or goddess.

Polytheistic: to describe a person who believes in polytheism.

Psychic: a clairvoyant individual; a person who utilizes extrasensory perception.

Reclamation Traditions: traditions such as Eastern European Wicca, Druidism, or Norse Paganism.

Regla de Ocha: see **Lucumi**.

Reincarnation: a belief that people are reborn after death and live more than one life.

Rite of Passage: a ritual or ceremony to observe a transition in life.

Ritual: formal religious or spiritual actions to effect change or celebrate an event.

Sabbat: one of eight major holidays in Wiccan or other Pagan traditions; together they make us the Wheel of the Year.

Sacred bundles: a collection of items used in a spiritual and holy way.

Sacred fires: fires that are built with a spiritual intention.

Sage: (1.) an herb burned for purification during ceremonies, for example, white sage (*salvia apiana*) or sagebrush (*artemesia tridentata* or *artemisia ludoviciana*). (2.) when capitalized, a term used to mean a man who is an Elder.

Seer: one who has visions, predicts the future, or foresees events; a prophet.

Seidh: an oracle in Heathen or similar Pagan traditions; one who is a seer.

Seven generations: a term used to signify those who come after us.

Shamanic extraction: a spiritual method of removing and neutralizing foreign energy from a person.

Shaman: an individual who mediates between the seen and unseen worlds to bring healing and balance to people and the community.

Shamanism: ancient healing traditions based on the belief of multiple worlds and realities.

Smudge: (1.) burning plants or incense to purify a person or place. (2.) the act of cleansing an individual, a space, or a room.

Solitary: a person who practices Paganism alone and does not identify with a specific group.

Sorcery: (1.) a system of physical, emotional, and energetic practices used to increase vitality, heighten perceptions, and find freedom from debilitating habits and beliefs. (2.) the process by which an individual works to evolve into a Man or Woman of Knowledge, that is, an integrated person with wisdom and awareness.

Spiritism: a religious movement originating in Europe used to communicate with spirits; whether beneficent or maleficent, the spirits influence the world of the living.

Spiritualism: communication with the helpful spirits of the dead who want to talk with the living and want to assist us.

Stone circle lodge: see **Sweat lodge**.

Stregha: the study and practice of Italian folk magic or witchcraft.

Sundance: an indigenous ceremony done on behalf of the people.

Sweat lodge: sacred ceremony done in an enclosure with heated rocks and used for healing and prayer.

Talisman: an object charged with energy and typically used for protection.

Talking stick: a stick, feather or other object used to designate who has permission to speak.

Telepathy: communication through psychic or extrasensory means.

Thor's Hammer: a symbol worn by those who follow Norse, Heathen or other Northern European spiritual paths. A religious amulet of protection based on the legendary weapon used by

Thor, god of thunder.

Transcendent: beyond comprehension.

Underworld: one of the levels of reality.

Vice Archdruid: in a Druidic organization, a person who is second in ranking to the Archdruid.

Voodoo: folk magic and spiritual practices that evolved from the African diaspora.

Voudun: an initiatory religion based on West African traditions working with ancestor spirits.

White Buffalo Calf Woman: a sacred spirit woman who came to the Native American people now known as the Great Sioux Nations and taught them seven sacred rites.

Wicca: a nature religion based upon the pre-Christian folk traditions of Europe worshiping both God and Goddess. Although solitary practitioners exist, typically Wicca includes working with a dedicated group and includes initiations within the group.

Wiccan: a person who practices Wicca.

Witch: (1.) a practitioner of Wicca or witchcraft. (2.) someone who believes that nature should be respected or worshiped, and practices old traditions such as European folk healing, herbalism, and spellcraft.

Appendix 6: Suggested Readings

Aburrow, Yvonne. *All Acts of Love and Pleasure: Inclusive Wicca.* (Avalonia Press, 2014).

Adler, Margot. *Drawing Down the Moon: Witches, Druids, Goddess-Worshippers, and Other Pagans in America* (Penguin Books, 2006).

Banutu-Gomez, Michael. *Africa: We Owe it to Our Ancestors, Our Children, and Ourselves* (Lanham, Maryland: University Press of America, 2005).

Blanton, Crystal, Editor. *Shades of Faith* (Megalithica Books, 2011).

Bonewits, Isaac. *Real Magic: An Introductory Treatise on the Basic Principles of Yellow Magic* (Red Wheel / Weiser, 1989).

Brown, Joseph Epes. *The Spiritual Legacy of the American Indian* (Crossroad, 1984).

Buckland, Raymond. *Buckland's Complete Book of Witchcraft* (Llewellyn Publications, 2002).

Corrigan, Ian. *Sacred Fire, Holy Well: A Druid's Grimoire* (ADF Publishing, 2009).

Cunningham, Scott. *Wicca: A Guide for the Solitary Practitioner* (Llewellyn Publications, 1989).

Day, Kenn. *Dance of Stones: A Shamanic Road Trip* (Moon Books, 2013).

De LA Torre, Miguel A. and Edwin David Aponte. *Introducing Latino/a Theologies* (Orbis Books, 2001).

Dorsey, Lilith. *Voodoo and Afro-Caribbean Paganism* (Citadel, 2005).

Fatunmbi, Awo Fa'Lokun. *Ìbà'şe Òrìṣà (Iba'se Orisa): Ifá Proverbs, Folktales, Sacred History and Prayer* (David G. Wilson, Original Publications, 1994) .

Fortune, Dion. *Mystical Qabalah* (Weiser Books, 2000).

Gardner, Gerald. *Witchcraft Today* (Citadel, 2004).

Harner, Michael. *The Way of the Shaman* (HarperOne, 1990)

Henes, Donna. *The Queen of My Self: Stepping Into Sovereignty in Midlife* (Monarch Press, 2004).

Hutton, Ronald. *The Triumph of the Moon: A History of Modern Pagan Witchcraft* (Oxford University Press, 1999).

Kardec, Allan. *The Spirits' Book* (1857). Retrieved May 7, 2017. From http://www.allankardec.com/Allan_Kardec/Le_livre_des_es prits/lesp_us.pdf .

Linde, Nels and Judith E. Olson-Linde. *Taking Sacred Back: The Complete Guide to Designing and Sharing Group Ritual* (Llewellyn Publications, 2016).

Lifton, Robert Jay. *The Broken Connection: On Death and the Continuity of Life* (Washington, DC: America Psychiatric Press, 1979).

Lincoln, Bruce. *Emerging from the Chrysalis: Rituals of Women's Initiation* (Oxford University Press, 1991).

Livingston, Gretchen. (2014, December 22). Fewer than half of U.S. kids today live in a 'traditional' family. Retrieved January 26, 2017, from http://www.pewresearch.org/fact-tank/ 2014/ 12/22 /less-than-half-of-u-s-kids-today-live-in-a-traditional-family/.

Mead, Margaret. *Culture and Commitment* (Garden City, New York: Doubleday, 1970).

Miller, Timothy, Editor. *America's Alternative Religions* (State University of New York Press, 1995).

Mosley, Pat, Editor. *Arcane Perfection: An Anthology by Queer, Trans and Intersex Witches* (Cutlines Press, Kindle only, 2017).

Murrell, Nathaniel Samuel. *Afro-Caribbean Religions: An Introduction to Their Historical, Cultural, and Sacred Traditions* (Temple University Press, 2009).

Myers, Brendan. *The Earth, the Gods and the Soul: A History of Pagan Philosophy from the Iron Age to the 21st Century* (Moon Books, 2013).

Rael, Joseph E. *Beautiful Painted Arrow: Stories and Teachings from the Native American Tradition* (Element Books Ltd, 1992).

Smith, Wilfred Cantwell. *The Meaning and End of Religion* (Minneapolis: Fortress Press, 1991).

Starhawk. *The Spiral Dance: A Rebirth of the Ancient Religion of the Goddess* (HarperOne, 1999).

Starhawk and M. Macha NightMare. *The Pagan Book of Living and Dying: Practical Rituals, Prayers, Blessings, and Meditations on Crossing Over* (New York: HarperOne, 1997).

Strmiska, Michael, Editor. *Modern Paganism in World Cultures: Comparative Perspectives* (ABC-CLIO, 2005).

Teish, Luisah. *Jambalaya: The Natural Woman's Book of Personal Charms and Practical Rituals* (HarperOne, 1988).

McGaa, Ed. *Mother Earth Spirituality: Native American Paths to Healing Ourselves and Our World* (Harper, 1990).

Miller, Timothy, Editor. *America's Alternative Religions* (State

University of New York Press, 1995).

Myers, Brendan. *The Earth, The Gods and The Soul: A History of Pagan Philosophy from the Iron Age to the 21st Century* (Moon Books, 2013).

Neihardt, John G. Neihardt. *Black Elk Speaks: Being the Life Story of a Holy Man of the Oglala Sioux* (State University of New York Press, 2008).

Reference List

Banutu-Gomez, Michael. *Africa: We Owe it to Our Ancestors, Our Children, and Ourselves* (Lanham, Maryland: University Press of America, 2005).

Bonewits, Isaac. "The Advanced Bonewits' Cult Danger Evaluation Frame (Version 2.7)" *NeoPagan Net* (2008). Retrieved April 10, 2016, from http://www.neopagan.net/ABCDEF.html.

Bureau, U.C. (n.d.) Library. "Population." Retrieved May 2, 2017, from https://www.census.gov/library/publications/2011/com pendia/statab/131ed/population.html.

Edwards-Tate, Laurie. "Weekly column in the Washington Times Communities by Laurie Edwards-Tate" *At Your Home Familycare* (originally "Anthropologist Margaret Mead addresses today's aging issues") (posted February 3, 2012). Retrieved Jan 6, 2018 from http://atyourhomefamilycare.com /washington-times- communities/anthropologist-margaret-mead-addresses-todays-aging-issues/.

Fatunmbi, Awo Fa'Lokun. *Ìbà'ṣe Òrìṣà (Iba'se Orisa): Ifá Proverbs, Folktales, Sacred History and Prayer* (David G. Wilson, Original Publications, 1994).

Henes, Donna. "On Finding Myself Middle Aged with No Role Model I Could Relate to Because I am Not a Crone" from *The Queen of My Self* (2005). Retrieved February 2, 2014, from http://www.thequeenofmyself.com/a-queen1a.shtml.

Henes, Donna. *The Queen of My Self: Stepping Into Sovereignty in Midlife* (Monarch Press, 2004).

Lifton, Robert Jay. *The Broken Connection: On Death and the Continuity of Life* (Washington, DC: America Psychiatric Press, 1979).

Lincoln, Bruce. *Emerging from the Chrysalis: Rituals of Women's Initiation* (Oxford University Press, 1991).

Livingston, Gretchen. (2014, December 22). "Fewer than half of U.S. kids today live in a 'traditional' family." Retrieved January 26, 2017, from http://www.pewresearch.org/fact-tank/2014/12/22/less-than-half-of-u-s-kids-today-live-in-a-traditional-family/.

Mead, Margaret. "Culture and Commitment" (Natural History Press/Doubleday & Company, Inc., 1969). Retrieved December

26, 2013 from http://mx.esc.ru/~assur/ocr/mead/mead.htm.

Pew Research Center. "Appendix C: Defining the Religious Groups." *The Future of World Religions: Population Group Projections*, 2010-2050 (Pew Research Center, 2015). Retrieved June 15, 2017 from http://assets.pewresearch.org/wpcontent/uploads/sites/11/2015/04/PF_15.04.02_ProjectionsAppendixC.pdf .

Pew Research Center. "Chapter 1: The Changing Religious Composition of the U.S." *Religion and Public Life* (Pew Research Center, 2017). Retrieved June 15, 2017, from www.pewforum.org/2015/05/12/chapter-1-the-changing-religious-composition-of-the-u-s/.

Pew Research Center. "The Future of World Religions: Population Growth Projections, 2010-2050 North America." *Pew Forum*. (2015). Retrieved June 15, 2017, from http://www.pewforum.org/2015/04/02/north-america/.

Pew Research Center. "Spotlight on Other Religions" *The Global Religious Landscape* (Pew Research Center, 2012). Retrieved June 15, 2017, from http://www.pewforum.org/2012/12/18/global-religious-landscape-other/#spotlight.

Starhawk. "Peace, the Environment, Global Justice and Magic" (2015). Retrieved January 8, 2015, from http://starhawk.org/.

Tutu, Desmond and Mpho Tutu. *The Book of Forgiving: The Fourfold Path for Healing Ourselves and Our World* (HarperOne, 2015).

US Department of Agriculture. "Ag and Food Statistics: Charting the Essentials" (2014).

Index

In the Index, we have included the names of contributors, famous individuals, and Elders. In addition, people who were quoted but were not contributors are here. The index also includes terms, traditions, resources, and organizations that are of interest.

Egyptian-Themed Magic
From Megalithica Books
www.immanion-press.com

Sekhem Heka by Storm Constantine

Drawing upon her experiences in Egyptian Magic and the energy healing systems of Reiki and Seichim, Storm Constantine developed this new system to appeal to practitioners of both magic and energy healing. Incorporating ritual and visualisation into a progressive journey through the seven energy centres of the body, Sekhem Heka can be practiced by those who are already attuned to an energy healing modality, as well as those who are simply interested in the magical aspects of the system. Sekhem Heka is designed to help the practitioner work upon self-evolution and self-knowledge. Each of the seven tiers focuses upon a particular Ancient Egyptian god or goddess, including practical exercises and rites. ISBN pbk: 9781905713134, $21.99, £12.99

Graeco-Egyptian Magic by Tony Mierzwicki

Graeco-Egyptian Magick outlines a daily practice involving planetary Hermeticism, drawn from original texts and converted into a format that fits easily into the modern magician's practice. Graeco-Egyptian magick represents the last flowering of paganism before it was wiped out by Christianity. It blends ancient Sumerian and Egyptian magick with the relatively more modern Greek and Judaic systems. It includes a recreation of a planetary system of self-initiation using authentic Graeco-Egyptian practices from the first five centuries C.E. This is a practical intermediate level text aimed at those who are serious about their spiritual development and already have grounding in basic spirituality, but beginners who carefully follow the instructions sequentially should not be deterred. ISBN pbk: 1905713037, $21.99, £12.99

The Travellers' Guide to the Duat by Kiya Nicoll

Planning a trip to the Egyptian spirit world? Like any responsible traveller, you want to know something about the history, geography, and politics of your destination. You want to know what documents you need to have in order for customs and immigration, what precautions to take, how to book a boat tour, where to stay, what to eat, and when you'll get the most interesting sightseeing opportunities. Laced through its humorous presentation you will find extensive information about ancient Egyptian religion and magical practice. Renditions of ancient spells in modern poetry mark each section, showing the ancient magical texts in a new light. The Beautiful West awaits! Book your tour today! ISBN pbk: 9781905713738, $19.99, £10.99

Recent Titles from Megalithica Books

Zodiac of the Gods by Eden Crane

A new interpretation of the Egyptian Dendera Zodiac, this book explores character analysis for each sign, revealing your relationship with the deity presiding over your month of birth. The book also offers a primer for Egyptian magic, focusing upon the deities of the year. The vivid pathworkings enable you to connect with these ancient gods and goddesses, and work with their energy to influence and improve your life, helping you realise your goals and desires. ISBN: 978-1-912241-03-3 Price: £11.99, $16.50

Pop Culture Magic Systems by Taylor Ellwood

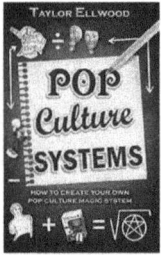

Discover how to construct a system of magic around your favourite pop culture. Learn what a the essential elements of a magical system are to help you shape your pop culture into a viable spiritual practice, to get positive results and explore deeper spiritual truths. If you want to level up your pop culture magical practice, this book will be your strategy guide! ISBN: 978-1-912241-00-2 Price: £9.99, $12.99

Reiki Subversives Manual by Karl Hernesson

Introducing a radical new approach to energy healing. Become a Reiki warrior and urban healer to heal yourself, your community and the Earth – even if you're not attuned to Reiki. This book includes a basic method for using Earth energy, as well as a process to connect to Reiki, so you can begin urban healing yourself. Heal your environment and connect with the healing power of the planet. ISBN: 978-0-9932371-3-3 Price: £11.99, $16.50

www.immanion-press.com

www.ingramcontent.com/pod-product-compliance
Lightning Source LLC
Chambersburg PA
CBHW021501090426
42739CB00007B/410